thebreak-updiet

a memoir

Annette Fix

Womyn Books
Dana Point, California

thebreak-updiet

© 2008 Annette Fix

Womyn Books
Dana Point, California

Cover Photography by Alex Gumerov
Cover Design by Angela Mackintosh
Interior Book Design by Peri Poloni-Gabriel, Knockout Books

Library of Congress Control Number: 2007931298
ISBN 13: 978-1-934518-39-7

Printed in the United States of America

Orange Curtain Publishing has elected to print this title on 50% post-consumer recycled paper with the recycled portion processed chlorine free.
As a result, we have saved the following resources:

13 trees
9 million BTUs of total energy
1,167 lbs of greenhouse gases
4,843 gallons of water
622 lbs of solid waste

(calculation courtesy of www.papercalculator.org)

Orange Curtain Publishing is a member of Green Press Initiative, a nonprofit program dedicated to supporting publishers in their efforts to reduce their use of fiber sourced from endangered forests.

For more information, visit www.greenpressinitiative.org

10 9 8 7 6 5 4 3 2 1

For media inquires and special discounts for bulk purchases,
please contact: info@orangecurtainpublishing.com

www.orangecurtainpublishing.com

For my broken-hearted sisters,

hopeless romantics,

seekers of princes,

believers in happily-ever-after,

and queens of their own castle.

table of contents

acknowledgements

I want to thank the people who affected my life enough to be immortalized in this book. If you recognize yourself in the stories, it is because of something you said or did, good or bad, which brought me to where I am this very moment. Without you, this book would not exist.

My greatest appreciation goes out to my family, friends, and fellow creative creatures who have fed my muse a steady diet of reality cookies. Donnamarie Vaughn—whose keen insight made me answer all the hard questions. John Kim—for the countless late night conversations about the wonders and frustrations of the process, those recipes are for you. Wendy Kamenoff—thank you for reading my stories and laughing and crying in all the right places, and especially for encouraging me to trust that the truth is enough. You've been a wonderful teacher and friend. Agent Wendy Sherman—for being the first industry professional to champion my work. Your affirmation kept me going. To the Wednesday Writers—Sandi Battista, Donna Todd, and Laurie Thomas for listening patiently while I pounded the clay, and for offering suggestions to smooth out the rough spots. Angela Mackintosh—you are such a prolific and creative genius, you inspire me. I look forward to continuing our friendship and working together on future projects. Michelle Montoya—for being my best friend and chief secret-keeper since seventh grade, and for never suggesting that I come up with a Plan B. Wonderboy—you are truly the best part of me. Thank you for always making me laugh and helping me keep things in perspective. Stefan—my dear, sweet prince, thank you for believing in me. You are loving proof that the universe expanded to meet my expectations. Without you in my life, I would be unfinished.

part one

kevin and the
kübler-rossian
process

the sky is falling

The cordless phone rang. Once. Twice. With my eyes still glued shut, I fumbled through the layers of bedding to find it.

"Hullo?" The word came out in a mumble as I surfaced from the depths of a dream.

Slivers of sunlight peeked between the blinds and cast pinstripes of pale gold across the room. I blinked to life and stretched beneath the flannel sheets.

"Did I wake you?" Kevin's voice, flat and cool, cut through the background bustle of the golfers in the pro shop.

"Mmmm…good morning." I cradled the phone against my ear and rolled onto his side of the bed.

I loved Kevin's daily wake-up call. Sometimes I kept my eyes closed and pretended he was still beside me, poking me in the back of the thigh with his early morning hard-on.

"Annette, we need to talk."

His tone switched on stadium lights inside my head.

"I just can't do this anymore. I've felt this way for a while now…"

His voice sounded so far away, each word was shrinking and fragmented, nearly inaudible. Time stopped. My throat constricted and my morning brain struggled to make sense of the waking nightmare.

Kevin continued to explain why our relationship had to end, but the only thing I heard clearly was, "I'm sorry." He said it again and again until the sound rushed in my ear like wind through a tunnel. Until the word *sorry* had no meaning.

"Don't do this," I whispered.

The ceiling swam above me. I blinked and my eyelids overflowed. Warm tears ran into the tiny hollows of my ears.

I cupped my hand over my mouth to hold back the choking sobs. I knew there was nothing I could say. He sounded so cold. I knew I'd already lost him.

The conversation ended as quickly as it began; I couldn't even say good-bye. Kevin hung up and the dial tone echoed in my head. My sobs, finally free from any witness, turned into wails bearing claw marks. Nooooo. Whyyyyyy? It became a rocking, incoherent mantra.

A soft rap on the bedroom door was almost lost in my sobs.

"Mom? Are you okay?" Josh peered into the room, his hand still gripping the doorknob.

I wiped the curtain of wetness from my cheeks and patted the space beside me. I tried to level my voice. "Good morning, Wonderboy. Are you ready for school?"

Josh sat on the edge of the bed and leaned to hug me. At twelve, he was small for his age, and reed thin, all elbows and knees. He pulled back and searched my face intently. "What's wrong?"

I couldn't tell him and then just send him off to school to deal with it. "I'm okay. Do you want me to help you with this?" I ruffed his soft, dark hair. "You're going to be late if you don't get moving."

"I need more gel, I'm out. Can you be sure to buy the blue kind like we got last time?"

I nodded to assure him that I knew the proper color choice was imperative for his social acceptance. "Did you have breakfast and brush your teeth?"

"Yep." Josh smiled with his lips pulled taunt like a manic clown.

"Good job." I kissed the top of his usually spiky head and nudged him off the bed. "Have a good day. I love you."

"Love you too."

Josh's steps thundered down the stairs and I heard the front door slam.

Alone in the house, I felt abandoned in a cave of cold shadows; the silence pressed painfully against my chest. A fat, single tear rolled down each cheek. I couldn't believe Kevin left me.

He left me.

I curled up like a wounded child and cried hard for hours. Weak and dizzy, the catching breaths pulled me into an exhausted sleep.

When I awoke, my head throbbed so much my eye sockets hurt. The sun had shifted, signaling the afternoon descent toward sunset. I rolled over and glanced at the clock. Josh would be home soon.

I stumbled weakly down the stairs to the kitchen and went through the mindless motions of boiling water for instant oatmeal. After forcing down two spoonfuls, I couldn't swallow. It caked like moist sand around the lump in my throat. I pushed the bowl away.

Why didn't I fight? I should've begged him to stay. I should've insisted he tell me what I did wrong. Maybe it was pride, maybe a little bit of defeat. It wasn't the first time I'd ever been dumped. But somehow, I thought my relationship with Kevin would make it all the way to happily-ever-after.

That's all I ever wanted.

devastation omelette

1 devoted heart
3/4 cup lame excuses
1 Tbsp. rotten timing
1/4 cup minced sorrow
Add disbelief to taste

Break devoted heart. Beat with lame excuses from live-in boyfriend until emotions peak. Pepper with rotten timing.

Combine sorrow and disbelief. Add to scrambled heart and pour into scalding pan of emotional devastation.

Fry over open anguish until misery sets.

Yield: Total nausea.
Unlimited servings.
Nutritional Value: None.

Guaranteed 5 lb. weight loss.

sanity stops here
Wednesday, October 24

Josh had already left for school. I noticed his breakfast dishes rinsed and stacked beside the sink. I'd have to buy an alarm clock to keep from oversleeping. There would no longer be any wake up calls.

I lifted the cordless phone from the charger and ran my finger over the number one—the speed dial button for Kevin. I couldn't imagine starting the day without hearing his voice. I wanted to call, but what would I say? What *could* I say, without sounding completely pathetic?

We would eventually have to talk. At some point, he would want all of his clothes and personal things. He'd need to rent a moving truck to take the furniture that was his and we'd have to figure out what to do about the lease—still eight months left and in both of our names. I didn't even want to think about what it would take to deconstruct our entire life together. A wave of dizziness forced me to lean against the edge of the counter. I hadn't eaten anything since those two spoonfuls of oatmeal.

I set the phone back into the base and scuffed across the kitchen like an un-showered asylum patient, wearing one of Kevin's old T-shirts and my Eeyore slippers. I opened the refrigerator. The chill pimpled my bare legs while I stared at the wall of food. Each jar and bottle meticulously aligned. Labels facing forward. Each cube of Tupperware stacked in neat pyramids.

How could Kevin leave me? Everything in our relationship was perfect.

A choking sob knotted my stomach and I knew I couldn't force down a single bite. I let the door swing closed and reached to straighten the towel hanging from the handle. Turning my back against the refrigerator, I slid to the floor and hugged my knees to my chest.

What is: Unhappiness?

I'll take "Failed Relationships" for $800.

The top three lamest break-up lines are on the board…

Survey says: #3 I just want to be friends.

#2 I love you, but I'm not ready to get married.

And the #1 answer: It's not you; it's me.

So, what did I win in this shitty game show medley? A free trip back into the dating pool. At thirty-four. What a prize.

I rubbed my forehead. Twenty-four hours of ceaseless crying had taken its toll. I rose from the floor and noticed my reflection in the microwave door. My hazel eyes peeked from between puffy lids. Kevin always said my eyes turned green when I cried, but I couldn't remember ever having cried so hard or so long.

I guess I should back up a little and mention how this particular relationship disaster started. I'm fighting the urge to use the phrase *Once Upon A Time,* but as a certified hopeless romantic, it did feel like a fairytale—at least in the beginning.

If there is such a thing as love at first sight, then that's what I felt when Kevin and I met. Everyone says you can't meet a decent guy in a bar, and certainly not in a strip club, but Kevin was different.

I saw him sitting at the tip rail with one of his buddies. I was working the lunch shift and they were still wearing their golf shoes. The blonde guy looked completely out of his element, but I recognized his dark-haired friend as a regular.

"So, how many holes did you guys make it into this morning?" I tossed out my first sexual innuendo de jour to both of them, but kept my eyes locked on the cute blonde.

The dark-haired guy flipped me a twenty. "Take this guy to the couch," he said. "His name's Kevin. Don't hurt him." The guy's laugh followed us as I led Kevin away by the hand.

Once we settled side-by-side on the red vinyl cushion, I was close enough to smell the sunshine on his skin, a warm, tangy scent. Kevin had wholesome, boy-next-door features and I was willing to bet he'd been crowned Prom King in high school.

"What's your name?" he said.

"Beth," I said, smiling like it was true.

I know, not exactly a typical stripper alias, but it was the only practical name I could come up with when I auditioned for the job. Somehow, I just couldn't see naming myself after a small defenseless animal, major U.S. city, or a semi-precious jewel.

"My friend says dancers don't tell guys their real names. Why did you tell me yours?"

I shifted on the couch and moved closer. "Beth *is* my stage name, my real name is Annette."

I peeked up to look at him and our eyes connected. His were magnetic— an electric blue that glowed against his tan skin. Kevin's hair had a slight curl to it that he obviously fought to control. I reached out to touch a stray curl.

Kevin sat ramrod straight with his hands gripping his thighs. "This is the first time I've ever been to a place like this."

"So, you're a virgin? I love virgins." I couldn't keep the smile from spreading across my face.

It was true. Doing a private dance for a guy who'd never had one was infinitely more fun than dancing for a regular customer; there was such a feeling of innocence in the way they watched you that first time.

I could tell Kevin was uncomfortable, so I made small talk: told him about my aspiring screenwriting career, my son, and asked him about his job and his life. At least an hour passed while we laughed and talked.

"Hey! Did I waste my twenty bucks or are you going to do a dance for my friend?"

Kevin and I leaned over and looked down to the far end of the couch. Kevin's friend slouched low on the seat with a beer in one hand, and Sasha, a busty blonde, shimmying her sequined bra above his face. He motioned for me to stand up and twirled two fingers like dancing legs.

I stood and stepped in front of Kevin. "I guess I have to earn my money..."

"You don't have to dance for me if you don't want to."

"I want to," I said.

The next song started and I moved my body to the tempo while I slipped out of my floral-print dress. His eyes passed from the small swell of my breasts encased in a matching bikini top, down my lean torso. I swayed my thong-clad hips like a hypnotist's watch. A few times, I dipped in and hovered my lips seductively close to his. Close, but not touching.

I studied Kevin's face as I danced. Fleeting expressions moved through a range I'd seen so many times before. Embarrassment. Curiosity. Arousal. The emotions ran on a loop for the duration of the three and a half minute song. When it ended, I wiggled back into my dress and flopped casually onto the couch beside him.

We picked up the conversation where we had left off, the topics skipped tracks from tangent to tangent, two people excited to know each other. In his company, the afternoon disappeared.

"Will you dance for me again?"

His question surprised me. I so badly wanted to tell him I'd do back flips to the moon if he asked.

"Sure."

The second dance was different than the first. The sense of awakening was gone. Longing had taken its place. His or mine, or both, I didn't know which.

Happy hour started and Kevin said it was time for him to leave. All of a sudden, neither of us knew what to say. He couldn't ask for my number. We were both awkwardly aware of how that would look considering his situation and my work environment.

"Well, if you ever want to learn how to play golf," he said, digging a business card out of his wallet, "you could come by the course for a lesson."

I took the card from his outstretched hand. After we exchanged a hug, Kevin stepped through the exit. He turned once and lifted his hand in a still wave before the door closed behind him.

I stood in the dim club, music pounding around me, and tucked his card into my small, silver moneybox. I couldn't care less about golf, but I couldn't deny that there was more than chemistry between us.

During our five-hour conversation, there was a connection. A feeling. A belief. Something that defied logical description. Something that spoke from my core saying, this is THE ONE. The other half of Aristophanes' divided whole. The match. My true soul mate.

Sadly, there was a sick, cosmic joke in all of it.

Life is unfair on so many levels.

How could Kevin dump me two weeks before our anniversary? What kind of sadistic prick breaks up with his girlfriend right before an anniversary? It would have been the two-year anniversary of our first date.

Well, technically, it wasn't really a date. It was a golf lesson.

I had scheduled the lesson for the first Monday of November, a week after I met Kevin. But that morning, I awoke to a giant red pimple, blinking like a beacon on the end of my nose.

When he met me, I was wearing stage makeup in perfect, soft, pink lighting. Which meant taking a golf lesson in broad daylight, while I sported a zit the size of Jupiter, was definitely not going to happen.

I called the golf course and asked the guy in the pro shop to reschedule my lesson for the following Monday.

When that morning came, it was overcast, cold, and spitting rain. I stood at the window and watched the drizzle darken the black canvas top of my convertible Celica.

The natural wave of my hair would never last out in the damp weather. I'd look like a walking warning about the hazards of sticking a fork into a light socket. So, I called to cancel, again.

I was surprised when Kevin answered the phone. His voice sounded as crisp as that fall day. "No way. You're not canceling today. I've been looking forward to seeing you since last week," he said.

"But the weather looks—"

"It's not really raining over here," he said quickly.

After we hung up, I stepped into the bowels of my walk-in closet.

What do you wear to a golf lesson when the instructor is married and you wish he weren't?

God, I'm such an idiot.

I stared at the racks. The colors, organized in perfect tonal harmony, striped the length of the dowels: red, pink, orange, yellow, green, blue, purple, white, brown, black. I flipped through each color category one at a time. The plastic tube hangers clicked like typewriter keys: strapless, spaghetti strap, tank style, sleeveless, short sleeve, three-quarter sleeve, long sleeve. I reached the end of the rainbow, and still didn't have anything to wear.

Why was I even going? Good question. Absurd answer: Because being near him, even to whack a stupid white ball with a metal stick, was better than never seeing him again.

I turned to the shelves. Since it was cold and rainy, I figured I'd pull a pair of sweats out of the stack. But that wouldn't work. At every country club, the women always wore tennis skirts or plaid pants. At least, that's what I remembered from watching *Dynasty* back in the '80s.

My wardrobe contained nothing remotely close to plaid pants and I had no idea where to buy a tennis skirt. I finally settled for one of my University of La Verne hoodies, an Anaheim Angels baseball cap with my ponytail pulled through, Avia cross-trainers, and a white mini skort.

Voila. Suburban country club chic.

Judging by how many times the maintenance guys circled the practice green in their little carts, I must've looked either very all right or definitely all wrong.

It was hard to concentrate on chipping the golf ball onto the green. Kevin was so damn beautiful. Whenever I looked at him, it was difficult to draw a full breath.

He was patient as he guided my hands to swing the club. Gentle and warm. I could feel the heat coming from his body when he leaned close to adjust my grip. I wanted so much to turn around, press up against him, and taste his lips. I knew it wasn't an option, but it was sweet torture just thinking about it. My heart hammered so hard that it felt like the only organ in my body.

When the golf lesson ended, I noticed the quick, thirty-minute lesson had become two languid hours.

Kevin returned my club to the bag on the back of the golf cart and climbed into the driver's seat. "Would you like a tour of the course?"

"Sure," I said too quickly. Anything to spend more time with you.

He guided the cart along the winding path to the back nine. The grounds were immaculately manicured and framed on both sides by a densely wooded stand of trees.

It was a soundless, secret place created in a dream. The cart path led over a bridge spanning a small creek and curved along rolling hills. Moist grass filled the quiet valleys with the smell of sweet earth. As Kevin drove, the cool air brushed along my bare legs, but the shiver I felt came from deep inside and had nothing to do with the weather.

Kevin pulled the cart behind the pro shop and parked. "Would you like to grab something to eat? I cancelled my other lessons for the day."

"Sure," I answered instantly. It seemed like the only word I could manage.

We settled into a cozy booth at a sports grill a mile away from the course. After browsing the menu, I couldn't decide what to eat, so Kevin ordered a picnic of appetizers.

Growing up. College. Dreams. Life. We laughed and talked and gorged ourselves with fried finger foods. The hours passed like minutes.

"I want to tell you something," Kevin said, "but I don't want you to take it wrong."

"Okaay," I said, not sure where he was going with his disclaimer.

"Remember I told you when we met three weeks ago that I was married?"

I swallowed hard around a jagged tortilla chip. "Yeah."

13

It was so much easier just to block it out and enjoy his company—wishing life was somehow different.

"Well, I don't want you to think this has anything to do with you." He lowered his voice, "I asked my wife for a divorce."

My head swam and my eyes darted to his ring finger. The wedding ring was gone.

Kevin leaned forward, his forearms braced on the lacquered wood table. "You said something the day we met that stuck with me. And it made so much sense."

I wracked my brain, trying to think of what I possibly could have said that was so profound. I replayed the pieces I could remember of our long conversation. The tavern noise receded to a soft hum. I must've been staring at him blankly.

"You said life is too short to be miserable."

"I was talking about life in general, I didn't mean for you to divorce your wife!"

Somehow I felt sickly responsible and secretly happy all at once. If he wasn't happy with her—maybe he could be happy with me.

"Don't think I did it for you," he said. "It's been on my mind for the last few years, but that night when I got home, I knew I finally had to do it."

I felt like I was slowing down at a car accident on the freeway and craning to see if anyone was wounded.

"How did she react?" I couldn't stop myself from asking.

Kevin twisted a napkin in his hands. "It was really hard." He stared at the table. "When I told her, she fell on the floor crying and threw up."

The image of that day wet his face with tears. His voice cracked as the story tumbled out. Kevin seemed so lost, torn between feelings of obligation over the time invested in his marriage and his desire to leave.

"I tried. For so many years, I tried, but I can't do it anymore," he said.

I moved beside Kevin and wrapped him in a hug that was both close and fierce. I wanted to take away his pain. My heart ached for Kevin and I dared to let it beat a quiet, hopeful rhythm for the possibilities of a future with him.

When Kevin came to me that day, I benefited from what had resulted in Joanne's sorrow. I took her place in his life.

Two years later, I finally felt her raw, bleeding loss. Now, it was my turn to spend my days crippled and vomiting emotion.

And somehow I thought I deserved it.

guilt stew

1 tender woman
16 oz. good intentions
1 rebounding man
2 lbs. desire

Simmer good intentions over flames of gentle affection.
Add man, woman, and desire.

Scald woman with false hopes of a future.
Remove man, let all love drain.
Garnish woman with grated nerves.
Serve over self-loathing biscuits.

Yield: Complete regret.
Unlimited servings.
Nutritional Value: None.

Guaranteed 3 lb. weight loss.

makeover madness
Thursday, October 25

"Sorry, Mom. See you later. Love you." Josh shot a quick peck onto my cheek then jumped out of the passenger seat and ran up the sidewalk to the schoolyard. Getting caught up in morning cartoons had made him miss the bus.

I grabbed my cell phone out of my purse, scanned the internal phone-book, and punched the call button. The ringing echoed from somewhere on the dark side of Saturn.

Each morning after Kevin left, I moved in a haze. Barely functional. I couldn't focus on my writing. And I certainly couldn't go to work at the club.

"Maggie, can you squeeze me in t-today?" My voice tripped over the hard, permanent lump in my throat.

On the drive to the salon, I confronted my new reality. So much for my Happily-Ever-After story. Kevin was supposed to be my Prince Charming. We were supposed to ride off into the sunset together the way every fairytale ends.

Disney can kiss my ass.

Along the street, every stoplight turned red. The cars were going too slow. People weren't even bothering to signal lane changes.

And screw Uncle Walt for making me believe in princes. I don't think he ever considered the kind of heartbreak he crafted into his stupid fairytales. There would always be that one day in every girl's life when she'd finally discover it was all a lie. A sick, twisted, fucking lie.

Buildings and cars streamed past my window, the car on autopilot. Kevin. His smile. The feel of his hands on my skin. The way he kissed the worry creases from my forehead. I loved his robust laugh—it was sunshine, breaking through my emotional clouds.

So many memories. So many moments I would never forget.

Kevin stepped out of the master bathroom completely naked. I lounged across the bed, admiring his perfect symmetry while he stood at the sink. He turned and posed with mock drama, standing with his body on full display.

When I dragged my eyes back up to his face, I noticed Kevin wearing my pink cotton headband, and there was mischief in his smile.

He ran across the room and stood in front of me, twirling and dancing in place like Jennifer Beals from the movie *Flashdance*. He screeched the "Maniac" song in falsetto, his bare feet pounded faster and faster to the tempo. Kevin's nakedness, in frantic motion, swung wildly, smacking against his thighs.

On that blue day, I rolled off the bed and we collapsed onto the carpet together, laughing so hard I almost peed in my pajamas.

God, how can I go on living without him?

Tears pinpricked my eyes. I'm not going to cry. I refuse to cry. I twisted the rearview mirror to check the mascara around my blurry eyes. A look of glassy desperation stared back.

I pushed through the doors of the salon and saw Maggie applying hair gel to her wilting, gothic spikes. I walked past the receptionist, straight to Maggie's station and she turned the chair to meet me.

"Just a trim today?" Maggie snapped the drape around my neck and our eyes caught in the mirror.

"Cut it off," I said.

"Oh m'god, he's gone." It was almost a question, but not quite.

That's when the carefully controlled tears finally spilled down my cheeks.

She set down her scissors and looked squarely into my face. "I won't cut a single hair unless you promise you're not cutting it off to spite that rat bastard."

"I just need a change."

That was all Maggie needed to hear. She clipped while I choked out as much of the story as I could. My eyes ached from the brightness of the harsh flourescent lights and the force of my tears.

When she finished, I slipped on my sunglasses and stared at the caramel-colored halo of hair on the floor. Twelve inches. Gone. It had been over a decade since my hair was this short.

Kevin loved my long hair. But that was when he loved me.

kiss my A.D.H.D.
Friday, October 26

I rolled my mouse to the taskbar and clicked the green, lowercase, script *f* icon shaped like a filmstrip. The Final Draft software opened to my working document: a family feature spec script intended for Disney.

The cursor blinked, a nagging throb on the page. I re-read what I had written the week before and tried to get back into the story.

It was all so fucking happy. I could almost hear chipmunks singing campfire songs.

Tears blurred my carefully formatted words into waves of alphabet soup. I closed the document and opened my LifeJournal software. I began writing what sounded more like a plea directly to Kevin than a diary entry.

The phone rang, disturbing my pseudoliterary flow of sorrow. "Mrs. Fix—" a woman's voice began.

"It's Ms. I'm not married now and never have been." My curtness covered the catch in my voice.

"MS. Fix, I'm calling about Josh. We'd like you to come to the school."

My stomach clenched. "Is he okay? Did something happen?"

"We'd like to discuss your son's academic performance. How about after school? Today. At three o'clock?"

I glanced at the clock. That would give me forty-five minutes to shower, dress, and drive to the school.

"That's fine. I'll be there."

In the shower, I let the water run over my face to rinse off the sticky tears.

When I pulled into the school parking lot, a rainbow of students poured out of the classrooms and jostled toward the buses. I saw Josh sitting slumped on a low block wall near the office. His head bowed, he bounced the toe of one skate shoe against the cement.

I stepped in front of him and he didn't even look up. "Hey Wonderboy, what's going on?"

"Do we have to go in there? They're just going to tell you how stupid I am." His voice dragged like his shoe.

"Then I'll have to tell them how wrong they are."

I had my arm around his shoulder when the secretary led us into the conference room. *They* had taken their positions on one side of a long table. Principal. Guidance Counselor. And four of Josh's seventh grade teachers, the absurdly cartoon personifications of Math, English, Science, and Social Studies. With their fake smiles and shuffling papers, they looked like a wall of human constipation.

I felt a slight tremor straight to my core. How could I possibly make it through the meeting without completely falling apart? Us versus Them. My parents attended meetings like this with me, but back then, I was invincible.

Principal started by clearing his throat. What a cliché. If I didn't feel so much like throwing up, I would've laughed.

He introduced everyone on the Them team, all of whom I'd already met at Back-to-School Night. Principal formed a steeple with his fingers and studied me across the table.

"Josh seems to be having problems," he said.

The room erupted in a machine gun of charges.

"He's failing his class work *and* his tests." Social Studies patted her stack of worksheets, the top page crisscrossed with red ink.

Science managed a weak smile that faded before he spoke. "Josh is always polite and helpful, but rarely wants to participate in class."

"He disturbs my class by constantly being out of his seat and telling jokes," English said.

"He is completely unable to concentrate," Math said.

I lifted my hand to stop the barrage and turned to Josh. "Why don't you take a walk while we finish talking."

The change in focus gave me a minute to settle my composure. I was almost visibly quaking and wanted to cover it quickly. I let out a long sigh, hoping it sounded like impatience with the situation instead of the release of anxiety that it was.

Josh flashed me his typical look: an innocent, wrongly accused and facing execution. I nodded toward the door and he left without comment.

It was his first semester and clearly, they hadn't had time to figure out how to deal with Josh yet. When the door closed behind him, I directed my attention to English.

"Josh has always been very strong-minded. I'm a single mother, so he's had to grow up without a father…"

A slight expression crossed her face, but she didn't say anything.

I'd seen the look before. Raw judgment. I brushed it off and continued, "And he's more independent than most boys his age. I taught him to cook and do his own laundry when he was in third grade."

Out of the corner of my eye, I saw an eyebrow rise on the stoic Principal— his only physical movement since the meeting began.

I took a deep breath. "So, obviously, he requires strong direction. If Josh is out of his chair, you need to tell him you'll nail his butt to the seat if he even moves before class ends."

English recoiled like she'd received an invisible slap. "I don't speak to my students that way," she said.

"Well, then I don't know what to tell you. Because I don't have any problems with him at home."

"Perhaps he needs medication," Counselor said. "We've found that students who have Attention Deficit Hyperactivity Disorder really benefit from Ritalin."

A flat, humorless smile pressed my lips together. Don't even go there, lady. "There's nothing wrong with Josh. If you check his file, you'll see that his elementary school already tried to label him."

It was a battle at his last school, constantly defending my position against cognitive testing. I finally gave in, just to prove what I already knew—my son didn't need medication. "If you care to look, you'll see Josh doesn't have A.D.D. or A.D.H.D. No dyslexia. No learning disability. And no processing problems."

Counselor opened Josh's file, shuffled through the stack, and paused to scan the report. I recognized the cover of the document I'd signed last year allowing the school district to test him. She turned to Principal with a slight shake of her head. "Josh doesn't qualify for any special education programs."

I leveled a solid gaze across the table, encompassing the judge and jury. "So, what are you going to do to teach my son?"

They looked at one another blankly as if I'd asked them to prove the world was round.

"We can put him on Friday letters…" Math looked to each of the other teachers.

Counselor went into further detail for my benefit, somehow managing to sound condescending at the same time. "That is a note, signed by each teacher at the end of the week, notifying you of discipline problems, missed assignments, failed tests, detention, et cetera."

And that helps…how? The logic wasn't there.

"Why don't you send home a Monday letter, telling me what Josh needs to do for the week and I'll make sure it gets done?" My quaking feeling had stopped completely.

"It doesn't work that way," English said. A smug curve turned the corners of her lips.

I leaned forward in the chair and locked eyes with her. "And why not?"

Principal stepped in like a referee. "The teachers are too busy to print up their lesson plans for individual students. It takes away from the learning time of the other students."

Was he serious? Bullshit, ass-covering pseudoexcuse. Had the man never read a college class syllabus? Are middle school teachers busier than university professors? What the hell is wrong with this picture?

My right leg twitched and bounced uncontrollably under the table. "Somebody needs to start thinking outside of the box," I said, trying not to completely lose it.

I looked from one face to another and could see it clearly. Without so much as a ripple, they were going to let Josh slip quietly and unnoticed between the cracks in the system. I measured my tone carefully. "Please have the secretary make a copy of my son's records. I'm withdrawing him from this school."

Principal looked excited to play his trump card. "The standard protocol is for the new school to request his records and they will be mailed at that time. To the school."

I reached across the table and pulled Josh's file and a pen from in front of Counselor. I scrawled our address on the cover in oversized letters and slid it across the table to Principal. "Here's your request. I'll be homeschooling." I stood and walked out of the room.

When Josh rose from the bench in the hall, I put my arm around his shoulders and we stepped outside into the ocean-chilled air.

"So, what happened? What did they say?" Josh stopped walking and waited for my answer.

I was the lioness who had fought an entire pack of jackals to save the life of her young cub. My hands shook and the pulse in my head felt like it would burst through my temples.

"I've decided I'm going to homeschool you." The reality of my decision was starting to sink in. "It will be fun, we'll do all kinds of cool stuff," I said.

Josh's forehead wrinkled. "Are you sure? Who's going to teach me math? You suck at math."

"We'll get a tutor if we have to." I forced a smile. "Don't worry, we can do this."

no scent negative associations
Saturday, October 27

There's an old aphorism that some women change boyfriends like they change their underwear. It doesn't work that way with me. I change perfumes whenever my relationships fail.

Contradiction. Uninhibited. Poison. Past boyfriends could be defined by each of these. When a relationship ended, I swore I'd never trust anyone wielding both a smile and a penis ever again. Then I met Kevin, and *never* felt like a really long time.

Kevin was supposed to be a fresh start, full of promises for the future. Unlike the others, Kevin believed in the South Orange County fairytale—the custom tract home, the Lexus SUV, the 2.5 private school honor students, and the incontinent Golden Retriever.

Kevin was *Allure* by Chanel. Soft, warm, and subtle—until he left me. I needed a new perfume. Something without memories attached.

Josh balked ten feet in from the entrance to Nordstrom. "Mom, can I go get a soda at the food court? It stinks in here." He always chose to escape unless it was a store that sold baseball equipment or computer games.

"Can I?" He reluctantly followed me deeper into the store, awaiting my answer.

"No soda. But you can have a lemonade." I handed him a five-dollar bill. "Bring back the right change."

He sprinted toward the doorway into the mall and dodged between the displays like he was running the gauntlet.

I wandered along the perfume counters, fingertips trailing the glass, stopping to sniff samples.

A well-preserved sales shark with a helmet of over-sprayed hair hovered nearby. "Can I help you find something?"

"Not right now, I'm just smelling." I coughed and waved my hand through a fog of perfume.

"Of course..." the woman trailed off, as if finishing her sentence was a waste of time.

My eyes moved across the many displays. Unique bottles always caught my eye first.

Classique by Jean-Paul Gaultier. Nice bottle—a dress form with part of the glass decorated in the shape of a full bustier. I sprayed my wrists and rubbed them together to warm the scent on my skin. I hate those paper tabs; you can never tell how the perfume really smells.

I caught sight of my reflection in the mirrored wall. Someone else was wearing my clothes and my face. I reached up to touch my hair. It was short and weightless. Do I like my hair like this? I tilted my head a little to the side. Would Kevin like my hair like this? The tips tickled the top of my shoulder. I slowly shook my head. The bob swung gently against my neck, a heavy curtain of hair no longer waved along my back.

The sales shark circled and cleared her throat with mock delicacy. "Would you like to buy that?"

Buy it? You mean staring in the mirror catatonically for who knows how long, while clutching a bottle of perfume isn't good for business?

"Yes, please. A set with perfumed lotion," I said.

While she rang up the purchase, Josh appeared beside me with his cup of lemonade. He squeaked out an elaborate tune with the straw by dragging it up and down through the bisected hole in the plastic lid. It sounded a little like the *Gilligan's Island* theme song.

I flashed Josh my stop-that-before-I choke-you look.

"Okay, let's go." I tucked the bag handles into the crook of my arm and walked toward the exit. I paused beside the door and waited for Josh to open it.

He looked at the door and then at me. "Why are we standing here?" He took a deep pull on the straw that ended in a damp slurp.

"Don't you think it's about time you start holding doors open for ladies?"

"You're not a lady, you're my *Mom*," he said.

I've decided that it's the little moments of child rearing that remind me the process is the next best thing to enduring a root canal.

"Humor me," I said.

i write, therefore i am
Sunday, October 28

I stacked the projects in neat piles on my desk and opened my Day Runner to the month-at-a-glance view of November. Deadlines. The writing jobs were marked in green ink—for money. The bills due were red—which basically meant, somebody please shoot me on or before this date. There was more red than green. Always.

I pulled out a blank piece of paper to organize my writing related tasks.

to do list:

1. **Write marketing brochures for computer technical support company and refrigeration systems company.**
    Boring. Guaranteed to knock my creative muse unconscious with bone-dry freelance work. But it bills out at $100 an hour, so that's good CPR.

2. **Meet with start-up magazine publisher to discuss layout and design.**
    Goofy, sweaty guy with the bad idea of creating a magazine for strip club patrons. But he pays for my editorial input—which makes him my new best friend.

3. **Meet with photographer to select stock images for the debut issue.**
    Watch in disgust as photo guy uses a program on his computer to manipulate pictures of women into the "perfect" specimens—further perpetuating eating disorders in young girls and unnecessary plastic surgery in women who try to measure up to images of women who don't really exist.

4. **Write inane features and articles that appeal to mammary-obsessed males with double-digit IQs.**
    Why? Because I'm paid $1,000 a week for it and I'm riding the cash cow until it's butchered by reality.

5. **Come up with a pseudonym.**
    So no one can trace this creative disaster back to me.

I sighed and leaned back in my chair. I may as well stand naked on a street corner with a sign that reads *Will Write For Food* stapled to my forehead.

Writing prostitution. Are real prostitutes too tired at the end of a workday to enjoy sex for personal pleasure? I did know that working as a topless dancer made going out dancing at nightclubs less than appealing.

I pushed aside the freelance to-do list and opened the screenwriting software to my Disney spec script in progress. I watched the cursor blink at the tail of the last sentence I'd written. I wanted to focus on my screenwriting, but it would be a long time until that would pay the bills. The freelance stuff really needed to be done first, but it felt mindless to slap adjectives together so Joe Consumer would buy whatever Company X was selling.

A frustration tantrum was building. Feeding my creative writing muse was like supporting a 900-pound, spoiled gorilla that eats everything. Conferences, seminars, how-to books by every guru in the business, writer's retreats, pitch fests, workshops, networking breakfasts, trade subscriptions, entertainment industry organization memberships. None of it was cheap. Yet, I'd give it all up, right after I gave up breathing.

I squeezed my eyes shut and tried to reach that quiet space of creative peace. I found Kevin's face embossed on my mind in the darkness behind my eyelids.

God, I love him so much. For his beauty, the kindness in his soul—and for his potential. I believed we could accomplish anything through our love and support of each other. He wanted to play golf on the PGA Tour. I wanted the world to embrace my stories. I knew if we worked together, we could make it happen.

I still believed that. But somewhere along the way, he stopped.

grid iron vs. nine iron
Monday, October 29

I heard the phone ring once. Josh called downstairs, "Mom, it's for yooou."

I gave the spoon a final lick, threw away the last of the chocolate pudding cup containers, and reached across the counter to pick up the cordless phone. The sound of Josh hanging up the other end clattered in my ear.

"Hey girl!" Heather's perky voice practically bounced through the line. "Let's go out for Monday Night Football."

I was tempted to pretend she had the wrong number, but she already heard Josh, so reciting the only sentence I knew in Vietnamese wouldn't have worked.

"We can order something greasy and watch the guys...um, I mean, the game," she said.

"Thanks anyway, but I don't think so." Because honestly, I'd rather stay home, lock myself in my room, and cry facedown on the floor until I'm completely feathered with carpet fuzz.

"Well, at least let me buy you a cranberry juice. It'll take your mind off what's-his-name," she said.

Impossible.

"I'm not taking no for an answer. You need this. I'll meet you at the Aliso Viejo tavern in twenty minutes," she said.

If I got into my car right now and drove south at eighty-five miles an hour for twenty minutes, how far away could I get from the AV tavern? Not quite to the Mexican border, probably only to the Camp Pendleton Marine Base.

"Don't even think about standing me up," she said.

It might be good to go out. Kevin doesn't work on Mondays. Maybe he'll come down to hang out with some of his buddies, maybe they'll go to Monday Night Football at the AV tavern, and maybe he'll walk in, see me again, and realize how much he really loves me, and maybe he'll ask me to marry me right there in the middle of the bar in front of everyone. It could happen.

"Okay, I'll go."

When I hung up, Josh leaned on the kitchen counter wearing his let's-make-a-deal face. "Since you're going somewhere, can I have Adam over for dinner?"

"I don't care, but you have to make sure his mother knows I won't be here to supervise."

Josh rolled his eyes. "I don't need you to watch. I've made spaghetti a hundred million times."

I pulled him into a headlock. "Make sure she knows," I said.

"Ack...okay, I will," he choked out the words.

When I turned into the sports bar parking lot, I scanned the aisles looking for Kevin's steel blue truck.

Maybe he's not coming.

Maybe he's just not here yet.

The tavern was filling fast, but I saw Heather waving her arms at the bar like an airline traffic flagman, her short auburn hair bounced with her movements.

"Hey," Heather hugged me tightly and released quickly. "Look at you—your hair. Forget the hair—you're so skinny!"

"Compliments of the break-up diet," I said.

"How much weight have you lost? Are you eating at all? You look sick."

"Eight pounds so far."

"In a week? I wish Derek would break up with me." Heather patted her rounded hips.

No. You don't.

My eyes filled with tears, and my nose tingled, threatening to run.

Heather saw my total breakdown only seconds away. "Let's order some drinks and greasy food." She waved to the bartender and wrapped her arm around my shoulder like the wing of a mother hen. "Are you hungry? Have you eaten anything today?"

"A chocolate whey protein shake with a Hershey bar blended in it for breakfast and five chocolate pudding cups before I got here."

"YEEEAAH! Birdie!" A guy's voice boomed louder than the football announcer on the big screen.

I turned to see three random guys crowded around a video game that stood wedged in the corner between the dartboard and the pool table. It was *Golden Tee*.

Kevin's favorite.

He loved to rout his buddies on the golf course and on the electric greens of that video game.

It still baffled me how grown men could get so wrapped up in video games. There should almost be a screening question prior to the first date—Bachelor #1, Which do you do more often: A. Play video games? Or B. Masturbate?

Kevin played *Golden Tee* whenever we stopped at the neighborhood tavern, always trying to top his last score. He slept and breathed golf in any and every form he could find. Kevin's passion for the game was tangible—the very core of his being radiated the classic mystery of the fifteenth-century game.

So beautiful.

As I peeked over Kevin's shoulder, he spun from the screen to face me. "Did you see that shot, Annette?" He picked me up and twirled me in a kiss.

As usual, Carter and Stan groaned in defeat, but they never stopped trying.

"The next round is on you guys," Kevin said.

Stan went to the bar to order another round of Samuel Adams while Carter dug into his pocket for quarters to buy the next round of golf.

I perched on a barstool near the drink rail and watched Kevin enter his initials in the electronic scoreboard. I poked my straw into the melting ice at the bottom of my glass, slurping the last of the watery remains.

My eyes roved over his tan, lean frame. He turned from the machine and matched my gaze. Kevin walked over and stood between my knees, dotting my forehead and the tip of my nose with kisses. Kevin's lips moved over mine. His kiss blocked out everyone and everything around us. He whispered against my ear, "I love you, Princess."

"That's cranberry juice with a lime, right?" Heather said, dragging me back to reality.

"Uh, yeah…" I pulled out of the fog. "…and light ice."

Will I ever be able to go places I've been with Kevin and not think about him?

A weight of emotion pressed heavily on my chest. The sounds of people drinking, talking, and cheering the game, came as muffled vibrations in my head. I let my eyelids slide closed to block out the room.

"Are you tired?" Heather set her hand lightly on my shoulder.

"Yeah, I think so." My tears began to brim.

"Maybe it's too soon to go out," Heather said.

"Maybe a little."

does mapquest give life directions?
Tuesday, October 30

I jotted notes while Josh peered over my shoulder.

"Thank you for all your information. You've been a great help," I said into the phone before hanging up.

The local contact for the HomeSchool Association of California seemed to be a nice lady. She explained how to file an R4 form with the Department of Education and suggested a list of resources for purchasing textbooks and study guides. There were so many decisions to make. But as a certified education junkie, I was pretty excited about the possibilities.

I turned to the computer screen and went back to browsing the Irvine Valley College online catalogue. "I think I'll enroll us in a language class," I said more to myself than to Josh.

Josh sat on the floor at my feet. "Language? Don't you mean an English class?" he said.

"No. I mean like ASL—an American Sign Language class. That would be fun. And I think it would be easier for you to start with that instead of a foreign language."

Josh looked at me like I'd just grown a third eye. "What good is learning sign language?"

"I dunno. I guess I can always use it to yell at you in public so no one else will know what I'm saying."

"Yeah, that's real funny." Josh rolled his eyes. He pulled the notebook off the desk and scanned the handwritten list of subjects. "Mom, I want Kevin to teach me the pre-algebra. Can I ask him when he gets here?"

A knot instantly tightened in my chest. "I don't think so, sweetie."

"Why? Do you think he won't want to?"

I knew it would come up this week, but I still hadn't prepared what to say. I stood up from the desk chair and motioned for Josh to sit beside me on the edge of the bed.

"You know Kevin has been staying at the company apartment because the drive is so far..."

Josh nodded.

"Well, he won't be coming home on his days off anymore. He wants to live there all the time now."

I bowed my head slightly, hoping Josh wouldn't notice the tears welling in my eyes.

"So, we're moving to Los Angeles with him?" Josh's voice sounded both hopeful and confused.

"No, honey. Kevin and I aren't going to be in a relationship anymore." My tears spilled over.

Josh leaned to wrap his arms around my shoulders in an awkward hug. "It's okay, Mom." He squeezed a little harder. "It's okay if it's you and me again. We don't need him anyway."

I knew his dismissive comment came from his deep loyalty to me. And maybe a desire to mask his own disappointment. Josh liked Kevin, so much that he had even tried to learn to play golf, though I knew he'd rather play baseball. They were both people-pleasers whose quiet emotions ran deep.

I started to say something to draw Josh into a conversation about it, but the stony look on his face made me swallow the words. I silently welcomed his simple statement of closure because if I didn't have to talk about it, he wouldn't discover how weak I really felt.

When Josh left my bedroom, I opened a blank journaling template and began to type. The thoughts poured onto the screen.

How could I possibly go on without Kevin? The end of my Cinderella story left me holding a handful of frog piss. And what the hell was I thinking when I pulled Josh out of school? I'm a moron. How could I possibly teach him anything of value? Maybe I should just embrace the Orange County stereotype: get a boob job, a lobotomy, and hunt for a rich husband—

My cell phone rang "Ding Dong the Witch is Dead"—it could be Valerie, Bonita, Heather, Jaimee, or Chelle—one of the gal pals in my witch posse. I took a break from my diary rant and answered the call.

"So, how are you holding up?" I could hear Valerie's nails tapping a rapid staccato on the keys of her adding machine.

I looked beside my computer monitor at the empty jar of fudge topping, a sticky spoon handle leaning against the inside rim.

"Fine, I guess. Just had lunch and I'm writing in my journal about you."

"Oh, really? So, what does it say?" she asked.

I read the page-long entry to her. She laughed through it—right up until the part about the boob job and the lobotomy.

"Hey, no fair taking shots at me when I'm not around to defend myself." Valerie pretended to be angry, then her tone quickly changed. "That was some funny shit though. You should make that into a book."

"You think so?" Everything I'd tried to write lately sounded like crap.

"Either that or go get a real job," Valerie took her jab to counter the boob smack.

Ever since college, we playfully boxed. Now, in the real world, she was an investment analyst. And as an English major, I was highly qualified to suggest an order of french fries and the opportunity to supersize it.

"Seriously, do you think it would make a good book?" I asked.

"I think you are the only person I know who can make misery funny. I'd buy it."

"Well, maybe I will…" I leaned back in my chair and chewed the inside of my lower lip.

"So, what's the deal with the homeschool thing? Are you really planning to do it? Who's going to teach Josh math? You suck at math."

The call-waiting function on my phone beeped.

"Hang on a sec," I said.

I switched lines. "Craig! Um…I'm on the other line, can you hold?" I squeaked like a strangled mouse. "I'll be right back."

I clicked over.

"Val, it's the producer for the Disney project, oh shit, oh shit. I'll call you back."

My mind raced. I had no new pages to give to him. My muse checked out after Kevin left and I didn't have shit.

I clicked back on the line, "Hi…" The word came out like I was recovering from a marathon.

"Annette, I want to go over some script notes with you, do you have a minute?"

"Yes, of course," I said.

While Craig talked about the pacing in Act II, I stared at the patterns on the scraped ceiling.

I couldn't do it.

There was no way I could possibly write the happy, fluffy, family comedy he wanted. The thought of it made me want to vomit.

"Craig…" I broke into his flow of comments. "I am so sorry, I can't finish this project." I took a breath and continued, trying to get my explanation out before the tears came. "I'm having a hard time dealing with some emotional family stuff, and I know the script will suffer. I can't do this. I'm really sorry."

Craig gently pushed for details. In our first few meetings, we had shared stories about our personal lives, so it wasn't hard to continue. Soon, the complete story tumbled out. In my incoherent babbling, I even admitted I worked as a dancer to pay the bills.

Career suicide. My professional credibility died on the line.

He listened quietly and waited until I finished before responding, "If there's anything I can do, let me know. Don't worry about the script, I have other things in the pipeline. Call me whenever you're ready to take another run at it."

After we hung up, I looked back at the journal page filling my computer screen. The cursor blinked and I stared. Would chronicling all of my break-up misery actually make a good book?

all hollow eve

Halloween
Wednesday, October 31

I heard the sound of Josh's running feet pounding down the stairs. He jumped into the living room and posed with his most menacing glare. "So, how do I look?" He cradled a plastic machine gun against his chest.

"You look great. That costume is perfect," I said.

His man-sized, pin-stripe suit was far too big, but still a lucky find. The thrift store also had a worn pair of wingtips for three dollars and a black fedora for five. A quick stop at a costume store for the black, mock shirtfront and white necktie finished off the look. Josh's slight Italian features sealed the image.

One tween gangster—$25. No retarded Butterick costume pattern to sew—priceless.

Josh grabbed his black plaid pillowcase and headed to the door.

"Don't eat anything until I check it," I said.

"Aw, Mom—"

"I'm serious." I grabbed his retreating coattail.

"Okay, okay, let go. I promise already." He drew an invisible cross on his chest with his index finger and bolted out the door, slamming it closed in the rush of his wake.

I wandered through the living room and stepped over the lounging dog bodies. Nina's long legs and lean form stretched out like a supermodel during a

Sports Illustrated photo shoot. Her paws twitched, perhaps chasing the electric rabbit around the Greyhound racetrack from her youth.

Buddy aimed a lick at my ankle and thumped his tail as I passed. He expended most of his puppy energy wrestling with Josh for over an hour. Adopting the abandoned Rottweiler/Shepherd puppy was a good choice. Rough and tumble enough for a growing boy, even if he was originally a Valentine's present for Kevin.

Kevin. Without him, the house felt hollow.

I paused in the doorway of the kitchen. The night before, Josh and I had carved two funny-faced jack-o'-lanterns for the front doorstep. Now, on squares of paper towels, the pumpkin seeds spread out, nearly dry. I had rinsed them meticulously and lined them up in careful rows. They were ready to salt and bake.

I don't even like pumpkin seeds. And neither does Josh. Kevin likes pumpkin seeds.

With a sweep of my arm, I scattered them into the sink, rinsed them down the drain, and ground them to pieces in the garbage disposal.

I pulled a large plastic bowl from the cupboard and opened the bags of candy bars into it, ready for the parade of greedy little monsters.

Is it a good thing or a bad thing to only buy Halloween candy I like? I poked my fingers into the bowl and tossed the different chocolate bars like a garden salad. I always wonder about the cruel intentions of people who buy candy no one likes.

In the weeks that follow the big night, the ten pounds that Josh collects gets picked over. Then the crappy stuff sits in the bottom of the bowl until Easter when I finally throw it out.

Who says I haven't established any family holiday traditions?

I popped in a DVD of *The Wizard of Oz* and sat cross-legged on the floor between the dogs with the bowl of candy bars in my lap. I turned up the volume on the TV to fill the empty house with voices. The wind began to blow. A tornado was coming. I unwrapped a mini Snickers and popped it into my mouth.

I wished a tornado would carry me far away.

The doorbell rang. Halloween munchkins called out, "Trick or Treat" and peeked into the entryway from the partially open door.

Follow the yellow brick road.

Buddy's eyes lit up. Someone had delivered giant pet toys right to his doorstep. He ran barking and skittering across the entry tiles. Buddy drooled and bumped the children around as I filled their bags with candy. A motherly Bo-Peep scooped up her woolly-headed lamb when Buddy began gnawing on the child's cotton-stuffed tail. Nina kept her distance, watching the chaos from the safety of the living room.

Up and down like a pogo stick, I answered the calls for candy treats. After each round, I retreated to the mental void offered by the great and powerful Oz and the bowl of chocolates. I stared at the screen. The images danced light and dark in front of my eyes. Kevin's absence was tangible.

Dorothy promised there was no place like home.

For her maybe. Mine was a prison of loneliness.

Josh burst through the door, the bulging sack of treats over his padded shoulder. "Mom, check out how much I got already." He dumped the pile onto the dining table. "I'm dropping this off, so I can go and get more." He shook the last of the candy out of the pillowcase.

"Did you eat all that yourself?" Josh pointed to the cemetery of candy wrappers around me on the carpet.

I combed the wrappers into my hand, counting as I went. Fifteen. Sixteen. Seventeen empty wrappers.

Well, it's only like eight regular size candy bars. Which only counts as 3.5 dairy servings according to Jenny Craig. Or maybe it was my Aunt Jenny who said that.

"Don't eat all my candy while I'm gone," Josh said on his way out the door.

I guess that depends on whether there's anything good in the pile or not.

I sat at the table and began checking the wrappers, separating his candy into categories: Chocolate. Hard candy. Gum. Chocolate. Hard candy. Gum.

elementary, my dear watson
Thursday, November 1

After spending the morning helping Josh diagram sentences in his new grammar workbook, I finally sat down to go through the mail.

I pulled an envelope from the pile on my desk, slid my finger under the flap, and felt a biting slice. Damn, a paper cut. Sawing off my hand with a dull butter knife would hurt less than a paper cut puckering the skin on my knuckle. I pressed the curve of my finger to my lips and licked the reddening sliver.

I scanned the cell phone bill. I obviously needed a better minutes plan. The bill for last month's usage was higher than my car payment.

Note to self: Call to cancel family plan. We aren't a family anymore.

Kevin's portion of the bill was higher than normal. I'd have to call and let him know how much to send to cover it. My eyes flicked over the numbers: me, his Mom, work, his golfing buddies. One line jumped off the page.

Ninety-nine minutes.

He never talked on the phone that long—except to me. Who else would he talk to for ninety-nine minutes?

In New York?

Who the hell does he know in New York that he would talk to for ninety-nine minutes? My finger traced across the line to the date.

The night before he broke up with me.

Bile roiled in my stomach.

There was another call to the New York number just minutes before the call to me that morning. That morning when he said he couldn't be with me anymore. I felt flushed and dizzy. The numbers blurred like heat rising from summer asphalt.

Maybe it's just a coincidence.

I shuffled through the rest of the pages. There were calls to that number striping every page. I grabbed the phone, stopping with the handset halfway between my ear and the cradle.

I had to call the number.

But what if a woman answered?

That wouldn't prove anything.

My rational mind argued the case about as successfully as the prosecuting attorney in the OJ trial. I punched autodial number one.

Kevin answered just one ring short of voicemail. "What's up? I'm really busy. I'm in the middle of giving a lesson," he said.

"I just got the cell phone bill. Who lives in New York?"

"I don't have time to go into this right now," he half-whispered.

I stressed each word succinctly. "Who the fuck were you talking to in New York for ninety-nine minutes and again in the morning right before you broke up with me?"

"Geez, what are you doing? Sherlock Holmesing the phone bill?" he asked.

"Who is she?"

"Annette, don't do this. It's just a friend." He sighed heavily. "I can't believe you're doing this. Did you call the number too?"

Hmmm...let's see, what would I say? Hi, I'm Kevin's completely devastated, psycho ex-girlfriend. Um, by any chance, did you have something to do with him dumping me, you fucking bitch?

"No," I said quietly. "I didn't call the number."

I've got far too much pride for that.

"Annette, do yourself a favor. Do me a favor. Don't make this into something it's not."

It really isn't his nature—to be like that. Am I being foolish? Kevin would never cheat. And how could he cheat with a woman who lives three thousand miles away? My thoughts raced around the room mocking my angst.

"Look, I've got to get back to work, just send me the bill so I can pay it. I'll talk to you later, okay?" He hung up.

But none of it felt okay.

doubt cake

2 lovers, separated
1 unbleached cellular phone bill, well-sifted
1 imported woman's phone number
8 oz. unsweetened excuses
1/2 cup suspicion
1/4 cup distrust

Beat 1 lover with anxiety until stiff, then boil in betrayal until completely softened to tears.

Blend suspicion and distrust, sprinkle liberally with excuses.

Pour mixture into pan greased with intuition.
Bake until frustration sets.

Serve cold. Topped with crushed nuts of ex-boyfriend, if regionally available.

Yield: Overall queasiness.
Unlimited servings.
Nutritional Value: None.

Guaranteed 3 lb. weight loss.

the chicken dance
Monday, November 5

"You'll never guess in a million years where I'm going. It's something I told you I'd never consider doing in this lifetime." I juggled the cell phone and merged onto the freeway, flicking the blinker signal.

"Oh my gosh, you're going to a therapist, I'm so proud of you!" Bonita squealed through the phone.

Maybe now she would stop nagging about it. "You'll be happy to know that the head mechanic I'm going to has a PhD and says she does hypnotherapy, homeopathic healing, Reiki, and all that new age crap. As long as she doesn't get all mumbo-jumboey on me, I'll try it," I said.

"You'll be so glad you did. Make sure you call me when it's over and tell me if my diagnosis was right."

Bonita, the self-appointed armchair psychiatrist in our group of friends, took the liberty of researching all the various neuroses in the DSM IV that she thought applied to each of us and gave her diagnosis at Valerie's last dinner party. I regularly joked that Freud had been reincarnated as a petite Latina.

I figured Marisa would appreciate the irony of me going to a therapist. She knew I thought the most irritating and overused Orange Countyism was any sentence that began with: "My therapist says...."

But with the way things were going, maybe seeing a therapist wouldn't be such a bad idea.

I ranted non-stop for forty-five minutes, pouring out my feelings about Kevin.

The therapist's analysis: Kevin and I had a "teepee" relationship, both leaning against each other for support.

"And that's not healthy," she informed me, wagging her finger, and sending her plump arm swaying. "If the relationship is to prosper, you both need

41

to stand straight beside each other and pursue your own career goals while maintaining a loving and supportive association."

It sounded simple enough. Too bad he dumped me before we got that far.

"Okay, Doc. What can I do to fix him so we can get back together?" I said.

"We need to work on you," she replied.

So, she hypnotized me. Or at least, I think she did. Or at least, I think she thinks she did. I'm really not sure.

She started out by turning on a lilting, flute music CD. I thought it was a little goofy, but I was trying to go with it. She lit a scented candle and dimmed the lights. I reclined in a soft leather chair. An actual couch would've been just way too much to get over.

Voice low and monotone, she began walking me through a lush garden toward the temple of my mind. "Now, picture your temple," she said in a soothing tone.

I had just started to relax, but that comment sent my brain into a tailspin. It was like rummaging in my closet to pick an outfit. I couldn't decide what my temple should look like.

She had already left the doorstep of my temple and was talking about something else, but I was busy creating and mentally erasing different structures.

A Spanish mission. That's not it.

A white church with a steeple. No, definitely not.

An English country cottage. Nope, don't like roses.

I finally decided on a palm-frond hut on the beach with a doorstep to the ocean. Then I ran to catch up with her in my mental pineapple garden.

Maybe I watch too much TV, but I thought a hypnotist could make you do the chicken dance and you wouldn't even know it. I heard everything she said—once I got past the temple thing. I heard her take a drink from her cup, and even shift positions in her chair. Maybe to fart, but I didn't smell anything, except that stupid candle. Which is good. Maybe that's what it was for. Camouflage.

"You are content, empowered, and motivated," she said.

Then she did that count backward thing to wake me up. I felt like popping my eyes open and saying: "Okay, I'm back. You can stop counting now." But I didn't want to hurt her feelings, so I blinked a few times and stretched.

I thanked her, we hugged, and I mumbled something about calling her again. It was like the cliché of a bad date.

As I was driving down the freeway, I thought about the experience. It was the weirdest thing. I don't think I was hypnotized, but I can't explain the sense of peace I felt inside. I decided to test it out to see if it worked, so I called Kevin.

"Hi," I said after a long pause.

"Uh, hi," Kevin said, clearly not sure where the conversation was going. "What's up?"

"Um...not much." He sounded intentionally vague. "How are you doing?"

"I'm fine. What about you?"

He hesitated a minute. "I'm good."

"Good. Well, I'll talk to you later," I said.

"Okaay." Kevin still sounded baffled.

I hung up and let out a deep breath. The hypnotism worked. I was okay talking to him.

It was the first time since we broke up that I could talk to him and not burst into tears. It felt like progress. It felt good. I wondered how many times I would have to go back to therapy to keep that feeling.

fear, the other white meat
Friday, November 9

The roller coaster car rocketed past us. Every seat held screaming riders. I followed it up the tracks with my eyes and shook my head. No way. Magic Mountain's "The Riddler" didn't look like anything I wanted to entrust with my life. With my luck, the seatbelt would break and I'd be shot head first into a hotdog stand.

"C'mon, Mom, don't chicken out now."

"Where's the Dumbo ride?" I looked around. "That's more my speed."

Josh made a sound like a leaky car tire. "That's Disneyland." He waved his arms. "This is more fun."

Yeah, getting the piss scared out of me and throwing up my nine dollar and seventy-five cent veggie burger sounds like a blast.

Josh wanted an amusement park day for our mother/son date. It was his choice this time around. Obviously, this was my punishment for the trip to the natural history museum.

We mugged for pictures in a photo booth. I planted a kiss on his cheek in one shot. In the rest of the photo strip, Josh either had his eyes crossed or his tongue sticking out. Typical.

He pulled on my arm, "Hurry Mom, we have to get to the next ride before the line gets longer."

Somehow I made it through the day and didn't die.

Within a half hour of returning home, Josh fell asleep on the living room floor watching a Jackie Chan DVD. Buddy and Nina lay stretched out beside him. I stepped through the obstacle course of bodies to retrieve the remote and click off the TV.

The silent house made me feel restless and the room held a damp chill. I reached for a throw blanket to cover Josh, but it only covered to the back of his knees, so I flipped the switch on the fireplace.

Instant flames. No logs. No newspaper. No matches. No fuss. No ambiance either, but at least I wasn't crouched over a pile of wood shavings clicking two rocks together.

I wandered into the kitchen and stared into the gaping 'fridge. I bypassed the real food and pulled a jar of hot fudge topping off the door rack, popped the safety top, and dug in. A thick wad of fudge clung to the spoon. Each lick smeared my tongue with smooth, sweet chocolate. I held a strip of cool fudge in my mouth until it melted—creamy and satisfying. I sat on the carpet in front of the fire and ate the entire contents of the jar while staring into the flames.

Kevin always said eating the fudge straight out of the jar was disgusting. God, I miss him so much.

My cell phone rang, interrupting my thoughts. *The Addams Family* theme ringtone signaled that it was either my mother, my sister, or my cousin.

"Hey, what're ya doin'?" Cousin Melissa exhaled a breath that sounded like it held a plume of cigarette smoke. "Let's go hang at the Yard House in Irvine Spectrum."

"Nah, I think I want to stay home tonight."

"It's Friday night," she informed me like it mattered. "Get off your ass and let's go out."

"No, really, I'm planning to take a bubble bath and read."

"Bullshit. You're gonna sit in a tub of water until it gets cold and cry about Kevin. You better get ready, I'm coming over."

"I'm not going," I said.

She ignored me and kept talking. "You can drive us there, so I can get drunk. Oh, and I'm spending the night, so change the sheets. I don't want to sleep in your old, dried-up tears."

Family. You can't stand them, but you can't kill them.

Black suede boots. Black skinny jeans. Black V-neck top. Mascara. Lipstick. Done.

I shook Josh's shoulder. "Hey, Wonderboy, wake up. Let's get you upstairs to bed."

"Huh?" Josh wiped the drool from the corner of his mouth. He blinked and rubbed his eyes open. "Why are you all dressed up?"

I hooked a thumb in the direction of Melissa who leaned against the doorway. She fiddled with the belt of the black leather jacket cinched around her narrow waist.

Buddy nudged Melissa's leg, looking for someone to rub his head.

"Go away, dog. You're getting hair on me." She pushed against him with her knee.

"Hey Cousin Mel." Josh lifted a droopy hand in her direction. "Have fun, Mom." He plowed a kiss along my cheek and staggered up the stairs, dragging the blanket behind him.

Buddy left Melissa and galloped up the stairs ahead of Josh. Nina quietly followed.

"Goodnight baby, I'll be home in a few hours. Call me on the cell if you need anything."

"G'nite," I heard Josh call out just before the flop of his body hit the mattress.

Melissa smoothed her platinum blonde hair and rubbed her pink, glossy lips together. "Aren't you glad I'm getting you out of this zoo?" She stepped out the front door into the glow of the porch light.

I locked the door behind us. "Yeah, I'm sure it'll be fun," I lied.

turkey fest
Wednesday, November 21

"I called-in to ditch work. Let's go bar-hop." Jaimee's tone sounded like she was preparing for a ten-day vacation instead of one night out.

"I don't know..." I paused with the phone cradled on my shoulder.

I'd have to call off work too. And dealing with drunk guys at a nightclub was too much like being at work—minus the tips as an incentive. And going places with Jaimee made me feel invisible.

Tall, and darkly exotic, she immediately attracted attention. Jaimee could make a burlap sack look like haute couture, but her six-pack abs were always displayed between the standard clubbing gear of low-rise jeans and a body-hugging, cropped top. I knew exactly what people thought when they saw us together: the carousel horse and the wooden pony.

kevin and the kübler-rossian process

"We have to go out tonight," Jaimee whined. "The night before Thanksgiving always goes off the hook."

I switched the phone to my other ear and made an audible groaning noise in my throat.

"C'mon, go with me. I don't want to go alone," she said.

"Okay, fine. I'll go."

We hung up and I dialed the number for the club. I had to yell to be heard over the music. "Sunshine, transfer me to Nate."

He picked up on the first ring. "Yeah?" His voice rumbled from his chest like it emerged from the depths of a canyon.

"Nate, this is Beth. Take me off the schedule for tonight. I'm having some trouble with my eyes."

"What's wrong with your eyes?" I could hear his smile tugging at the end of the question.

"I can't see coming in to work tonight," I said.

It was a joke we shared over the last five years. Nate was the most laid-back manager I'd ever worked for. Corporate middle management could've taken employee relations lessons from him.

"Haven't seen you in a couple weeks. You back in writing mode again?" he asked

"I wish. I just need to get out tonight. I'm on the schedule for Friday, Saturday, and Sunday. From nine until two. I promise I'll make it in."

Nate had plenty of girls who wanted to make money, so he never made a big deal over call-ins. A part-time job working as a dancer was an unfortunate necessity, but until I became rich and famous from my writing, it would help pay the bills. And best of all, it was flexible.

I waited in the parking lot of Del Taco. It was a halfway point between our houses, just off Interstate 5 at Alicia Parkway.

47

Jaimee pulled up in her slick, black BMW and I slid into the smooth leather seat.

"I brought that belt you wanted to borrow," she said, motioning to the glove box.

I pulled out the belt and worked it through the loops of my jeans. The rhinestone buckle glittered in the passing streetlights.

Jaimee merged at the Y to the 405 Freeway North toward the Newport Beach 55. Destination: Josh Slocum's, Dennis Rodman's nightclub.

"I wonder if Kevin is coming down to his Mom's tomorrow." With my forehead resting against the window, I watched the ribbon of asphalt slide under the car.

Maybe I should pop by to visit. Or maybe I should just poke a fork in my eye. That would be equally painful.

"I think you should stop wondering what he's doing and get on with your life," Jaimee said as she pulled off the exit. "You need to get over it."

"Like you're over your ex?"

"Well at least I'm trying. Why do you think I wanted to go out tonight?" she said.

At the club entrance, we flashed our pink VIP cards to the gatekeeper. Rodman's freaky face was nowhere to be seen, but it was only 11:30—still early. We weaved our way toward the bar. The music pumped and a melding of bodies bumped together rhythmically on the tiny dance floor.

Jaimee squeezed between the mass of people waiting at the bar to flag the bartender. Several guys turned to check her out.

I watched a parade of twenty-something hoochies pass. The mandatory attire for the evening seemed to be thong underwear pulled high enough to pass for a back brace and breast implants the size of geography globes.

I'm old and grossly overdressed. Now I remember why I never go north of the Y.

A gorgeous nightclub panther appeared from behind my right shoulder. "What're you doing here all by yourself?" he asked. His dark hair stood up, perfectly gelled into dangerous-looking spikes.

I couldn't help but notice the size of his arms. The curve of his biceps strained against the armholes of his black knit shirt. A tribal band tattoo ringed one arm. My eyes followed the shirt stretched smooth across the square muscles of his chest and down to the outlined bars of his abs.

Maybe twenty-five years old—max.

When I dragged my eyes back up to meet his, he smiled. It was a smile that said he knew exactly how good he looked.

With our gaze locked, he flicked the tip of his tongue out just enough to show off the silver toggle pierced through it. He caught the toggle between his front teeth and jiggled it slightly before letting it retreat back inside.

Did he just make a blatant offer of oral sex?

A slight smile played at the corner of his mouth. His eyes slowly roved over my frame, coming to rest solidly on my lips.

I felt my body flush and tingle.

"Finally!" Jaimee stepped beside me, a glass of cranberry juice in her outstretched hand. "I swear that was the slowest bartender."

"I'll be right back." I motioned toward the bathroom and launched into the crowd.

I stepped into the dim shoebox and took a deep breath to shake off the encounter with Junior the Tongue Stud; I definitely wasn't ready to go down that path. I leaned toward the mirror to touch up my lipstick and see how the Botox had settled in.

My Achilles Heel: I don't want to be old. In South Orange County, visible aging is considered a serious affliction. Inside the Newport Beach city lines, I'm pretty sure it's against the law.

Jaimee heard Botox called a miracle cure for wrinkles and she twisted my arm to get me to go with her to the dermatologist a week ago to try it.

Okay, so maybe she didn't have to twist too hard.

There is definitely something to be said about a woman who will actually pay hundreds of dollars to have a doctor inject a deadly bacterium into her face just to avoid having wrinkles.

I'm not a needle person, so it took a rubber stress ball squeezed in one hand, and Jaimee's hand in my other, to keep me from taking a knee-jerk kick at the doctor's nuts. The needle pricks didn't really hurt, but every time he pierced the skin, my forehead squeaked like a sautéed onion. I could hear it inside my head and the sound made me shudder.

When the Botox started to kick in, my left eyebrow sat a quarter of an inch higher than the right. I had an involuntary perplexed look on my face for two days. During which time, I contemplated sneaking into the dermatologist's house and killing him in his sleep. Then it evened out.

I finished applying lipgloss to my peach-colored masterpiece and leaned closer to the mirror to touch up my lashes. I lifted my eyebrows and went slack-jawed in the typical trout-mouthed application of mascara. Then my forehead seized up.

What the hell?

Both eyebrows were stuck in the upright and locked position like an airline tray table. I looked like someone had just surprised the shit out of me.

"No! No! No! No!" I smacked my forehead with my palms trying to get it to let go.

I can't go out there looking like this.

An image flashed in my head of the dermatologist standing blindfolded in his office, a bottle of vodka in one hand, and a Botox needle in the other, playing a game of Pin-The-Eyebrow-On-The-Old-Lady.

Fucker.

Now what am I going to do?

A few minutes later, Jaimee pushed open the door. "Annette, are you—" She stalled when she saw my face. "What happened? You look...scared."

"My forehead is stuck." The complete absurdity of my situation balanced my emotions precariously; my eyes filled with tears.

"Holy shit." Jaimee stifled a giggle. "That sucks."

We burst out laughing together.

"Here, let me help." Jaimee paddled my forehead with her fingertips while holding the back of my head with her other hand.

It looked like a Benny Hinn spiritual revival. The only thing missing was some zealot yelling: "You're saved."

I pulled away from Jaimee when two girls entered the bathroom. "How are we going to get me out of here?" I whispered.

"Just walk behind me and keep your head down," Jaimee said.

We pushed through the crowd toward the front door. Junior the Tongue Stud didn't notice when we passed. He was too busy chatting up one of the contestants for Miss Rocky Mountains in her thong suspenders.

Outside, Jaimee rushed the valet to get the car. I could feel my forehead beginning to release. Within seconds, the cramp, or whatever it was, completely disappeared.

"It's gone." I reached to smooth my hand from one temple to the other. "I'm sorry to ruin the night, did you want to go back inside?"

Jaimee surveyed the parking lot. "Nah, it looks like everyone is leaving anyway. Let's just go back to Del Taco and go through the drive-thru. I'm starving."

The valet pulled up and opened Jaimee's door. Before she could get in, a staggering Colin Farrell wannabe invaded her personal space. "Hey, you're fiiine. Where ya goin'?"

"Excuse me." Jaimee plucked his hand from the frame of her car, climbed in, and closed the door.

"Yeah, you think you're hot shit, well that's only a 3 Series BMW, so try to get over yourself," he spit-sprayed the side window with his slurring.

Who says there are no princes in Newport Beach?

norman rockwell slept here

Thanksgiving
Thursday, November 22

Josh sprinted from the car to the front door. As I climbed out of the seat, I juggled the keys and my purse. "Don't just barge in. Knock first," I called out to him, bumping the car door closed with my hip.

"Mom, I practically lived here. Sandi won't care if..." The sound of his voice faded as he ran inside.

I entered the living room just in time to catch the reunion.

"Look at you, you're so big." Sandi hugged Josh tightly against her apron. "Tom, come look at Josh, he has little hairs on his face."

"How's it going, big guy?" Tom pulled Josh into a hug and clapped his back. "Don't you have an important birthday coming up?" Tom pushed his wire-rimmed glasses up the bridge of his nose and settled himself back on the couch.

"Only twenty-one more days 'til I'm a teenager."

Visiting the Loomis family was like time travel back to the 1950s.

It was the kind of family I always wanted, but never had. Meals together, the entire family gathering to watch the classic movie channel in the evenings. On the weekends, Mom baking, the kids making crafts, and Dad puttering in the garage. It was all so perfect.

Perfectly enviable.

Norman Rockwell would've blown his load all over the canvas sketching a Loomis family scene.

Josh and I were invited into their world when Sandi answered an angst-filled ad from a struggling single mother seeking reliable childcare for a six-month-old baby boy.

"I'll only watch him for a few weeks until you find a permanent sitter," Sandi said.

How can twelve years pass so quickly?

After all the greetings were exchanged, I sat and swiveled on a wooden stool, breathing in the smells of Sandi's cooking. It had always been like this. She moved around the small kitchen like she moved in her own skin. The gray hair dusting her temples was the only marker of passing time.

I watched Sandi sprinkle flour into the bubbling gravy and stir it with a large spoon.

She turned to face me. "I'm glad you came, we're all glad you came. It's important to be with family for Thanksgiving."

"I should drive out to visit more often…" My half-promise sounded weak as soon as the words crossed my lips.

Josh and I had only moved sixty miles away, but somehow the time just flew by. Sandi's house was a safe haven, my surrogate family. I almost forgot how much I'd missed them.

Her smile told me she understood.

In the early years, I knew I served as a walking cautionary tale for her daughters. They had the chance to observe the trials of a young woman who was living outside of their Mormon lifestyle. Way outside. But it didn't bother me because Sandi treated Josh with the same love that she showed for her own children. After time, the distinct lines of our differences faded. Sandi became a mentor, a mother, and a friend.

Her daughters, now with families of their own, moved between the hot stove and the dining area, setting the long table, and tending to their spouses and gurgling babies.

Josh sat on the carpet and set up a block tower with three-year-old, Shay. "Is she my niece or am I her nephew?" he asked.

"You're her uncle," Tina, Sandi's eldest daughter said.

"I can't believe I'm an uncle three times already." Josh watched the two babies crawl across the carpet.

I sat quietly and soaked it all in. I wanted this. Kevin and I could've had this.

We sat down as a family to a hand-passed parade of All-American tastes. The conversation buzzed around me like the hum of a favorite song. I felt so close to everyone and yet so far away.

The tangible love in the room left me feeling more alone than ever.

envy pie

Crust:
1 box pre-made pale green covetous dough

Filling:
3 cups pre-soured craving berries
1 cup pre-sifted jealousy
2 tbsp. pre-softened longing

Mix jealousy and longing by hand until thick, hard lump forms in your throat. Slowly crush craving berries into mound of narcissistic pulp.

Roll pastry dough until emotionally flat, press firmly into pan pre-greased with unfulfilled dreams. Pinch edges.

Dump filling like a rejected girlfriend into unprepared crust.

Burn at an insanely high temperature. Prick center with something sharp to determine level of lingering hunger.

Serve alone.

Yield: Intense yearning.
Unlimited servings.
Nutritional Value: None.

Guaranteed 2 lb. weight loss.

five hours in purgatory
Monday, November 26

"I'm coming by to pick up the last of my clothes, the golf pictures in the living room, and a few things from the garage. Are you going to be around?"

Absently, I wrapped the phone cord around my index finger until it turned magenta. I hadn't seen him in over a month. "I'll be here," I said quietly as my stomach twisted and bucked.

"I was hoping maybe you could be somewhere else while I'm there. It would be easier for me," Kevin said.

Fuck easier. What part of this is supposed to be easy for me?

I should have said it, but "Okay" came out of my mouth instead. I think I meant: "Okay, I understand it will be easier for you." But it really didn't matter because I had no intention of going anywhere. I hoped that maybe if Kevin saw me again, he'd change his mind.

"I'll be leaving here in about ten minutes," he said before hanging up.

As soon as the handset hit the cradle, I ran to the closet and scanned the racks. I wanted to look good, but didn't want to look like I was trying too hard. That would be too humiliating.

I changed outfits five times, finally deciding on something that was simple and casual. I surveyed my reflection in the mirror: a pair of relaxed-fit Calvin Klein jeans that showed I'd already lost fifteen pounds in a month, and a powder blue T-shirt that hugged my petite, braless curves. No shoes, just barefoot. I fluffed my hair, brushed my teeth, tinted my lashes with mascara, and dabbed a light coat of clear gloss on my lips.

Perfect.

Outside, I looked pulled together and in control. Inside, I was an emotional train wreck.

I padded down the hall to the homeschool zone. The third bedroom that we originally intended as a guest room was easy to set up with a computer desk, overstuffed reading chair, and a row of bookcases. I gave Josh free rein to decorate the walls with his skateboard posters.

With his back to me, I saw Josh engrossed in playing a game of *Myst* on the computer. "Done with your homework yet?" I asked.

He jumped like he'd been shocked with a cattle prod. "Geez Mom! You scared the crap outta me!"

"Guilty conscience?"

"No, I finished. See all this that I did." He handed his essay and two work-sheets to me. "I did the Aleks math program too. You can check the hours log online if you don't believe me."

"I'll take a look at it later. I just wanted to tell you Kevin is coming by to pick up some of his things."

I saw Josh's lips pull together in a taunt line. His eyes narrowed slightly. "I don't want to see him. He left and he made you cry." His whole body quivered with tension. "I hate him."

I had no idea what to say to Josh's outburst, so I stepped beside his chair and stroked the top of his head. He leaned against my abdomen and I held him quietly for a moment. I couldn't tell him his feelings were wrong, but I wouldn't fuel them either.

"You don't have to be here, if you don't want to," I said softly.

Josh stood up from the chair. "I'm gonna ride my bike to Carl's Jr. and get a burger," his voice cracked slightly, "then wait for Adam at the bus stop." He grabbed his jacket off the chair and left the room. "Call me at Adam's when he's gone."

I wandered back into my room and flopped across the bed to wait. It would take Kevin at least an hour to drive down from Los Angeles. I opened a book and tried to pass the time by reading, but the words blurred across the page. The time passed with me staring at the binding between the same two pages, feeling sick to my stomach and wondering what it would be like to see him again.

When I heard the front door open and Kevin call up the stairs, my body flushed hotly, making my hands shake when I closed the book. Kevin came around the corner of the landing and stepped into the bedroom doorway.

Seeing him crushed my heart and my lungs felt too tight to breathe. I walked over and looked up into his clear blue eyes. In a passing thought: I wondered if he'd say anything about my short hair.

"Hi." The word escaped my lips in a breathy whisper.

Wordlessly, Kevin wrapped me into a hug. Pressed up against him, I could feel the length and warmth of his body through his clothes. The familiar feeling, the shape of his back in my hands, was bittersweet. I buried my face into his shirt and inhaled his scent.

So many memories, so many possibilities—I couldn't let go.

We sank to our knees on the floor. Minutes passed and the tears flowed between us.

"I am so sorry." He touched my damp cheeks with his fingertips. "I never meant to hurt you."

"Kevin, I love you so much, please don't do this." Sobs choked my plea into choppy gulps.

His apologies ran unchecked. "I tried. I did. I tried, but I can't anymore. I'm so sorry, please don't hate me. It's so hard for me to do this, it's killing me." His eyes begged me to understand.

"Then why?" I looked into his eyes while teardrops printed exclamation points on my T-shirt.

He rose from the floor and scrubbed his eyes with the palms of his hands. "This is why I didn't want you to be here. I knew this would happen."

Kevin walked into the closet and began gathering his polo shirts from the hangers. I stepped beside him, lifting several from the dowel.

"Don't help, Annette. I can't handle that. You don't need to help me pack." He paused with an armload of clothing and looked into my eyes. "Just stop."

Kevin walked out of the room and down the stairs to his truck.

I sat on the vanity counter with a pile of his shirts across my lap and waited for him to return.

There had to be a way to make him stay.

Kevin came in and reached to take the mound of shirts. I placed one hand atop the pile to stay his motion.

"Tell me why. Tell me why I'm not the one."

I had to know.

"Don't make me do this." His eyes filled with tears and he shook his head.

Sobs tore at my throat. "It's me. Isn't it? Something about me isn't good enough. Just admit it."

"No, Annette. I won't say that."

"Then tell me what it is!" I pushed against his chest.

Kevin gathered my arms together and pulled me close. I could feel the weave of his shirt absorbing my tears.

"Just let go," he whispered.

"I can't. It's been two years. You can't expect me to just go on like we never made plans for a future together. You said I saved you after your divorce. You *said* you wanted to spend the rest of your life with me…"

He was close. Close enough to kiss. The tip of my tongue slid out to wet my lips. Just once more. I wanted so much to taste his kisses and feel him want me.

"Things changed." Kevin pulled away and straightened his shirt. "Can't we just leave it at that?"

"Are you saying you don't love me anymore?" Kevin's sweet face swam in my blurred vision.

"I'm saying I had to start pulling away and turning off my feelings for you. Too many things weren't working."

"I don't understand. What wasn't working?" My mind scrambled to make sense of his reason.

"I can't give you and Josh what you need right now. I need to focus on my golf if I ever expect to make it on tour. And you need to focus on your writing so you can get out of that club."

I took a brave shot at levity. "Maybe it will work out for us in the future… sometime down the road…when we're both rich and famous." I tried to smile through my tears.

My comment released him from our emotional tug o' war. "Maybe it's serendipity," he said.

A raspy laugh clawed at my chest. That wasn't a typical guy thing to say.

I reached out to touch him intimately. "We could just have sex."

Kevin moved away from my hands. "You know we can't do that." He took another step back. "Because it would never be just sex."

There wasn't anything left to say, and there was nothing I could do to make him stay. My heart begged him not to go and promised I'd do anything just to be with him, but no sound crossed my lips.

Kevin collected his pile of shirts and left the room.

I couldn't bear to sit in our room alone, not as long as he was still in the house. I followed him downstairs to wait while he packed. I sat on the stairs and studied his every detail, touching him with my eyes on each pass he made through the door.

The November air chilled my bare feet numb. Huddled on the stair step, my body shivered uncontrollably. I moved to the marble hearth of the fireplace and sat holding a fistful of tissues. They disintegrated in my hands as I watched him carry away box after box of his stuff. I held back the sobs, but the tears flowed freely.

When the truck was full, Kevin readied to leave. I cast my eyes to the floor, studying the pale nubs of the carpet. My hair swung forward to hide my face. I couldn't watch him walk out the door for the last time.

Kevin kneeled beside me. The hiss of heat from the gas fireplace wasn't warm enough to reach the chill in the marrow of my bones. "Hey," he said, ducking to look at my tear-swollen eyes. "I just want to say one last thing."

I felt my heart breaking from the weight of sorrow pressing against my chest. I couldn't look into his eyes.

"I want you to know that I'm still going to pay half the rent until the lease is up. And whether you believe me or not, I will always cherish the time we spent together. You will always be special to me, and I will always love you."

My throat knotted tightly, I didn't respond.

I couldn't.

Kevin rose to his feet and walked away. Then I heard the door click softly behind him.

pine box or bust
Wednesday, December 5

I looked at the digital clock in the dashboard: 3:00 A.M.

The club was busy tonight. I was tired. Exhausted. It seemed to take forever to count up the ones and divide the money to pay out the house, the DJ, and the bouncers. Even the seven-mile trip home seemed to take longer than usual. The only part of the drive I remembered was waking up at a stoplight. I had no idea how many changing light cycles I'd slept through. I put the windows down, hoping the cold air would keep me awake the rest of the way home.

When I pulled into the garage, I thumbed the remote to close the roll-up door and laid my head back against the headrest. So tired. I didn't have the energy to move. I just wanted to rest a few minutes before going inside.

The carbon monoxide pumped into the chilly, cement garage, displacing the air. My eyelids felt heavy. My body slowly sank into the soft embrace of the bucket seat while the car engine continued to idle. Silence, like cotton, padded my thoughts, making them thick and slow.

It seemed like such a wonderful way to rest. The seat held me like a cradle. It would be easy to sleep, so quietly, so much peace...

But my screaming obligations shook me awake while my mind played out disjointed thoughts about the horrible consequences if I continued to let the engine run.

I wouldn't want Josh to find me.

Not like that.

Blue-faced with my tongue hanging out and my cute jeans full of feces pieces.

Responsibility was the only thing that always kept me going. Josh couldn't raise himself. If I'd ever made a commitment to anyone, it was to him. When he was only a few hours old, I promised that I would always be there for him. He had become the only constant in my life and I couldn't leave him alone.

If I died, Kevin would probably think I did it because he left. But it wouldn't be the truth. As far back as I could remember, the same darkness came for me every winter and made me feel tired all the time.

I switched off the engine and pulled the key from the ignition. The nail on my index finger caught in the key ring, tore to the quick, and snapped off.

"Damn!" I plunged my sore finger into my mouth.

I stumbled out of the car and pressed the garage door opener to release the gases into the night.

Silently, I padded upstairs in the stillness of the house and fell across our empty bed, still dressed in my clothes. Slumber came quickly and my near fatal mistake faded into a sea of foggy dreams.

teen birthday with a titty surprise
Wednesday, December 12

I think the tradition started with Josh's first birthday when I bought a Baskin Robbins roll cake with chocolate chip ice cream inside. He'd had one every year since.

I stepped out of the ice cream parlor and balanced cake number thirteen, while I juggled the keys to open the car door.

The seat? Or the floor?

Even after so many years, I never managed to get the cake all the way home without it rolling against the side of the box and messing up the frosting.

Josh was out front riding bikes with Adam and two other neighborhood boys when I arrived.

"Is that my cake? Can we have it now?" Josh laid his BMX bike on its side and reached out to take the box.

"Paws off. No cake until after dinner," I said, lifting it away from him. I felt the cake roll and bump against the side.

I left the boys to jump curbs and a homemade wooden ramp on the little street in front of the identical Crackerjack-boxes in our quiet, gated community.

After I stowed the cake in the freezer, I started dinner. Josh's favorite: Mexican lasagna—a 9x13 casserole, double-layered with white corn tortillas, tomatillo sauce, refried black beans, cooked brown rice, stewed tomatoes, diced green chilies, black olives, and jack cheese. I preheated the oven to 350 degrees and set the timer for forty minutes.

I'd have just enough time to get ready for work, eat dinner and cake with the boys, and go.

I took another lap around the club and scoped out the prospects for my next private dance campaign. December was always a busy month, no matter what night of the week. Husbands would tell their wives they were going out Christmas shopping, then spend thirty minutes in the mall and three hours at the local strip club.

I checked the time on my cell phone and decided to call Josh before it got too much later. It was too noisy out on the floor, so I wandered into the back dressing room.

"Hey Wonderboy, I'm just calling to say goodnight and make sure you brushed your teeth." I dug a mint out of the Altoids tin in my moneybox and popped it into my mouth.

"Not yet. I'm having another piece of my cake and watching *Dogma*, but it's almost over. Is work good?"

"I'm really busy, it's slammed tonight. I can barely keep up with all the drink orders."

One of the dancers touching up her makeup turned to me and raised her eyebrows.

The curtain into the backroom parted as Brandy pawed her way through it, her thin, bleached hair disheveled by the heavy velvet folds.

"Fuckin' clumsy sonofabitch!" She staggered and almost fell. "He tried to grab my tit and spilled his whole fuckin' beer on me." She stopped in the middle of the room to use the wadded dress in her hand to wipe the wetness from the large tattoo on her stomach.

I motioned with my hand for her to keep her voice down and pointed to the phone pressed against my ear.

Brandy scowled at me and reached out to steady herself with the edge of the makeup counter. She missed and stumbled into me, directing her crimson mouth less than six inches from my phone. "We're all fuckin' strippers, nobody's fuckin' quiet. It's a strip club. Fuckin' deal with it."

I backed her into the wall of lockers and held the cell phone against my bare abdomen. "Shut up," I hissed in an angry whisper, "It's my son." I glared at Brandy and walked away.

I stepped into a bathroom stall, closed the door behind me, and lifted the phone to my ear. "Hey Wonderboy, you still there?"

"What was that all about?" he asked, a sharp edge to his voice.

"Just some girl. She's drunk."

"I guess so."

There was an awkward silence.

"Well, I have to get back to work. Don't stay up too late. I love you," I said, struggling to sound as if nothing had happened.

"I won't. See you in the morning, love you too."

I slammed open the stall door and went looking for Brandy. I found her perched precariously on one of the wooden stools in the makeup area.

"What the fuck were you thinking?" I yelled. "That was my son. And he thought I was a cocktail waitress until you opened your big mouth."

"Well, fuck, you shouldn't be on the phone with your kid back here. What the fuck did you expect? Get over it, so now he knows. Big deal." She shrugged and looked away.

I wanted to reach out and choke the stupidity out of her. "Unbelievable," I said, turning on the heel of my platform stilettos.

I brushed through the velvet curtain. Four hours left in the shift.

Happy thirteenth birthday, son. Just thought you should know, Mommy is a stripper.

homeschool park days
Thursday, December 13

"What if they're all weird?" Josh's anxiety overflowed in his tone.

"I talked to the mom who organizes the group. She seemed really nice. I'm sure the kids will be nice too." I guided the car up the 57 Freeway toward the community park in Brea.

Josh squirmed in his seat. "Just because they're nice doesn't mean they won't be weird."

When we pulled into the lot, I parked my sporty little convertible in a line of minivans and SUVs. It reminded me of a kindergarten worksheet: *Which Object Does Not Belong?* Maybe Josh had it wrong. Maybe we were the weird ones.

Josh grabbed his baseball sports bag and his skateboard from the trunk. We walked up the grassy hill toward the covered picnic tables. A group of mothers sat on the benches and many small children played nearby. A group of older kids stood gathered around another table and took turns writing on a large scroll of butcher paper.

When we reached the crest, the entire group stopped and watched us approach.

"They're all looking at us," Josh said, barely moving his lips.

"Just smile and give them a chance." I stretched a grin across my face. "Hi," I waved to the group. "Which one of you is Glory?"

Glory, a plump Hispanic mother with a shock of dark curls, shook my hand and pointed around the picnic area, naming the members. During the dizzying introduction, I counted fourteen moms and thirty-one kids. Only five looked to be in Josh's age group, the majority ranged from toddlers through elementary school.

Glory explained to Josh that the older kids were working on writing a perpetual story—each child adding the next scene to something the child before had written.

Josh tilted his head and looked at me. His expression couldn't have been more telling of his thoughts. The look he gave me screamed: *You've got to be kidding. See! I told you they'd be weird.*

Despite his reluctance, I was proud of his display of manners. He smiled at Glory, set his bag and skateboard at my feet, and wandered over to join the juvenile storytellers.

Once Josh was settled watching the narrative project unfold, the group's attention turned to me.

"Are you a stay-at-home mom?"

"What does your husband do?"

"Where do you live?"

"How long have you been homeschooling?"

I didn't realize I had to interview to join a homeschool playgroup. I knew my situation was far from the norm. I felt uncomfortable being asked to hold it up to scrutiny by so many people at once.

"Well, I'm a single mom. We live in Aliso Viejo, and I just started home-schooling Josh."

I felt like a life-sized Show-and-Tell project. The questions just kept coming.

"What does your ex-husband think of you homeschooling?" asked a petite Asian woman holding an infant.

There it was. The same basic question that always came up one way or another. In Josh's early years, I answered in vague platitudes about accidentally putting the cart before the horse. After thirteen years, I just served up the answer without decoration.

"I was never married. Josh's father left when I was five months pregnant and I haven't seen him since."

There was a soft, collective 'Oh.' just like the sound made when a crowd witnesses a circus performer fall off her horse.

I waved it off. "But that was a long time ago. So it really doesn't matter, and I certainly don't need to worry about what he thinks."

One mother, Tammy, raised her hand to ask the next question. She had a warm smile and looked like the cliché of granola crunchy, all the way from her Birkenstocks to the thick braid of hair that hung like a rope down to the seat of her pants. "So, what do you do for a living?"

Out of the relationship frying pan and into the employment fire.

"I'm a writer." I shrugged slightly. "And I work part time in a bar."

I didn't want to admit that it also happened to be a topless gentleman's club. I detested having to mention the bar job at all. It always led to that unspoken assumption that I was only a writer wannabe. But the only way you could confidently say you were a writer was if you could provide an ISBN or production credits to back up your claim.

Everyone, everywhere, seemed to be writing a book or a screenplay. I cringed whenever I mentioned writing a book and a person's response was, "You are? Me too." Invariably, their next comment was "I think we should get together and collaborate on a project. You can help me write it, you see, I have this idea..."

"You should talk to Karen."

I missed Tammy's comment completely while I zoned out. "I'm sorry, what did you say?"

"I said you should talk to Karen. She's not here today, but she's writing a children's book about a homeschooled girl. You two should get together."

"Sure. I'd like to meet her sometime." The statement wasn't at all untrue. I enjoyed talking about the craft to anyone who was interested.

"So, what teaching method are you using?" Laura, a slim blonde in a blue tracksuit, handed a bag of Cheerios to her three-year-old, then turned to study my face for an answer.

"Method?" I shifted from one foot to the other. I wasn't sure how much method there was in handing Josh a stack of textbooks and threatening him with lethal injection if he didn't study them.

"Charlotte Mason? Montessori? Waldorf? Unschooling?" Laura looked at me like I truly had no idea what I was doing.

"Have a seat," Glory said.

The moms along one bench scooted over to make room for me. Then the conversation turned to an interesting debate over teaching principles and techniques. I was glad to have the focus off my personal life. I sat, listening intently, and cast my eyes over to the group of kids assembling around Josh.

He had reclaimed his sports bag and revealed the baseball treasures to the rest of the kids. Soon, a haphazard team formed a tight infield and outfield between the shady trees. I watched as Glory's oldest son tossed a gentle underhand pitch to Laura's seven-year-old daughter. Josh, on his knees beside her, helped her swing the bat. There were calls of encouragement all around, and three girls who decided to play cheerleader on the sidelines. Twin boys ran after the ball when the girl took a swing and missed.

It was good to see Josh interacting with something positive. There were no cliques. No age divisions. No pressures to have designer clothes. Just kids playing together.

Socialization. That was the big argument I'd heard against homeschooling. But it felt like a healthy environment—for both of us.

land shark on the loose

Christmas Eve
Monday, December 24

Candy bars, batteries, cologne, toothbrush—Josh's last minute stocking stuffers shifted in the bag as I turned my house key in the lock. I pushed the door open with one foot and felt along the wall for the light switch.

Snap. The room flooded with light. I gasped at the sight of a Christmas massacre. Crimson smears from hand-dyed ornaments stained the beige carpet. Broken glass bulbs littered the floor. Severed wires snaked in pieces, snagged in the fibers of the rug. Pine needles and gnawed branches were scattered around the room.

Buddy, with a wad of shiny tinsel hanging from the corner of his mouth, sat in the middle of the mess, wagging his tail.

Too stunned to yell, I stood surveying the damage. Everything from the middle of the Christmas tree to the bottom was completely stripped and destroyed. A few ornaments clung precariously to the top branches. The tree leaned at an awkward angle, held up by only the screws in the stand. The angel on top looked unsure whether to take flight or pray.

"Bad dog! Go! Get on your bed!"

I knelt to the floor and raked the frayed wires of the Christmas lights into a clump with my fingers. Buddy watched me from his cedar-filled pillow with that puppy look that wavers between "let's play" and "oh shit, I screwed up."

"Don't even look at me right now!" My voice echoed in the room. Tears clouded my vision. I dropped to the floor on my hands and knees.

Why did he have to leave me? Am I ever going to find someone who truly loves me enough to stay? Why does every holiday, every everything, good and bad, have to remind me of him? I blindly crawled along the carpet, collecting the broken glass in my hands.

The front door swung open. "Mom?" Josh rushed over and crouched beside me, "Are you okay? What happened?"

"Buddy—" I choked on a sob.

"Don't cry, I'll help you clean up. It'll be okay," Josh half-patted, half-hugged my quaking shoulders.

"We can try to redecorate the tree…"

"Don't do it for me, Mom. I'm thirteen now. I know there's no Santa Claus."

"Are you sure?" I sat back on my heels and searched his face.

"I don't really care if we don't have a tree set up, as long as I still get the presents."

The priorities of a teenager.

Silently, we took down the Christmas tree. Josh collected the mess in a trash bag while I removed the remaining ornaments and returned them to the garage storage bin.

We wrestled the 7 ft. Noble through the doorway and placed it on the curb. Bits of tinsel fluttered in the cool breeze.

'Twas the night before Christmas and all through the house...

santa works for the auto club
Christmas Day
Tuesday, December 25

I stared at the ceiling. There was no reason to get out of bed. Christmas was ruined. I couldn't imagine turning on Christmas carols and faking my way through the day. I rolled over and buried my head under the covers.

A soft rap on my bedroom door preceded Josh's face peeking between the door and the frame. "Mom, you awake yet?"

"Come on in, Wonderboy." I sat up and plumped the pillows behind me.

Josh crawled across the bed and curled up beside me with his head in my lap. "Can we open presents now?" he asked.

"I suppose so. But let's eat breakfast first." I stroked his soft, clean hair, enjoying the feeling of it without the crispy gel spikes.

"Do my back." Josh shifted on the bed and pulled up the edge of his T-shirt, exposing his lower back.

I started doing the tickle touch when he was an infant to get him to relax and fall asleep in his crib—the light, barely-there massage still had the power to put him into a near coma.

"See if you can figure out what I'm making for breakfast," I said, drawing the letters, spelling it with my index finger on his skin: G-R-I-L-L—

"Grilled egg and cheese sandwich?" he guessed, looking at my smile to confirm it. "I'll get the ketchup!" Josh jumped off the bed and ran down the stairs, yelling over his shoulder, "Hurry up, Mom!"

That was the one thing that was guaranteed: his favorite breakfast trumped everything else.

After breakfast, I watched Josh open his presents and dodged his question about why there was nothing for me. I just couldn't bring myself to buy my own gifts, wrap them, and then open them. To me, that felt more pathetic than not having any at all.

The plan for the rest of the day was to drive over to Bonita's: Josh could spend the day with her sons, while Bonita and I sat around eating the 500 pounds of Christmas cookies she baked every year. Usually, we had Valerie's help, but this year, she had flown home with her kids to visit family in Nebraska.

I maneuvered the Celica onto the 73 Toll Road North from the Aliso Creek onramp. The road was nearly deserted, so it would be a quick drive up to Bonita's condo in Costa Mesa.

Josh held a stack of his new DVDs on his lap. I knew the boys would fill the entire day watching testosterone-injected movies and playing violent video games—the teen boy activity equivalent of consuming junk food.

I accelerated on the incline toward El Toro Road and pushed in the clutch to shift from fourth gear to fifth. I felt a pop, like having a rubberband break under my shoe, and the clutch went all the way to the floor.

"Shit." I guided the car across one lane, braking to slow down. I stopped on the right edge of the roadway and turned on my emergency flashers.

"What happened?" Josh asked, a worried look pinching both of his eyebrows together. "Why are we stopping? What's wrong?"

"The clutch went out," I said, reaching into my purse for my cell phone.

"What are we going to do? Are we going to have to walk?"

I pressed the Call key for the first number in the internal phonebook: AAA Roadside Assistance. "We're staying here and I'm getting a tow truck."

"Well, this blows." Josh slumped low in his seat.

That summed it up pretty succinctly. Could anything else go as miserably wrong as the last three months of my life? Why couldn't something just go right for once?

"Is this payback for kicking a karma puppy?" I shouted out the window.

The look on Josh's face said a good Christmas gift for me would've been a silver-buckled, hug-me sweater.

The whole situation was almost laughable.

I nearly dissolved into hysterical tears when the tow truck driver arrived wearing a fluffy, red and white Santa hat.

resolution #1: no more obsessing about kevin

New Year's Day
Tuesday, January 1

I opened my eyes, blinked until I could focus, and then glanced at the clock. Almost noon.

Somehow, I had made it through New Year's Eve alive. Probably because South Orange County doesn't have any buildings tall enough to jump from. And I wouldn't have been able to climb to the top in my platform stilettos anyway.

Jaimee and I had decided to work instead of going out. Josh was at a slumber party at Adam's house, and sitting at home alone wasn't an option; it would've made me crazy.

There had been a skeleton crew: only six dancers, one bouncer, a bartender, two waitresses, and the DJ. Nate was the manager who drew the short straw.

The entire night, there were never more than twenty customers in the club, but it was a surprisingly good money night—almost as if free-flowing cash and free-flowing alcohol could help both the dancers and the customers pretend it was a celebration of a new year, instead of a night saying goodbye to a year without anyone significant to share it.

At the countdown to midnight, I couldn't chase the thought out of my head that Kevin might be kissing someone special and welcoming a new year with her. I was tormented by the visual of silver confetti swirling around them while their lip embrace was serenaded by "Auld Lang Syne."

He clearly wanted this old acquaintance to be forgotten.

The rest of the night passed slowly with that image playing like a skipping record in my mind.

Now, it was New Year's Day—the ritual. A day I usually spent evaluating the year before, all of the failures, and the resolutions that never quite made it past March.

Eat better. Exercise more. Spend less. Live slower. Be a better mother. A better friend. A better mate. A better person.

This year, I could leave out the better mate resolution.

I stretched out on top of the bed, notebook and pen in hand, and glanced around the room to assess my personal space.

71

Gaps. The gaps were too big. I rolled from the bed and spread my knick-knacks across the long dresser, trying to fill the empty space left when Kevin gathered his personal items. I picked up a picture of him; his brooding expression from an old modeling pose stared back. I set it facedown. Almost in the same movement, I picked it up again, and stood it upright in its original place.

Every private thing that belonged to him was gone. Only the furniture remained. Mismatched pieces of a bedroom set. Some his, some mine, waiting to be divided in another six months at the end of the lease.

Maybe then, once I'd gotten my life in order, when I wasn't working at the club anymore, and when I'd sold my book, maybe then, we would get back together.

But just in case, just in case we didn't, I needed a plan.

A Five-Year Plan.

I'd be empty-nested in five years. So, I'd devote myself to breaking into the publishing industry and at the end of those five years, if I wasn't a rich and famous author, then I'd sell everything and move to an island.

Maybe Fiji. Or I could backpack across Europe. I'd always wanted to do that.

There was a certain freedom in being alone.

There was a certain misery in being alone.

Well, there it was—My Five-Year Plan. Eat better. Exercise more. Spend less. Live slower. Be a better mother. A better friend. A better person. And move far away to escape my haunting failures.

a survey of sanity

Wednesday, January 2

I couldn't pass up the serendipity symbols. Kevin sent me his half of the rent check in a card. It usually came in an envelope alone, no note. Nothing. And it wasn't a holiday card; the card said *Thinking of You*.

I wondered how many cards Kevin read before he found one that said what he wanted to say. The check he sent for the rent wasn't the usual 50/50 split either. He wrote it for $1000 and left me to pay the other $895.

True, it was only a $50 difference, but why did he do it? It was almost like being a gift without really being a gift.

Was I reading too much into it?

Those two things alone were unsettling enough. Then I received an email from Meg inviting me to a girl's craft day get-together up in Los Angeles. The address of the event had the same cross street as the golf course where Kevin worked.

If I went to the event, I'd be less than ten minutes away from him.

All of that was far too much for me to pass off as just a mere coincidence. It was a sign. Serendipity. It meant I had to go see him.

I wanted to see him so much that just about any excuse would have sounded valid. I couldn't stop picturing us the way we used to be.

God, I miss the feel of his skin.

The whole thing could go in virtually any direction. Either Kevin would turn me down completely and say no.

Or we'd have dinner, and then I'd leave.

Or we'd have amazing sex and no dinner.

Or we'd have dinner, incredible sex, and then I'd leave.

Or we'd have dinner, fabulous sex, and I'd spend the night.

I wasn't sure how well I would handle any of the possible scenarios; I just knew I wanted to be with him.

I called my support network to get a second, third, okay—five opinions. I'm not sure if it was to validate my decision or to help talk myself out of it. The thought of seeing Kevin again made me quake like Northridge.

Valerie said she would do it—without hesitation. No surprise there. She was just as ballsy and could have easily been my Gemini twin, cosmically separated from me at birth.

Cousin Melissa said it was a stupid idea—that sleeping with him would set me back six months emotionally.

Jaimee said I was nuts—she'd never have the nerve to do it.

Heather was adamant that I was giving him all the power and control by showing him I would always be waiting in the wings for him.

Okay, so that's a bad thing?

Bonita announced that I had finally reached the bargaining stage of break-up recovery: the point where a woman continually tries to convince herself that if she behaves a specific way, it will reconcile the relationship.

I really didn't mind Bonita practicing her armchair psychology on me. So far, she hadn't come up with anything I hadn't already figured out about myself.

I decided the best part about being so self-aware was that it gave me the liberty to totally disregard sound advice in favor of following my emotional whims.

hope is a chocolate-covered turd
Sunday, January 6

So, of course, I drove up there to see him. I didn't get a chance to see his initial reaction though. One of his assistants saw me walk into the pro shop and called Kevin on his cell phone to give him a heads up. When he finally came in from the golf course, he seemed very composed, but I knew his heart had to be racing like mine.

He looked like shit. Kevin had at least a week's growth of stubble on his cheeks. After sharing an awkward hug, I reached out to tentatively stroke his jaw with my hand. "Nice bristles," I said.

Kevin managed a weak smile and cast his eyes to the floor.

He tried to grow a goatee once about a year ago, it was strawberry blonde, so I teasingly called him "red beard" until he gave up and shaved it off.

His skin was too pale, not at all its usual warm color. Kevin's haircut was at least three months old and was so long it curled against his collar. The top was far too pouffy.

I fought the urge to ask him if he was auditioning for an '80s flashback music video for The Stray Cats. He always hated my sarcasm though—said it was too mean spirited.

It was obvious he hadn't been taking care of himself; it gave me some hope that at least he wasn't dating. That was a good thing. It meant there was still a chance for us.

"How's work?" I said.

"It's okay. I've been busy." He looked around the pro shop. A group of cart boys watched our exchange with interest.

"Let's talk outside." Kevin pulled open the back door and we stepped out to the patio. "So, what brings you all the way up here?" he asked.

"My friend Meg lives up here. And she was hosting a creative craft day at a ceramics shop nearby, so I thought I would drop by here on my way home..."

It hadn't sounded this lame when I first practiced saying it.

"To bring you some of your golf magazines that came in the mail..."

But what I really want to do is go straight to bed with you.

"And to see if you might want to grab something to eat," I tacked on.

Kevin watched me intently while I floundered with my explanation for my unannounced visit. His eyes passed from my new, tan suede boots, up the snug legs of my new, rub-faded jeans. "Nice jacket," he said.

Also new. A plush, blonde, faux fur, thigh-length coat.

Just a few products of my out-of-control shopping frenzy earlier in the week. But not even shopping therapy made me feel as good as when I was wrapped in his arms.

But I couldn't tell him that.

"Thanks." I squirmed in the awkward silence. "So, are you hungry? Would you like to have dinner with me?"

Kevin ran a hand through his hair, leaving tracks from his fingers through the blonde waves. "Not this time, Annette. I already have plans to go out to dinner with some of the members. Maybe if you call first next time..."

A gentle, verbal spanking.

"Okay, sure, um…next time I'll call."

"I'll walk you to your car," he said. "I have to get going, they'll be waiting for me at the restaurant."

At the car, I handed Kevin his magazines. I wanted so much to hug him, to feel his arms around me, but he made no move to close the gap between us.

As I drove away, I watched Kevin in the rearview mirror. He walked toward the clubhouse. And never looked back.

a reason and a season
Tuesday, January 15

Sitting in front of my computer, I watched the cursor pulse like a heartbeat. Another journal entry. Another piece of the book.

I began to type.

> I don't know. I may be getting over it. It's been almost three months. I feel apathy. At least, I think it's apathy. Maybe this is what the acceptance stage feels like. I know I can't force Kevin to love me and stay with me. I still believe we could have a wonderful life together, but I know it can't work when only one person feels that way—

This is ridiculous.

I felt like I was Twelve-Stepping through Failed Relationships Anonymous. Hello, my name is Annette. I'm an obsession addict.

I minimized the journaling screen onto the task bar and logged online to AOL to receive my daily dose of positive reinforcement. The electronic voice announced that I had mail. Tangible proof that either someone loved me, or they were offering to increase the size of my penis.

It wasn't spam; it was an email from my best friend from seventh grade. My gal pals still rallied around to support my break-up recovery. Chelle did what she could from 80 miles away.

That was the beauty of the Internet, keeping friends connected, one urban legend at a time.

I clicked the Read Mail button.

Nettie,

I hope this helps, even just a little. Call me anytime if you need to talk.

Love you like a sis,

~ Chelle :-)

She sent me an attachment that opened to an essay about why people come into your life. For a reason, a season, or a lifetime. I'd seen it circulated in emails about a year ago. When I first read it, I knew Kevin was my lifetime.

Now after reading it again, I saw that I was only a reason to Kevin. It was my purpose to help him recover a sense of himself, get over his brutal divorce, and refocus his passion for golf. A convenient transitional woman to pick him up, dust him off, love him unconditionally, encourage his dreams, and then be tossed away like a semen-stained tube sock.

I'm not bitter. I'm realistic. Okay, and maybe occasionally prone to acts of sheer drama.

I know Kevin was my season: it was my time to learn that I was capable of feeling so much love for someone and giving so deeply. That thought helps me cope sometimes. Everything else is emotional autopilot.

Josh peeked his head into the room. "Mom, aren't you going to be late for work?"

I glanced at the clock on my computer monitor. "Yeah buddy, I'm going. Thanks for reminding me of the time."

Josh went back to whatever he had been doing and I scrambled to get ready to go. I was supposed to be at work and dressed to go on stage in two minutes, but hadn't even taken a shower yet.

I'd learned to deal with the fact that the hours slipped away whenever I thought about Kevin. But no one who really knew me ever expected me to be anywhere on time anyway. I'd already decided years ago that when I died, I'd have someone bring my body to the funeral late so everyone would know they were at the right place.

I picked up the phone and dialed the club. After nearly twenty rings, Sunshine's sing-song voice greeted me.

"Hey girl, tell Nate I'm running late, but I'm on my way."

"Naaate!" I heard her yell over the din of the music. "Beth's calling to say she's running late again!"

"Okay, I will!" Sunshine laughed when she turned back to the phone. "He told me to tell you only to call-in when you're going to be on time."

My Dilbert-Inspired Tip of the Day: The easiest way to maintain personal freedom is to nurture the boss' low expectations of you. Of course, there is also something to be said for being virtually unemployable outside of the strip club scene.

---

speed limit? what speed limit?
Wednesday, January 23

With the convertible top and windows down, we rode the air currents like waves with our outstretched arms. The 241 Toll Road lay wide open in front of us, while Josh and I played in the wind. The faster I drove, the more wildly our arms whipped and bucked. With my left hand and Josh's right, we could almost make the car leave the ground and take flight.

WHOOP. WHOOP. A siren chirped.

I looked in the rearview mirror and saw the flash of blinking cherry lights on the dash of a black and white patrol car. Then I glanced down at the speedometer: 85 mph.

Shit.

"Uh oh, Mom, you're so busted."

"Sit still and shut up," I instructed as I pulled to the side of the road.

"Can I see your license, registration, and proof of insurance?" The officer's face was a stone mask.

I leaned across Josh and dug through the glove box looking for the paperwork. I turned the entire stockpile upside down: fast food napkins, CD cases, hand sanitizer, tire gauge, and citrus body spray.

"What's your name, son?" the officer asked.

Josh looked at me as if he couldn't remember his name.

Don't look at me! Look at him!

"Uh...Josh, sir." His eyes fixed on the officer's holstered Smith & Wesson.

Sir? When have you ever called anyone sir? Excuse me, Officer, there is a pod person wearing my son's Etnies.

"Josh, do you think your mother deserves a ticket?"

Josh looked at me as if he didn't know what to say.

Don't look at me! And you better say no or you are soooo grounded.

"I think you should let her go. I'll make sure she doesn't drive fast anymore," Josh said.

That's my boy!

I handed the officer my information. He took a cursory glance and then handed it back to me. "Slow down and drive safely."

"You too," I said. "I mean, thank you."

Yes, thank you! I don't have to waste another Saturday watching that goofy Mr. Walker/Mr. Wheeler video in traffic school again.

hand in the cookie jar

Thursday, January 24

It was a long time to go without one. At least three months—maybe more like three and a half months. I wasn't even sure I could do it.

I stared at the ceiling. Maybe it would work if I closed my eyes.

C-o-n-c-e-n-t-r-a-t-e. Clear your mind. Relaaaax. Tune in to each and every sensation.

This is stupid. I opened my eyes and stared at the ceiling again. Why did it have to be so difficult? It's masturbation, not Tibetan astral travel.

I pressed my eyes closed and tried to focus on my own movements.

Okay...here we go...Okay...Okay...OOOOOOOOO-kaaaaaaaay...

When I opened my eyes, the room looked fuzzy and tinted blue. Pinpoints of light popped like tiny bubbles in front of my eyes. And then the phone rang.

Great timing.

I picked up the receiver and giggled. "Hello?"

You know the giggle. The sex giggle that sounds like nothing other than the result of sheer orgasmic satisfaction.

"Uh...you sound...busy. I didn't mean to... I'll, um, call you later," Kevin said.

My heart skipped a beat at the sound of his voice.

"It's not what you think." I laughed at his obvious assumption.

I shifted under the covers. "You caught me snapping off a round," I said.

"Are you serious?" Kevin's warm chuckle fused with my giggle of after-glow. The connection felt familiar and intimate and it made my heart ache.

"A girl's gotta do what a girl's gotta do." My faux levity wilted around the edges.

"Well, don't let me interrupt," he said. "I can call back later."

"Thanks, but I already finished."

"Oh."

A long pause hovered in the air like a nervous hummingbird.

"So why *did* you call?"

"I don't remember now," Kevin said quietly.

An ACME bomb of awkwardness landed and all I wanted to do was crawl under a rock and hide.

"Why don't you call me when you figure it out," I said. Then I hung up.

God, I must look so pathetic to him.

dog day sadness
Tuesday, January 29

"Mommmmmm! Buddy just peed on the carpet!"

I grabbed a towel out of the linen closet and ran downstairs. "Was the sliding door closed?" I flashed Josh a stern look.

Josh shoved the dog out the doorway into the backyard and slammed the slider. "No. It was wide open." He glared at the dog through the glass. "He stood right there in front of me, lifted his leg, and peed on the table leg."

I blotted up the wetness and then called the carpet cleaners to make an appointment. I decided to call Mom for advice. She'd bred, raised, and shown Russian Wolfhounds before I was born, so I figured she'd have some good suggestions to keep it from happening again.

Mom was predictably direct. "That dog is out of control. You should've never bought him for Kevin. Or the least he could've done is take that damn dog with him when he left you."

Nothing quite like a little motherly compassion to help me get through a tough time.

"Buddy's such a sweet dog. I know he'll be wonderful once he's past his destructo-puppy stage." I bent to pick up a chunk of drywall he chewed off the corner of the kitchen entryway. "Maybe I can wait it out."

Just the thought of giving up Buddy felt like losing another piece of Kevin.

"Then you need to take him to obedience school or send him to a trainer. Those are really your only options at this point," she said.

I didn't have the emotional energy to deal with any of it.

After I got off the phone with Mom, I decided to call Kevin. The knot in my stomach tightened with every ring of the phone. I carried it upstairs to the bedroom so we could talk privately. I knew Josh would be upset if he discovered I was considering getting rid of the puppy.

"Hi," I said without introduction.

"Hi," Kevin echoed.

I wondered if he felt as uncomfortable as I did.

"I called to see if that guy at the golf club still wants Bud-dy." My voice cracked and I knew it was only a matter of seconds before I'd begin sobbing. "Please ask him and get back to me as soon as you can. I just can't keep him," I said, rushing to get off the phone.

"I'll find out and let you know. Is everything else okay?" Kevin asked gently.

"It is what it is," I said, gripping the receiver tighter. I longed to hang up and end the emotional torture of hearing his voice, knowing the words *I love you* would never cross his lips again.

Kevin pressed a little more. "Are you sure you're okay?"

"I'm not any different from the way I was back in October. I have to go now." When I said goodbye, he was quiet. "Just say goodbye, Kevin."

"Okay." He sighed and there was a long pause before he finally said it. "Goodbye, Annette."

I hung up and sank to my knees, rocking, with my arms wrapped around my body.

Will the pain ever go away?

The phone rang a few minutes later: it was Kevin, crying. "I'm so sorry for hurting you and for leaving you with the dog," he said.

"It doesn't have anything to do with Buddy," I whispered past the lump in my throat.

Josh must have let Buddy back inside the house because I noticed the puppy now lay curled on the floor at the foot of the bed. Looking sweet, soft, and oblivious, he pulled himself more tightly into a ball and closed his eyes.

I sniffed. My nose ran almost as quickly as my tears, but I tried to sound forgiving and rational. "Kevin, you shouldn't cry. You didn't do anything wrong. I can't force you to love me and stay with me, I know that."

"I just want you to be happy," he said.

"I was happy," I said softly.

He wouldn't let me off the phone. His apologies flowed while the room swam in a blurry haze and my head throbbed.

"We have nothing more to talk about. I know it's over," I said.

"Are you sure you don't need anything?"

Only you—I wanted to scream over and over until he finally understood. But instead, I said, "Dealing with the break up is my problem and it doesn't affect you."

"Just because I'm not with you doesn't mean I don't care about you."

I couldn't stay on the phone any longer. A painful choking feeling seized my chest, making it impossible to breathe. Kevin kept repeating that he was sorry. I couldn't listen any longer, so I said goodbye and hung up.

Pushing the emotion aside, my rational mind began to churn. It was my coping tool, but at that moment, I welcomed it openly.

I'd been bargaining with myself for too long. He wasn't waiting for me to get my writing career going and move to Los Angeles. That was my twisted fantasy. He was done.

Thanks for picking me up and showing me I can love again, but it's time for me to go. Sorry I hurt you. Now get over it.

I was only a bridge from where he was after his divorce to where he is now. Unfortunately for me, that bridge was made up of my heart and soul.

adrift soup

5 cups futility broth
1 lb. wandering thoughts
16 oz. can of diced emotional vacancy
2 tbsp feelings of loss

Preheat hollow container. Fill with seasoned futility.

Peel wandering thoughts and discard sense of purpose.

Add emotional vacancy.

Simmer in limbo. Stir pointlessly without any sense of direction.

Ladle over aimless dumplings and garnish with feelings of loss.
Serve lukewarm.

Yield: Another penicillin project for the 'fridge.
Unlimited servings.
Nutritional Value: None.

No Guaranteed weight loss.

And you don't even give a shit.

the wish list
Tuesday, February 12

I started The List when I was nineteen. My friends always asked why I bothered keeping a list of everything I wanted in a guy.

Why? Because it made sense. And according to Bonita, my obsessive list-making also happened to fit my DSM IV profile.

My rationale was that if I determined ahead of time what I really wanted, and what was really important to me, then I'd have a better chance of actually finding it, and not wasting time and emotional energy dating Mr. Wrong.

It was my Obsessive Compulsive Girl's Guide to Dating.

Everyone who had ever heard about my list insisted I would never find a guy who had everything I wanted. Could that be why, at thirty-four, I was still single?

Over the years, I had added to the list, but never subtracted. As I learned more about what made me happy, I used it as a blueprint for my perfect mate.

Only by dating a few gazillion Mr. Wrongs, could I have come up with the list for what makes a man Mr. Right-For-Me.

THE LIST

Intelligent	Physically fit/Active
Well read	Outdoorsy/Adventurous
Good sense of humor	Health conscious
Attractive	Family oriented
Politically similar	Environmentally aware
Spiritual, but not religious	Animal lover
Financially stable	Optimistic
College Educated	Thoughtful/Generous
Ambitious/Goal oriented	Attentive/Affectionate
Self-confident/Assertive	Trusting/Trustworthy
Socially competent	Addiction free
Good communicator	Disease free

Kevin was the only guy I'd ever met who had everything. I pulled the original list out of my filing cabinet one day to show him. The page was old and yellowed. Changes in the maturity of my handwriting over the years sloped down the length of the page. Kevin laughed when I assured him that he was the perfect guy. Everything I ever wanted.

Now that he was gone, I didn't think anyone else existed who was better for me than he was—I mean is.

Am I doomed to settle?

zen & chocolate
Wednesday, February 13

> *Everything that has a beginning has an ending. Make*
> *your peace with that and all will be well. —Buddha*

The Complete Idiot's Book to Living Buddhistly. Zen Stuff for Totally Clueless Dummies. Seven hundred pages later, they both said the same thing and I just wasn't feeling "well" with it.

Somehow I don't think Buddha ever got dumped; otherwise, he'd know there's no such thing as peace the day before Valentine's Day when you're alone.

This is the last major holiday in the first Chinese year of The Break-Up. Kevin managed to hit every one of them in rapid succession: Halloween—no couples costumes, Thanksgiving—no lover to be thankful for, Christmas— no mate to sing Christmas carols and exchange presents with, New Year's Eve—no partner to celebrate with the beginning of another wonderful year. And now, Valentine's Day—with everyone walking hand-in-hand like they are about to board Noah's Fucking Ark.

I sat in the corner of the living room on Josh's videogame rocking chair, overdosing on Hershey's Kisses and feeling like a loser.

Buddha, I'm definitely not well with it.

I was sure that if I saw another pink and red, heart decoration, I'd kill something. On the phone today, Bonita said, "Congratulations, you're now officially out of the bargaining stage and into the anger stage."

I can't believe Kevin was stupid enough to ruin such a good thing. It played over and over in my head like a loop. I pushed myself up from the foam rocker and gave it a sharp kick, turning it onto its side.

"What a moron!" I screamed to the empty house.

I snatched the bag of Kisses and thrust my hand inside, grabbing a handful.

"Don't you realize you're screwing up our destiny?" I threw the chocolates across the room like so many foil rocks.

Mind-boggling.

"How can you be so stupid? Stupid! Stupid! Stupid!" I yelled.

I knelt to pick up one of the stray Kisses. Then I crawled across the floor picking up the others. I gathered my thoughts and the scattered chocolates.

This residual break-up crap was affecting my happiness. I compared every new guy I met to Kevin and they all came up lacking. I tried to move on, but how the hell was I supposed to do that when I had the best guy out there?

It's over for me.

I leaned against the wall and stretched out my legs with the candy in my lap.

Demographic reality check. I was in my midthirties, which meant that shopping for guys in my dating pool was like sorting through the remainders on the clearance table at Walmart: they were either hideous looking, they didn't fit, or they were damaged.

Never married.

Teenage son.

No plans for additional birthing.

I mentally pie-charted my options: At least 85% of single guys in their thirties would rather not date a woman who already has a child. At least 99% of single guys in their thirties wanted to get married and have children of their own. I absently divided the chocolates into rows along the length of my legs to build a 3-D graph.

My math got a little fuzzy here, but that might leave an odd 1% of single guys who would even be remotely interested in signing up for the mentor-manning of a teenage boy and then D.I.N.K.ing toward happily-ever-after, which leaves me with the divorced guy option that usually comes complete with phone calls about alimony payments and a brood of small children more than five years away from empty-nesting.

I wasn't exactly ready to sign up for that.

That's it. I know it. I'm doomed. Doomed to live alone in a dilapidated old house, reading romance books, wearing chenille sweaters, and feeding forty stray dogs. Okay, so it's a slight tweak to the old spinster cliché, but I can't wear wool sweaters—much too itchy. And I'm not really a cat person.

Thanks, Kevin. I hope you have a Happy Fucking Valentine's Day too.

bitter shake

3 cubes of iced contempt
1 cup sour cynicism
1/2 cup fresh resentment
1 tsp. sarcasm

Crush cubes of contempt harshly until edges are sharp.

Add cynicism and resentment. Puree until attitude is completely irritated and snippy.

Top with shaved sarcasm.

Serve in chilled, empty vessel shaped like a broken heart.

Yield: Ratty mood.
Unlimited servings.
Nutritional Value: None.

No Guaranteed weight loss.

You're in maintenance phase now.

girlfriend in a box
Sunday, February 17

I brushed a lock of hair from my face with the back of my hand. Up to my ass in cardboard boxes and packing paper, I sorted through the contents of the garage. I packed Kevin's PGA books neatly into a box, labeled the side, and taped it closed.

It's past time to move on.

I separated the boxes; his on the left wall of the garage, mine on the right.

Josh opened the walkthrough door leading into the house and peered into the garage. "I thought I heard noises. What are you doing?"

"I'm packing up the rest of Kevin's stuff, so it's ready for him whenever he comes to get it."

Josh leaned against the doorframe and looked at me. "You should throw it all away." His tone was a blend of bitterness and hostility.

"I can't do that. It wouldn't be right to—"

"Yeah, whatever." Josh rolled his body off the doorframe and closed the door.

I thought about following him inside, but decided against pushing the confrontation. We both felt it: the house had become nothing more than Kevin's overpriced storage unit.

When I turned back to the task, I came across a worn, heavy box in the back corner of the garage. It was sealed and labeled *Marriage in a Box* in Kevin's handwriting. His tangible memories of ten years with Joanne.

I stood staring at the box.

Then I reached for a new cardboard box and taped the bottom closed. The creased flaps of the top formed a gaping mouth. I pulled a sheet of packing paper into my hand and wadded it into a ball. One piece at a time, I filled the empty box.

The tape skipped on the roll as I pulled it across the final closing seam. At the end, the serrated edge of the roller bit through the sticky ribbon.

I pulled the cap off a Sharpie pen. The black marker squeaked out each letter as I scrawled *Girlfriend in a Box* on the side.

Now Kevin can have two boxes.

part two

**the
dating
pool**

hello mrs. robinson!

Saturday, March 9

I grew up in Fontana: home of the Kaiser Steel Mill, the Ku Klux Klan, the Hells Angels motorcycle gang, and the Valley Boulevard trailer parks—a place very much like where *Deliverance* was filmed. Not exactly an enchanted forest brimming with charming princes.

In high school, my best friend, Chelle teased me about dating a freshman when I was a senior. I always went for the younger guys. There was just something about the sexiness of a baby face and the sense of fun that attracted me. Or maybe it was the fact that they were too young to be on parole yet.

As a gag gift for my eighteenth birthday, Chelle bought a license plate frame for my convertible '74 Volkswagen Thing that read: *Want Some Candy, Little Boy?*

I finally had to remove it. The playful message attracted too many men in pickup trucks making vulgar V-fingered hand gestures with their sloppy tongues poking through.

But enough with the skip down banjo road.

I wouldn't have brought it up, but tonight I met this really cute young guy at the club.

Totally adorable. Tousled blonde hair that fell over one eye. And he was tall, so tall he could've used the top of my head for a place to set his beer. Just looking at him conjured up visions of my very own Statue of David—built to scale.

When I first saw him, he stood in a group of four guys gathered around the pool table, drinking beer and sneaking peeks at the private dance area. Of course, I couldn't let that go on without saying something.

"So, which one of you boys is planning to bust open the piggy bank and spring for a private dance? Because I know you didn't come in here for the cheap beer." I posed against the pool table in a way that put my bare abs and legs on display.

The short, stocky guy patted the front pockets of his jeans and lifted his hands in mock surrender. "I'm tapped out," he said.

I looked at the others.

The two guys holding the pool cues simultaneously pointed at each other. "He will," they both said in unison.

This was going nowhere.

The tall blonde dug his right hand into the depths of his front pocket and pulled out a wrinkled twenty-dollar bill. "This is all I have," he said.

Young guys were rarely worth the effort to spend working them for a private dance. But if I felt playful and the night wasn't too busy, I'd flirt for a little while. It never failed; the next time they came in, they always bought at least one dance from me, and then they were hooked.

"Okay, big spender, what's your story?" I asked.

His name was Garrett. And he was a freshman running back for the Florida State University Seminoles. Unfortunately, he blew out his knee at practice, so he didn't know if he'd to be able to play again.

We had an easy conversation and there was obvious chemistry. I'm sure it didn't hurt that I couldn't stop picturing him naked.

Hotel room. Horizontal rodeo.

The get-to-know-you conversation progressed. He asked my age and I told him thirty-five.

True, I had a little less than three months until my birthday, but I tried to get used to it, so I wouldn't freak out when it actually arrived.

"Wow!" Garrett looked completely surprised, but he quickly changed his expression, trying to recover. "You don't look that old, I mean, not that that's old or anything."

"So how old are you?" I plied him with my sexiest smile.

"Can you keep a secret?" Garrett pulled his driver's license out of his wallet and handed it to me.

"1985!" He was born the year I graduated from high school. "That makes you..." I dusted off my mental subtraction flashcards.

"Eighteen," he said.

"How the hell did you get in here?" I looked at the beer bottle in his hand. I figured he was a bit younger—maybe twenty-five, but my brain hadn't managed to do the math.

"I'm six-seven. Nobody ever cards me."

I could almost hear the ratchet of the handcuffs, feel the scarlet letter *P* stamped on my forehead, and see the gavel slamming down, declaring me a pedophile and a menace to the virtue of extremely tall prepubescent boys.

For a minute, I still considered the rodeo option—there was something to be said about the fantasy of green-breaking a young colt...

My conscience adopted a falsetto voice and scolded me like Garrett's mother would for even thinking about molesting her little boy. I guess it's a good thing I'm not a high school English teacher or I'd be on the eleven o'clock news.

In the end, I went home alone and masturbated. Junior was only in my head, but he did a good job anyway.

for love or money?
Wednesday, March 20

Is it a bad thing that my dating pool is a strip club? And does that mean I'm swimming in the shallow end?

Some women swear against dating men they meet at work. For me, it's like a buffet. Where else could I find so many eligible guys all in one place? And it certainly cut out the awkward conversation that always came up when it was time to tell a guy I was interested in dating that I worked part-time as a topless dancer. That little bit of useless trivia had a tendency to send them packing. If the revelation of my single motherhood didn't already do it, the combination was usually relationship suicide.

Although it was the goal of some girls I worked with, finding a sugar daddy wasn't my nature. Put me in a room full of rich men and one poor guy—and I'd fall in love with the poor guy every time. It had always been that way. In finishing school, I must've missed Gold-Digging 101. Actually, to the discerning reader, I'm sure it's pretty obvious I missed finishing school completely.

So, I met a guy. Yes, another one at the club. But this one was visiting from Texas. He made me laugh when he told me stories from his childhood on "the spread" he called it. He grew up playing polo. Then he let slip that his family had more money than God and a vacation house in the Cayman Islands.

His gaze was direct. "I want to take care of you," he said.

Now that sounded tempting. I'd never been faced with it as a serious offer, so I wasn't sure how to respond.

"I'll have to think about it," I said.

I couldn't even fathom what it would be like to have someone else take over. No worries. No financial concerns. I could finally focus on my writing and maybe even take a vacation.

Just the thought of reclining on a beach in the Caribbean, reading a dog-eared bestseller, with Josh swimming in the turquoise ocean, while back home a maid cleaned my obscenely large house—pinch me. It sounded like a dream.

But then there was the moral dilemma: could I look at myself in the mirror every morning, knowing I got together with this guy just for security and luxury?

Women do it every day…

I know I'm in justification mode, but look at that busty blonde with the IQ of a pencil. She ended up with her own reality show and a big weight-loss endorsement deal. All that, and she started out as a stripper. Now, tell me again she really married that old geezer for his big, juicy wiener. Um…highly doubt it.

I thought I deserved a little luxury in my life. I'd like to be able to give Josh that kind of life; he deserved it too.

I don't know if I could do it though. What about love? And Prince Charming? The white horse? The sunset and happily-ever-after?

Can you get all that if you sell out?

bdsm, the new pink-collar job
Tuesday, March 26

I leaned back in my chair and contemplated my most recent journal entry. Selling out. That moral gray area. Can making serious life decisions based on the monetary outcome still result in ultimate happiness?

W.W.J.D.? What Would Jung Do?

The trill of an Instant Message notification reminded me that I was still logged online. I pulled up the AOL program from the task bar and saw a dialogue box had popped onto my screen.

I often deleted random IMs without bothering to reply. Occasionally, if I were feeling particularly feisty, I'd respond to the age/sex/location query by typing an off-putting description of myself: I'm a SWF, 53 yrs. old, 4'11", 350 lbs., with black frizzy hair, freckles, buck teeth, and a limp. That little visual usually made the IM intruder look for cybersex elsewhere.

I read the dialogue box on my screen.

> **From: BluldGy**
>
> huge career opportunity. flexible hours. great money.

What could I do? Of course I had to respond. I've always been a sucker for blue eyes and multilevel marketing scams. So I typed back.

> **From: SecretsbyBeth**
>
> Wow! A real, live cyber pimp. Today must be my lucky day.
> Can Trixie be my official prostitute screen name?

I couldn't help myself. Bored with my self-analysis, I decided to toy with the guy for some juvenile amusement.

> **From: BluldGy**
>
> there is no sex involved. you make your own schedule. meet interesting people. make $200-$400 an hour.

Okay, now I was seriously curious. What job could possibly pay that well, not involve sex, and be marketed on the Internet through random, unsolicited IMs?

I just had to know.

> **From: SecretsbyBeth**
> Ok. I give up. What are you selling?

His response came back quickly; he must've already had it typed in.

> **From: BluIdGy**
> i train women to be professional dominatrix.

A giggle bubbled up from my chest. It was a huge career opportunity with flexible hours and great money, where I could meet interesting people, tie them up, and spank the living shit out of them? My laughter echoed through the room. I couldn't believe the guy was trying to soft sell a totally freaky job as a bondage babe.

> **From: SecretsbyBeth**
> So, I guess that makes you like Devry Institute of Spankology? Do you provide a certificate of completion and job placement too?

His response came back in all caps—the online equivalent of a shout.

> **From BluIdGy:**
> BRAT. YOU BEHAVE.

Now he was playing a dominant role and I was supposed to be submissive? This just had too much comic potential to pass up.

I grabbed the phone and called Valerie at work. "Check this out—" I coughed into the phone, choking on my laughter. "This guy sent me an Instant Message…"

I read the volley of IMs to her. I heard her ten-key clattering in the background and could picture rolls of adding machine tape engulfing her entire desk. When I got to the dominatrix part, her tapping nails stopped.

"What?" Valerie's single word sounded like tires screeching to a halt. "He *trains* people to do that?" She lowered her voice. "That guy is a wack job."

I mulled it over. The thought of making $200-$400 an hour was tempting.

"Val, go with me on this for a minute."

She'd been my personal investment diva for a decade, knew the pathetic condition of my financial portfolio—and was used to indulging my flights of fancy.

"Okay, if I actually decide to do this, I mean, it's a lot of money," I said. "And how hard could it really be? I tell some rich, fat, balding, corporate weasel that he's a worthless slob, and whack him on the ass with a riding crop. Then I make him promise to give his sexually harassed receptionist a huge bonus or I won't let him come back to see me for another can of whoop-ass."

"You're kidding, right?"

"I saw *Exit to Eden* with Rosie O'Donnell. It didn't look like such a big deal," I said. "But what would I write on my taxes?"

"I don't think the IRS has a category for someone who spanks people for a living," she said.

Another dialogue box popped onto my screen.

> **From BluidGy:**
>
> you will come to a D/s party saturday night with me as my sub. i will collar you and show you the lifestyle. you will be safe there with me. no one will touch you.

The party sounded interesting in an *Eyes Wide Shut* sort of way. But there was no way I'd wear a dog collar and be anyone's submissive anything. Not in this lifetime.

"Val, what are you doing Saturday night?"

Maybe it was my tone that made her hesitate. "I don't know…" she said. "Why?"

"I was just wondering if you want to go to a bondage and discipline, sado-masochistic, dominant/submissive party with me."

"Are you fucking nuts?" she whispered. "Did that freak invite you to a party?" Her voice spiked. "I'm not going! And you're not going either!"

When I didn't respond right away, she lowered her voice. "Are you?"

"C'mon, go with me," I said. "We never do anything fun." When she didn't say anything, I tried another angle. "We can go shopping first to buy something cute to wear. A corset, vinyl pants, you know, do the whole Barbie thing and go dressed to blend."

"I gotta go," Valerie whispered. "One of the partners just walked in. Call me later so I can talk you out of this."

I hung up with her just as another IM popped up.

> **From: BluIdGy**
> these links are for you. read them and learn.

Curious, I clicked through the links he sent embedded in the message box. One link led to The Deviants' Dictionary. It was like a Webster's Unabridged, pervert edition. I followed another hyperlink to a "Negotiation List" for "The Rules of Play."

It was totally fascinating. This bizarre subculture. This strange and exotic lifestyle that I knew nothing about. It would make absolutely great story material. I could do an undercover exposé, sort of a behind-the-scenes look at female spankstresses. I was positively giddy at the thought of finding just the right words to describe the atmosphere, the people, the gray matter of why and how the lifestyle exists.

I clicked on the last link; it led to a series of pictures. Graphic pictures: a gallery of men and women—naked. Leather masks and ball-gags binding their faces, cages and body harnesses restricting their movement. Strange medieval looking machines probing into private areas, blindfolds and shackles, and soft pink skin with puckered red welts.

A tremor ran through my body. That clearly wasn't a world I wanted to explore—not even for $400 an hour and material for a really great story.

When it comes to sexual flavors, I'm as vanilla as it gets. Okay, so maybe that makes me boring. But I've decided to celebrate my flannel pajama boringness and leave the butt plugs and butterfly boards to more adventurous girls.

murphy's law of the universe
Thursday, March 28

I always end up with the retarded shopping cart. I think there's some sort of cosmic message in there somewhere.

"Mom, can I go look at the watches?" Josh had already turned toward the glass cases filled with cheap jewelry.

"I suppose. Catch up with me when you're done."

I pushed the wobbly cart along the wide aisle, fighting the crooked wheel dragging it to the left. I checked the detergent section and decided a man must've designed the layout of Super Kmart. Otherwise, the Simple Green would be over in the aisle with the cleaning supplies, not in the automotive department.

So, I traveled through the sporting goods section, feeling like Sacagawea leading a trek into the unknown.

Hmmm...look what I found. A guy—in his natural habitat.

Blonde spiky hair. Our eyes connected. I smiled. He smiled. Nice smile. I looked away.

What was I looking for again? Oh yeah, Simple Green.

I picked a bottle off the bottom shelf and put it in the cart. Spiky Hair walked past me. I stood for a few minutes breathing in the smell of his cologne.

Safari. Kevin's cologne.

Why does it always seem like when I'm finally trying to move on, some little thing like a reminder of the way Kevin smelled sucks me right back in?

I turned the cart around and followed Spiky Hair through the store, just to smell the cologne. I followed him down several aisles, inhaling deeply. He stole a few curious glances over his shoulder.

With my eyes half closed, I sniffed again. A few short intakes and then a long draw, maybe a little too loudly. His head turned with a jerk. The look on his face clearly asked, "Did I step in dog shit?" I smiled awkwardly and turned to feign extreme interest in the bunion pads on the shelf near my cart.

I continued to follow him, but kept a reasonable distance until he reached the cashier. Then I pulled my cart up behind him and closed my eyes. I breathed in slowly and quietly, trying to completely absorb the scent.

"Mom, what are you doing?"

My eyes popped open to find Josh peering closely into my face. He looked at me like I was a candidate for a weekend retreat to a rubber room resort.

"Why are you being weird?" he whispered.

I shrugged and turned to the magazines and booklets in the rack dividing the checkout lanes.

"I'll be at the arcade by the exit." Josh walked away, shaking his head.

I looked over the tabloid titles. Ridiculous. Do people really believe those headlines? I glanced at the top shelf. *Cooking with Casseroles. No Bad Dogs. Zodiac Dating. How to Survive a Break Up.*

Hmmm....

I pulled the last one off the shelf and flipped through it. The pocket-sized therapy guide was crammed with common sense solutions to salve sadness. I continued scanning to see if there was anything I hadn't already figured out on my own.

I felt Josh's presence beside me. "Back already?" I asked without looking up.

"The *Area 51* game was broken. What are you reading?" He tilted his head to see the cover.

I angled it parallel with the floor to conceal the title. "Just a book."

Josh turned to review the rack of possible options. The booklets each had a distinct size, so he instantly knew which one I held.

He yanked it from my hand and turned it over to confirm the title. "You don't need this stupid crap!" He chucked it through the air and over the top of two checkout stands.

"Josh! What do you think you're doing?" I couldn't believe he threw the book. I was afraid to check to see if it hit anyone.

"You shouldn't be reading that. You don't need it. You're fine." He sounded angry and somehow a little hopeful. "I'm going to wait by the car." Josh turned and stormed toward the exit.

My heart hurt and my head was full of Kevin, again. But at least I found the Simple Green.

deviled egg powwow

Easter
Sunday, March 31

I laid it out to Valerie while we sat on her patio under a canopy of stars. It was one of our typical nights in her grassy backyard, despite the day-long celebration with the kids. Bonita already left with her boys and the evening was winding down.

Too lazy to go to the store for more fire logs, Valerie and I took turns burning newspaper inserts and paper plates in her potbellied stove.

"Here's the deal. I met a guy at work and he wants to play the sugar daddy game, but I don't think I can do it," I said.

I've come to the conclusion that every heartbroken creative needs a left-brained realist as a best friend.

Without knowing the details, "You'll grow to love him," she said. Valerie swirled her Merlot while she built her case. "When women are with guys who take care of them and treat them well, we can't help but fall in love. It's the way we're wired." She shrugged and took another sip of wine.

"What about your marriage?"

"I was never *in*-love with Jack, but I grew to love him. And if he hadn't turned into such a prick, I wouldn't have divorced him."

"I don't understand how you could spend that many years with someone you aren't in-love with. I'd die inside."

"Your problem is that you think everything has to be a fairytale." Valerie folded a paper plate into the shape of a pie slice and pushed it into the fire. "You have to be realistic. A relationship is really about the benefits that each person can get from being with the other."

I picked up another deviled egg and looked at the jiggly white part spotted a faint pink from the Easter egg dye; I wondered if the dye was carcinogenic. I stuffed the egg into my mouth, my lips bulging around it. Too big a bite, but I hated when the yellow stuff slimed my front teeth. It always made me feel like I had to go floss.

She could be right. Maybe relationships only work when neither person has to deal with being in-love. It's got to be easier that way.

loveless 7 layer dip

1 fresh man of fat wallet
1 premium female gold digger
16 oz. tub of evaporated creamed conscience
24 kt. diced princess posturing
1/4 cup chopped feelings of entitlement
1/2 cup sliced opportunity
1 drained bank account

Peel wallet to reveal lettuce inside. Layer gold digger on top. Smear liberally with creamed conscience. Mix princess posturing with feelings of entitlement. Spread thickly.

Cover remaining surface with sliced opportunity. Top with drained bank account.

Garnish with platinum AMEX. Serve frigid with crispy triangles of attitude.

Yield: Whatever you want.
Unlimited servings.
Nutritional Value: None.

No guaranteed weight loss.

You'd have a personal trainer he pays for, so it wouldn't matter.

fly fishing in cyberspace
Sunday, April 7

Don't ask me what propelled me to do it. Because it's always a suggestion from that well-meaning friend—the one who already has a boyfriend.

"What about signing up for that Internet dating service you hear about everywhere? I bet there are a ton of great guys on there," Heather suggested gently.

I laughed it off, but she persisted. "C'mon what've you got to lose? Just do it. While we're on the phone, log on, and go to that website."

Okay, twist my mouse finger.

We both went online and window-shopped via telephone. It was like browsing a home-shopping network for slightly used penises.

"What about the one that says, 'Great Catch'? Don't you think that he's kinda cute?"

I tried not to choke. "Heather, that guy is playing on team recession. His forehead is migrating to the back of his neck. You are kidding me, right?"

"Okay, so he's not as gorgeous as Kevin was."

"Is," I corrected.

I heard Derek yelling in the background. "Hey Heather, what're you doing?"

"Nothing. Nothing," she said.

I could picture her frantically clicking the computer window closed. It would be easier than explaining to her boyfriend why she was trolling Match.com.

"Annette, Derek wants to watch a movie, so I have to go, but you should keep looking. Who knows, maybe you'll find a really great guy."

She finally hung up to go enjoy her relational bliss, leaving me in relative peace to continue with my ex-boyfriend replacement therapy.

I scanned the sign-up requirements. To contact any of the potential life partners, I had to register and make up a profile.

Blink...blink...blink...the cursor mocked me. What do you say about yourself to attract a cybermate?

Single, white, female, thirty-four, cute, petite...um...neurotic woman is desperately obsessed with ex-boyfriend, needs new distraction to use for rebound relationship. No sexual relation opportunities included. I can't go there yet. We only broke up seven months ago.

You can't write the truth in a profile. It's like an ad for a used car. Nobody will want it when you reveal there are too many miles on it and it breaks down all the time.

I'm a used car. God, this sucks.

play that funky music white boy
Saturday, April 20

It was a balmy night, unseasonably warm. Just the way I like it.

The club was packed. Disco Saturday night—retro trendy, and more fun than the '70s were the first time around. But that was when I was dancing to the Bee Gees in hopscotch squares on the playground. So, what do I really know?

"Hey, let's hit the patio for some fresh air," Valerie yelled, flailing her arms to the "Y.M.C.A." song.

It was stuffy and the press of bodies marinated in beer made the idea of fresh air seem like nirvana. On the patio, I fanned a puff of cigarette smoke out of my face and wondered what was so fresh about inhaling the second-hand ass gas of someone's stale, unfiltered butt.

Valerie's immediate goal was to bum a smoke from a cute guy. Standard bar technique: right up there with not having to stand in line to get in, and never paying for her own drink.

When she turned up her laser-white smile, and sucked in a lung-busting amount of air to elevate her implants—Valerie was unstoppable.

"Got a light?" she purred at a Tobey Maguire clone and flipped her hair over her shoulder.

The poor guy didn't stand a chance.

"Uh, yeah…" he fumbled in his pocket.

"Oh, and a ciggie too?" she baby-girled.

Never failed. If I tried to puff up my chest like that, I'd chip a guy's front tooth with my sternum.

"Nine out of ten doctors say that silicon turns brown when exposed to nicotine." I picked a new jab for our ongoing boob wars.

"Piss off," she said for the millionth time.

Then this cute, lanky guy with a boyish grin walked over. "Can I get a jump?" His eyes locked onto Valerie. A lick of his strawberry blonde hair dropped over one eye. Charm on overdrive, he lit his cigarette off Valerie's and blatantly stared down the v-neck of her top.

Behind my right shoulder, "Filthy habit. Don't you think?" whispered into my ear.

I turned to find a Cheshire cat inhabiting the body of what had to be a musician. The ponytail was a dead giveaway and his leather trench sealed my first impression.

"Pretty impressive tag team action." I smiled at the set-up.

"You like it?" He slouched against the patio railing.

I gave him an obvious sweeping glance, noting his lean body and the sun wrinkles around his eyes. "It's almost one o'clock, I guess you'll do," I said.

A robust laugh burst from his lips. "And who says you're not my last choice?"

Touché. Quick and sarcastic. Not bad.

"So, Miss Congeniality, what's your name?"

"Annette. And the name on your mug shot?"

"I'm Tyler and that's my bass player, Shane."

Ha! I knew it. A musician. God, I'm good.

"Let's go dance." He motioned to his friend who was all over Valerie like a layer of moisturizer.

The song "Atomic Dog" bumped through the speakers while the band was on a break. Good DJ. Great flashback tune.

On the dance floor, the guys moved into the leg-hump position to freak with us. Timeless. Freaking was like a tribal mating dance from the dawn of man. You just knew that if a guy didn't have rhythm, he would suck in bed. Tyler had rhythm, and so did Shane. Valerie and I exchanged knowing smiles.

When the song ended, Tyler nodded in appreciation. "I like the way you move."

"Thanks, you're not too bad yourself," I said.

Tyler's eyes locked onto mine. "You're a stripper, aren't you?"

Shit.

"I'm a *writer*," I said loudly over the DJ chatter.

"I was born at night, but not last night." Tyler smiled. "I'm a track coach to pay the bills." He leaned close to my ear. "Just admit it. It's no big deal."

"Okay, so what if I am?" I said.

"Ha! I knew it. Only a stripper could move her ass the way you do."

Well, that wasn't true in my case. I could dance before I started working at the club. How else was I supposed to get hired?

"So, you're a stripper, then why don't you have a boob job?" He seemed genuinely puzzled.

"Because I don't need one. I have a six-foot personality in a five-foot-three frame. If I added boobs, it would just be overkill," I smiled sweetly.

"So, what you're telling me is that you are a terrible stripper and you can't afford it?"

"There are two types of men," I said sharply. "Butt men and boob men. I appeal to butt men and I'm perfectly okay with that."

Before he could respond with another flip comment, I pinned him with a question. "Which one are you?"

"Definitely a butt man," Tyler responded with a look that said he expected to find USDA Select tattooed on my ass.

"Good. Then shut up and dance."

The DJ cued up another song and Tyler and I moved together to the beat of the music. Our dance was almost a challenge to see who had the best moves. I stole a glance at Shane and Valerie. They bumped against each other in a typical nightclub mating ritual.

When the song ended, the cruel closing lights glared through the night-club. Barely sober guys steered their staggering drunk, late-night selections toward the parking lot.

It looked sad to me. I was three years stone sober and wondered if those girls would ever realize as I had—that waking up the next morning feeling poisoned just wasn't worth it.

Tyler and Shane stepped outside the exit and held a boys only summit. Valerie and I walked through the parking lot toward her SUV.

"Hey!" Shane called out. "Do you girls want to go get some breakfast?"

Valerie looked at me and shrugged. "What do you think?"

"Sure. I'll go if you want to go," I said. "Do you want to go? Because if you don't really want to go, that's okay, we don't have to go."

"I'll go," she said.

"Okay, we'll go," I relayed to the guys.

"Let's hit Harbor House. I'm dying for a peanut butter shake and chili cheese fries," Valerie cast her vote.

"It's too busy. Don't you remember the last time? By the time we got seated, we almost fell asleep at the table."

Tyler waved his arm signaling for us to follow him. "We'll take you to a place up in Newport at the pier. They have great croissant sandwiches."

We followed the guys from the Crazy Horse parking lot to Newport Pier. A line of post-nightclubers already formed a barricade in the doorway of the small bakery.

The Asian owner smiled broadly. "Come in, you eat." He waved everyone inside and slid a rack of fresh croissants into the glass display case. It didn't take long before the tray was completely empty.

With our sandwiches in hand, we walked the length of the pier. At the end, I leaned over the railing and watched the wave swells ebb and flow over the barnacle-crusted posts. I always felt such a draw to the ocean. The rhythm and energy and depth filled me with a sense of peace. I closed my eyes and felt a mist of salt spray on my face. Slowly and deeply, I inhaled the tangy scent.

"Let's walk down the boardwalk." Tyler took my hand, dusting the tiny croissant flakes from my fingertips.

Shane and Valerie walked ahead of us; we hung back and let the distance grow, then followed.

"So, tell me about yourself," I said.

Tyler's passion was music; his face lit up as he spoke. The stories of his travels and the promotion of his band fascinated me. It seemed so glamorous. I wondered what it would be like to be the lead singer's girlfriend.

I could just see it: sitting beside the stage with Tyler singing a ballad to me—about me—while the audience looked on with endearing smiles. Then I watched in horror as a skanky groupie unzipped his tight leather pants and gave him a blowjob behind the backstage curtain. That would be my luck. I blinked away the images, and concentrated on his story.

Tyler talked and I listened. He was the most interesting guy I'd met in a while. I hoped I'd get the chance to know him better.

too good to be true?
Tuesday, April 23

Our date started at Johnny Rockets; we shared a chocolate shake in a sundae glass with two straws. It was so 1950s it made me wish I had a poodle skirt.

The warm sand of Laguna Main Beach beckoned, and our conversation flowed easily from one topic to another, as we walked along the water's edge.

Tyler spoke mostly about his family. They were deeply religious and didn't approve of his music, but he still hoped one day they'd become more supportive.

"I wonder if it's always like that for all creative people." I shaded my eyes from the sun and looked out across the ocean. The white wash churned over our feet and splashed up the leg of my shorts.

When the water receded, Tyler bent to pick up a smooth stone and threw it in a high arc into a cresting wave. "I don't know, maybe," he said.

It was something I'd thought about a lot since Kevin left. He seemed to be the only person I'd found who understood that I couldn't do anything else but write. He felt that way about golf. And Tyler felt the same way about his music.

We continued down the beach and I studied Tyler's profile as we walked. It was slightly rugged—a manly look, so different from my usual baby-faced preference. It reminded me that time was passing and unfulfilled dreams still remained. I knew I wanted to spend my life with someone who felt the same drive to create. It seemed the only logical choice.

In a relationship with another creative, I'd never have to explain why I didn't have a Plan B: some sort of back-up career if I never made it as a writer. Another creative would understand. There is no Plan B.

Both lost in our own thoughts, we walked the beach in silence. I wondered how Tyler would be with Josh. It was such an uneasy balance—trying to find someone who would be perfect for my future, but also work in my present. I wasn't quite sure Tyler could be both; only time would tell.

Tyler checked his watch. "I'm glad we could hang out for a couple hours, but I have to take off and meet up with the guys for practice."

"I had a good time." It was a comfortable, relaxing date and I wanted to make sure we would do it again. "Maybe sometime Valerie and I can watch you guys practice. She's supposed to go out with Shane this weekend."

We walked to the corner and he pressed the crosswalk button.

"Yeah, maybe we'll meet you girls somewhere and all go out after practice sometime."

Back in the parking lot, we stood between our cars and shared a brief kiss.

"I brought you something." Tyler turned and reached through the open window of his Jeep. He lifted a CD jewel case from the glove box. "It's my demo CD."

"Wow. Thanks. I can't wait to hear it," I said, tucking it into my purse.

On the way home, I slid the CD into the deck. My car instantly filled with his sexy voice: a wannabe Jon Bon Jovi, circa 1986. Over the years, my musical taste had changed from rock to a more hip-hop flavor, but Tyler's music was nice. Being with him was nice. I wondered if it was all too good to be true.

he did what?
Thursday, April 25

Tyler invited me into his condo and offered to give me the grand tour. I pulled out my mental clipboard with the rating sheet for The List. We'd had plenty of conversations, but seeing how he lived would show me things about him that conversation wouldn't.

Dirty dishes piled in the sink, food crisping and congealing on the plates. Red flag: slob alert.

Pictures of family on the shelves of the entertainment center. A good sign, family oriented.

Extra pillows tossed artfully on the couch. Subtract Martha Stewart points for having both zebra and leopard prints.

He pointed down the hall. "Those two rooms are my roommates', they're still at work."

Bad sign: roommates. He might be a Peter Pan guy who hasn't outgrown his keg party days.

"My room is the loft upstairs." He motioned for me to walk up ahead of him.

Ten...eleven...twelve steps to the top. I counted like Rainman, and was curious if Tyler chose to walk behind me so he could check out my butt.

I looked around his small room. Nautical decorations. Okay, not great, but not bad. Outdoorsy is good. Thankfully, there wasn't a trout mounted on the wall.

A shrine of technology stood in the corner and he waved his hand like a product model. "This is my keyboard and recording equipment."

"It's nice," I said. Lame response, but I couldn't think of anything else to say.

"Want to hear the new song I'm working on?" He sounded like a boy who was hiding a frog in his pocket.

"Sure," I shrugged and looked around the tiny room.

While he fiddled with the buttons and levers, I scanned everything for signs of unobtrusive female markings.

No earrings left casually on the nightstand. No ponytail scrunchie on the floor, kicked slightly under the bed. Ssssssnifff. No lingering perfume spritzed "accidentally" into the curtains.

It looked good so far. No sign of other women, but I wasn't quite ready to put a checkmark in the monogamous box.

He punched a few keys and music filled the room. In the recording, his gravelly voice sang a wrenching ballad of lost love; tormented emotion growled in the lyrics.

Nice try. Show me your soft side and I'll be sure to fall over on your bed with my legs open.

"Did you write that?" I asked when the song ended.

"Yeah, and I wrote all the music for it and I played the instruments too. After I recorded it all, I layered it together." Tyler walked over and sat on the edge of his bed, patting the space beside him. "Come take a look at my book of songs."

A modern variation on the '70s ploy to get a girl naked by offering to show her some etchings?

I sat on the bed next to Tyler. He handed me the notebook and I flipped through the pages.

"Relax a little." Tyler pushed me backward onto the bed. My knees still curved around the edge of the mattress, my feet planted firmly on the floor. In one swift move, Tyler rolled on top of me. I was pinned beneath him with the songbook covering my chest like a shield.

Our noses almost touching, I looked directly into his eyes. "What are you doing?" I asked. Woodenly, my shell supported his body weight.

A few seconds passed. I wasn't sure if he intended to kiss me, but my stiffness certainly didn't invite any continued sexual advance.

Tyler rolled off of me and onto the bedcover. He propped himself up on an elbow. "So, what do you think of my songs? Did you listen to that CD I gave you?"

Yeah, good idea to pretend that didn't happen.

"I liked most of them," I said, "but a couple have electric guitar rifts that seem to go on too long."

So, now I'm a music critic, as if I know what I'm talking about.

I glanced at my watch. "I have to meet up with my girlfriends. I need to get going."

Tyler walked me to my car. We stood awkwardly for a moment until he leaned down to kiss me. It seemed okay to kiss him standing up. The bedroom thing was just too weird.

"I'll call you later," Tyler said. He loped across the parking lot and turned to wave.

After I drove away, I plucked my cell phone out of my purse and auto-dialed home. "Hey Wonderboy, I'm just checking in. What's up?"

"I was riding bikes with Adam, but he had to go in for dinner. So I had a salad, now I'm making some soup and a grilled cheese sandwich. Are you on your way home?"

"No, I'm heading over to do crafts with the girls," I said.

"How was your date?" I could hear the curiosity in his voice. "I listened to his CD. When can I meet him?"

After today's weird little episode, it would be a while. "I don't know. We'll see."

"I have to make sure he's not a jerk." Josh's teasing carried a twinge of seriousness.

At least we shared a common goal.

"Well, I'm here at the craft store now. I'll call you when I'm on my way home."

"Mom, wait. Can I have some ice cream after dinner?"

I smiled. Thirteen and he still made a point of asking first. "Yeah, buddy. You can have a small bowl."

117

I tucked my phone back into my purse and walked toward the back room of the Tall Mouse store.

I laughed when I saw Heather, Bonita, and Valerie all wearing T-shirts and jean overalls. I looked down at my own overalls and mused that we hadn't even called to plan it.

We set up the materials and watched the painting lesson from the craft lady. Then Valerie, Bonita, Heather and I sat gathered around the table trying to create art for art's sake. Stencils and bottles of paint in each girl's chosen palette lay scattered across the table.

"So then what did he do?" Valerie loaded her brush and dabbed into a flower-shaped stencil.

"Nothing. He just laid on top of me," I said.

"You're kidding?" Bonita paused and a drip of blue paint fell from her brush.

"He didn't say anything?" Heather asked.

"Nope."

"Well, what did you say?" Valerie cast her stencil aside and dipped into her yellow.

"I just looked at him, nose to nose, and asked what he thought he was doing."

"How embarrassing." Heather reached to rinse her brush and knocked over the small jar of rinse water. Bonita grabbed the roll of paper towels, trying to absorb the wetness.

Valerie scrambled to move her work. "Dating sucks," she said.

"Tell me something I don't know." I sighed and turned back to my painting project.

a ghost from bankruptcy past
Friday, May 3

You know the prickly feeling you get when you sense someone is watching you? Well, that was the feeling that crawled up the back of my neck.

I looked across the aisle and locked eyes with David in the mirrored back wall of the main stage. He sat at the tip rail with his back to me, studying me in the reflection.

When he saw my transparent surprise, he broke the gaze by feigning concentration on the topless dancer on stage.

Two years go by and now you're showing up? You sleazy fuck.

"Excuse me," I said to the customer I was sitting beside. "I see someone I need to talk to." The man nodded and thumbed another lime into his Corona bottle. "You go ahead, but come back later. I enjoyed the company."

I walked up behind David and leaned my hip against the chair next to him. "So, did you come in here to pay back the fifty thousand dollars you owe me?"

David chuckled in his trademark, sickeningly charming way. "I wouldn't say it's quite that much."

"Funny, that was the amount on my bankruptcy papers."

"You can't blame that on me. I didn't force you to give me that money. You did it of your own free will…because you loved me."

"It was an investment in your business and you bailed, asshole."

His eyes roved over my body: tan, lean, and exposed in a crimson velvet micro-mini skirt and halter-top. "You look good," he said.

"You look like shit. You got fat and you need a haircut. What is that, a mullet?" He looked like a shaggy, grunge magazine model gone slightly soft.

David responded with an easy laugh. "So, are you single now?"

"Yes...um...no…it's none of your business."

"Let me take you out to dinner," David said.

"Why? Because you already ran your new girlfriend out of money?" I didn't wait for his response. It was my turn next on stage. I pivoted on my heel and brushed through the dressing room curtains.

Ballsy prick. What was he thinking? I peeked through the curtain, hoping he took the hint and left.

It was time to switch into entertainer mode. After five years, it was easy, but it wasn't always that way. For the first year, whenever it was my time to

119

perform, I waited behind the curtain, shaking and feeling like I didn't know whether to pee or throw up. I was always afraid I'd fall in front of everyone. The only thing that would be more humiliating than falling—would be falling naked.

The DJ announced my name and started one of the songs from my playlist. I entered the stage with a slow strut, using the stripper drag-walk. Think Jessica Rabbit in eight-inch platform stilettos. My steps matched the tempo of the music.

David's eyes followed me across the stage as I flirted and played up to the customers at the tip rail.

I worked my way along the brass rail to David's seat. The plush, red thong of my outfit curved between the swell of my smooth, bare ass. I rolled and swayed my hips in front of him.

He was definitely an ass man. That I knew.

"I've been there," he taunted so only I could hear.

I turned like a coiled serpent. "And you'll never be there again."

I crossed to center stage and arched against the pole. Pulling the strings of my top, I let it fall to the floor. I locked eyes with David, challenging his gaze. Then I dismissed him with a flick of my lashes and ignored him while I finished my routine.

At the end of the song, I put on my top and went along the rail to collect my tips. When I reached David's seat, I brushed his money off the rail into his face. "Fuck off," I said, as the bills fluttered onto the floor.

I worked my way around the room collecting tips from the customers at the tables and offering private dances. When I reached the far side of the room, David leaned over my shoulder just as I stopped to chat with a customer.

"Excuse me, can I get a private dance with you?" he said. A twenty-dollar bill stood erect between the two fingers of his Boy Scout pledge.

I started to say no, but changed my mind and snatched it from his hand. "Yeah, I'll take your money." I walked away from him toward the lap dance area.

He followed behind. "Are you going to take your top off during the dance?"

"You know that's against club rules." I shot him a withering look over my shoulder.

"I thought you might make an exception—for me."

I ignored him and continued walking.

David walked fast to catch up with my stride. "Aren't you going to hold my hand to guide me there?" he asked.

I spun around to face him. "Talking will cost you extra." I pointed to the couch. "Sit down, shut up, and don't touch me. Those are the rules." I leveled the ultimatum. "If you don't like it—leave. And I keep the money."

David mimicked zipping his lips and lifted his hands in surrender.

The next song had a slow grind tempo: "Pony" by Ginuwine.

Perfect. One of my favorites.

I arched and undulated, my body moving to the music while he watched. I snaked my hips low and rhythmically just inches above his lap. So close, but not close enough for contact. David drew in a deep breath, letting it expel slowly. I knew he was fighting to control his response to me.

Time to turn up the heat.

I leaned in close and locked eyes with David. My gaze slid to his lips. The tip of my tongue left a damp shimmering trail along my bottom lip and I leaned in closer. I tilted my head slightly, letting my lashes brush my eyes almost closed. I dipped in to hover with my lips just a millimeter from his. The slightest move from either of us would cross the line to a kiss.

"Your three minutes are up." I pushed away from him with my hand in the middle of his chest.

"That was unfair." His eyes studied the floor. "You get off on having the power, don't you?" he said, looking up into my eyes.

David stood up and slid his hands down the thighs of his jeans, adjusting the fit.

"Maybe," I said fiercely. I tucked the twenty into my moneybox and snapped the clasp. "I know that's all you have in your wallet, now get lost."

David stepped deep into my personal space. "Annette, you're a smart girl. You and I both know hate isn't the opposite of love. Apathy is." A smile played around his lips. "I can tell you still care about me or you wouldn't be so mean-spirited right now."

"You're just a thief and I don't give a shit about you. Get out of my club," I said.

David pressed his business card into my hand. "Call me tomorrow. I just want to tell you something." He turned and walked toward the exit.

"I'm not buying whatever you're selling," I yelled after him.

reach out and smack someone
Saturday, May 4

I sat by the phone staring at David's business card cupped in my hand. Should I? I couldn't decide if I really cared what he had to say or not. Maybe karma had finally bitten him in the ass.

When I met him, David owned one business shirt. He washed it in the kitchen sink of his apartment each night, ironing it in the morning before going to work. So thin in the elbows, that shirt was nearly transparent. Not exactly the successful image a financial consultant at a major firm would try to cultivate.

David had just started with the company. He came from the same blue-collar background I did. We both had college student loans to pay off and dreams to be so much more than where we came from.

When his apartment lease was up, David moved into my rented condo and we often talked late into the night about our future. He knew, without a doubt, that within two years of building his business, he would be making a million dollars a year.

One evening, after returning from a business seminar, David had told me to close my eyes and hold out my hand.

When I opened my eyes, I found in my palm, a rubber stress ball colored blue and green like the Earth with the continents and oceans molded into the foam.

David looked into my eyes and said, "I know I don't have anything now, but I will. My business is closer to taking off than your writing, so if you help me now, when I make it, I'll help you so you can write full time."

And I believed him. I paid all the rent and the utilities. I bought the food. I gave him money for gas, put tires on his car, bought software for his work computer, and dressed him from head to toe in a brand-new Alfani business wardrobe with Jerry Garcia ties.

Monday through Friday, I woke up with David at four o'clock in the morning, cooked a hot breakfast while he was in the shower, and sent him to work with an ice chest full of food packed neatly in Tupperware. For lunch: a deli sandwich that took two hands to hold closed, a salad with homemade balsamic vinaigrette on the side. And for a snack: Globe grapes cut in half with the seeds taken out. The dinner containers held baked, boneless and skinless chicken breasts, steamed veggies, and red potatoes or white rice. Everything he wanted for his diet, and enough food to last through his long days and into the evenings of cold-calls when he solicited for new clients.

David told me his coworkers in the other cubicles teased him about the ice chest—just once—until they saw what was inside.

"All the guys wish their wives were like you," he said.

It felt good to hear. I continued to play the perfect pseudowife; I wanted to be that perfect.

Time and distance gave me a different perspective. I must've been totally delusional to think that farce was really headed toward happily-ever-after.

After so much time had passed, did it even matter what David had to say now? What could he possibly say to make up for using me? Nagging curiosity made me pick up the phone and key in the numbers from his business card.

David answered on the third ring and I jumped right to the point. "So, what did you want to say?"

He chuckled warmly. "What? No hello? No how are you today?"

"Cut the shit. If you have something valid to say, then say it."

It was easy to be a bitch to David. I could still feel the sharp sting of his words when he left me.

"Look, I wanted to tell you something because it's just something I feel like I have to do."

"And?" I said. I had no intention of making it easy for him.

He took a deep breath and launched into his explanation. "When we were together, I was really stressed about succeeding with my business. And you were so amazing. You did everything for me."

My time. My encouragement. My love. My money. He took it all. I met him at the club, but after our first year together, he decided I should quit. "You need to get a decent job where you use your brain instead of your body," he told me.

I quit for him, but I couldn't support David, Josh, and myself in South Orange County on seventeen dollars an hour as an executive assistant. Within six months, the collection agencies began calling. I was paying the rent with one credit card, buying groceries on a different credit card, and paying the credit card payments with cash advances from another.

That's when David left. He said my anxiety attacks about the bills made it hard for him to concentrate on his business. He hadn't given me a dime in almost two years together, but he had saved up enough money to get his own apartment at the beach when he moved out.

I snapped out of my reverie of the past. "Why don't you try telling me something I don't already know?" The pain of being taken for a ride never quite went away.

"Annette, try to listen for a few minutes so I can tell you how I really feel. I know you still think I'm a piece of shit, but let me just say what I have to say."

I tried to decide if I really wanted to hear it.

He took my silence as a sign to continue. "I've finally realized I was a total jerk and I'll never find another woman like you. I made a mistake. I hope we can be friends. I miss having those long talks with you and laughing with you."

He paused dramatically as if he were going to say something significant. "And I miss making love to you," he said quietly.

"Are you finished?"

"Well, yeah…I guess so," David said.

"Okay, now, I'm going to tell you something." Despite the bitterness tightening my throat, my long dormant anger sprang to life. "It's nice that you've had your little epiphany and maybe if it came with an offer to repay me, I might be more accepting. But since it's just a way for you to clear your conscience and try to get back in my pants, you can just shove your apology up your ass." My torrent of thoughts continued. "I don't want to be your friend. I don't even want to pretend I know you. You don't fit into my life anymore. Got it?"

I could hear his breath release in a soft sigh. "If you ever change your mind, you have my number…"

I hung up the phone and tore his business card in half, again and again, until only tiny pieces remained. The jagged confetti fluttered into the wastebasket.

And I continued to stare at the Earth-shaped, rubber, stress ball on my desk that serves as a reminder to never go for that ride again.

free to good home
Sunday, May 5

I opened the sliding glass door and called the dogs to come inside for the night. Buddy rocketed into the house and almost knocked me over. He ran circles around the room, dropped onto the floor, and pushed his body along the carpet with his back legs. What a clown. I laughed so hard I leaned against the wall for support.

Buddy bolted upstairs, dragging himself along the wall. Almost eighteen months old and still just a crazy puppy. Back down the stairs he rumbled, eyes glazed, tongue lolling from his mouth. I doubled over with laughter. He galloped over to me and wiped his body along the legs of my jeans.

Ugh! What is that smell? My nose wrinkled and my eyes began to water. SKUNK.

The dog bolted upstairs again.

"Buddy, get down here! Oh, no! Come!" I took the stairs two at a time. "Bad dog! Here boy, here boy!" On the landing, I dove for his legs and wrestled him to the floor. The chemical smell of skunk spray choked the breath out of me. I lost my grip on the dog and clung to the stair banister, dry-heaving.

Buddy ran toward Josh's room. I grabbed him by the tail and pulled hard, lunging forward to catch him by the hips with both hands. "Josh, wake up! Open your shower!"

Josh stepped into his doorway, hair plastered to one side of his head. He yawned and adjusted his *South Park* cartoon boxers. He looked at me and his face registered his confusion. "Mom, what are you doing on the floor on top of the dog?"

Buddy squirmed in my grasp. "Quick, open your shower. Buddy got skunked." I dragged the dog by the collar toward the doorway. He pulled back like a reluctant mule.

"Ewww, Mom, not in my shower! He stinks!" Josh cupped his hand over his nose and mouth.

"Help me. Now!" I flashed one of those parental looks that foretold the probability of pending death.

Josh held the door while I wrestled the eighty-five-pound dog into the shower. I turned on the water and hosed off Buddy using the hand-held sprayer. Josh stood in the doorway watching and plugging his nose.

"Hold him. I have to go to the store."

"You're kidding me, right?" Josh stepped backward and looked for a place to run.

Now I know why some animals eat their young.

"Hold the dog. I'll be back in a few minutes." I punctuated my words with a scowl.

On the way to the market, I dialed the vet's after-hours emergency number.

Can the concept of an emergency be subjective?

While the phone continued to ring, I remembered a story my dad told me once when I was sixteen. Our old ranch dog, Baron, chased skunks regularly.

So, one day at the recommendation of a neighbor, Dad went to the store and bought fifteen disposable douches to use to shampoo the dog. The grocery clerk looked curiously at his purchase, so Dad told her he was a pimp.

It's the kind of family story that stays with you for a lifetime.

I decided not to douche the dog, so when the vet's service answered, I asked the operator if there were any alternatives.

"Mix one quart hydrogen peroxide with a quarter cup of baking soda and one teaspoon of dish soap. Lather, rinse and repeat as many times as you need to," she said.

what's that smell?
Monday, May 6

I waited for Tyler in the parking lot of Barnes & Noble. I glanced at my watch. Twenty minutes late. It didn't bother me though. It's not like I would ever be crowned Punctuality Poster Girl.

I wandered into the bookstore, zigzagging slowly through the aisles. I stopped at a wall of books in the relationship self-help section. Most of the books seemed to be written for people who still had a relationship.

A little too late to buy one of those.

One title caught my eye. *The Rules: Time-Tested Secrets for Capturing the Heart of Mr. Right.* I picked it up and thumbed through the pages. According to the book, I'd been doing it all wrong—for years. It was no wonder I was still single. I decided to buy the book and implement *The Rules* immediately. I didn't want to let this one get away.

Tyler rang my cell phone to say that he was pulling into the parking lot. I finished my purchase and tucked the paperback into the bottom of my purse. The best-planned attack was definitely a surprise attack.

Tyler opened the door just as I stepped out of the bookstore.

"Hey, sorry I'm late. The movie's about to start, can you run?"

"Uh, sure," I said.

About as fast as a three-legged rhino in Birkenstocks.

We took off in a sprint toward the theater. My purse jostled against my ribs. Thirty-four and running in strappy sandals to watch Spiderman? I'd expect my son would ask me to do it, but not a guy I was dating.

Tyler and I settled into the darkness. No popcorn. No drinks. He didn't want to miss a single minute.

A radioactive spider bit Peter Parker and Tyler watched raptly.

"Do you smell that? What *is* that smell?" Tyler whispered, leaning over and wrinkling his nose.

I faked a stretch and took a sniff under one arm. Maybe my deodorant was on vacation after that run. "I dunno. What do you smell?"

"Something smells like a skunk," he said.

The darkness of the theater hid the redness of my face. Should I tell him? Yeah, there's a great idea. Um, by the way, that nasty smell of feral rodent ass gland—that's me.

"Really? I can't smell it," I said.

"You're lucky. It's nasty," he whispered back.

thick crust temptation
Monday, May 13

I stepped into his kitchen and set the pizza on the counter. Tyler had mentioned he had boxes of flyers for his band that needed to be folded and stapled, so I told him I'd swing by with pizza and a movie to help.

Okay, so my plan broke five of the rules—not counting the rule I broke when I called him instead of waiting for him to call me.

The flyers were scattered in random piles all around the living room. My OCD immediately flared up to near seizure proportions. I quickly dove in and organized the paper chaos into neat piles of flat, folded to be stapled, and already stapled piles along the length of his coffee table. I set the stapler at a left angle to the folded stack for easy stapling. Effortlessly, I moved flyers through the assembly line and stacked them into the open box waiting at the other end of the table.

Tyler watched my efficiency with an appraising look and then sat beside me to do the stapling while I folded. We watched MTV while we worked. The piles finally gone, the boxes held all the folded and stapled flyers.

I hopped up and went into the kitchen. "You hungry now? I'll serve the pizza." I looked in his cupboard for plates.

Tyler scanned through the channels with the remote. "Ooh, it's on again. I've been wanting to catch this documentary on The Mommas and the Poppas."

I made a face behind the kitchen partition. Borrrring. It was the last thing I wanted to sit and watch.

"Good idea. That sounds interesting," I said.

Two points. I let him lead and responded positively to his interests. I swear these rules are going to kill me.

The documentary dragged like a dog with no back legs.

When the credits rolled down the screen, Tyler glanced at the clock and jumped up. "I have to get ready for band practice."

I tried not to sound disappointed. "I'll let myself out. Call me after you guys finish."

"I'm going to jump in the shower real quick. You can wait here. Or you can join me." Tyler flashed a daring, teasing smile and walked into the bathroom, pushing the door only partially closed.

Join him? Yeah right.

The bathroom door, still two-thirds of the way open, was located directly across the small living room. About fifteen steps from the couch, I guessed.

I saw Tyler's bare hip and the length of his leg as he stepped into the shower. It was a sharp contrast—the tan torso and leg with the fair skin in between. I heard the shower spray against his body. The water rhythm changed in tempo when it rolled off and cascaded to the floor of the shower as he washed.

I looked down at the pizza cheese stuck on the plates. It looked like orange rubber.

What if I just stood up, took off my clothes, walked in there, and stepped into the shower with him? I wondered what he'd say.

Tyler didn't say anything. He pressed me against the tiles of the shower and our lips met. Hungry and insistent. His body was slick with soap. He turned with me and let the water cascade down our bodies while his hands moved sensually over my wet skin. His lips never left mine. He sought. And probed.

"I actually thought you might join me." Tyler stepped out of the bathroom, tightening the towel around his waist. He shook some of the dampness from his long hair. Droplets of water clung to his faintly chiseled torso.

Still sitting on the couch, I hugged a leopard pillow against my chest. "I thought about it."

"Oh well, your loss." Tyler said.

all dressed up and no one to blow

My Birthday
Saturday, May 25

A pedicure, sushi, and a movie—that was my choice for my thirty-fifth birthday. Bonita, Valerie, and I started a birthday tradition years ago; each girl decided what she wanted for her special day and the others would make it happen. My day passed, filled with laughter and chatter about everything and nothing.

"Are you going to celebrate with Josh tonight?" Bonita asked as we walked out of the theater. "My boys always make me a birthday dinner."

"We'll do it tomorrow. Josh has a barbeque and sleepover at his friend's house tonight. And Tyler is supposed to pick me up in two hours."

"Where's he taking you?" Valerie slurped the last of her large diet Coke.

"He said he's taking me over to Sing Sing, that piano bar at the Irvine Spectrum. He knows the owner, so he's going to get up on the stage, play the piano, and sing to me."

"Aw, that is sooo sweet," Bonita and Valerie said in unison.

"Tyler said he wants it to be a special night out for us. I have to get home and figure out what to wear."

We hugged goodbye and I rushed to my car.

I stood in my closet and pulled out my favorite jeans. Comfortable and cute. Low rise, stretchy—they made my butt look small and round. Black suede boots? Brown suede boots? Or tan suede boots? That depended on the colors in the top. I changed tops four times. Finally, I decided on a sleeveless v-neck top that had a lacy overlay in a deep red, charcoal, and beige floral design. I finished with a red, antique, teardrop bead necklace with matching earrings and a bracelet.

I glanced at the clock in the bathroom. Fifteen minutes late. Good. I'm ready. He'll be here any minute.

I stretched my damp towel over the shower door and put the deodorant and toothpaste back in the medicine cabinet. I spritzed some perfume into the air in front of me and walked into the mist flailing my arms to capture the scent lightly on my skin. I hung the other three tops in the closet.

Twenty minutes late. I began reorganizing my makeup drawer.

Maybe I should call him to see if he's almost here. I looked at the cell phone resting on the granite vanity next to my large barrel curling iron. I picked up the curling iron, started to fix an unruly curl, then set it down again. I grabbed the phone and scanned the internal phone book for Tyler's cell number.

It rang once and went straight to voicemail. "Hi, um, it's me. Just wondered if you got lost and maybe didn't have my number with you to call. Call me if you need directions again. See you soon. Bye. Call me."

I picked up the curling iron and decided to fry the ends of my hair again. That killed another fifteen minutes.

Maybe I should call him one more time. I snatched the phone, but dialed Valerie's number instead.

"I think I just got stood up," I said as soon as she answered.

"No, Tyler wouldn't stand you up on your birthday. He's probably just running late. Did you try calling him?"

"Yeah. It went straight to voicemail, so he must have his phone turned off. I left a message."

I sat down on the edge of the bathtub and cradled the phone against my shoulder. "I think I'm being stood up."

Just the thought of it stung. An uncomfortable giggle squeaked out. "I can't believe this."

"Maybe his cell phone is just out of range," Valerie said.

I looked at the clock again. Forty-five minutes late.

"I am. I'm getting stood up." I paced the length of the bathroom. "If I am getting stood up, I'm not staying home." The heels of my boots tapped woodenly against the tiles. "I'm all dressed. I actually have make-up on and I curled my hair. Twice." I stopped in front of the mirror and stared at my reflection. "I look too cute to stay home. Let's go out."

"I'm in my pjs in bed. I'm not going anywhere. But if you want to come over here and watch a movie with me, you can."

I sighed to release the squeezing feeling in my chest. "No, that's okay. I guess I'll just go to bed."

"Tyler's a dick and Shane didn't call me either. Call me tomorrow and we'll go shopping," Valerie said before hanging up.

I stared into the mirror and slowly reached up to take each earring from my lobes. I pulled the make-up remover from the cabinet and wiped away the earthy colors from my face. As if on rewind, each movement undid my preparations for the date.

Finally stripped bare, I pulled an old T-shirt of Kevin's from the closet, slipped it over my head, and I snapped off the lights. I didn't want to look in the mirror anymore. I slid between the sheets and tucked an arm under my pillow. Sleep came quickly: always a great escape.

My cell phone rang, vibrating against the nightstand. I rolled over and scrambled for it. The digital clock showed five minutes after midnight.

"Hullo?" I sat up, slightly disoriented.

"Hey, I just got your message."

I instantly came awake at the sound of Tyler's voice.

"I left my phone in the car when I stopped off to grab something to eat. I ran into the guys from the band, so we had some beers. We can still meet up for an hour if you want."

I pulled the phone away from my ear and stared at it. He was kidding, right? There was no way he could possibly be serious...

The audacity of his statement left me speechless for a moment. Then I just wanted to scream obscenities and poke sharp pins into a leather-jacketed Tyler voodoo doll.

My words, when they finally came out, were well modulated. "You are totally rude and inconsiderate. I can't believe you stood me up *on my birthday* and then call me acting like it's no big deal. You're an asshole." I stressed each word carefully. "Don't-ever-call-me-again." I hung up without waiting for a response.

I wonder if there is a rule book for guys about how to treat girls like shit?

pickled penis

1 self-absorbed prick
1/4 lb. coarse salt
1 cup white-hot angry brand vinegar
2/3 cup sweet as sugar
1/4 cup penis pickling spice

Detach penis from self-absorbed prick by chopping with a blunt spoon.

Sprinkle salt liberally over severed penis until it bubbles like a snail. Douse with vinegar.

Toss penis into pot with sugar, spice and nothing nice.
Boil vigorously. Pour remains into clear glass jar. Cap tightly.

Set jar in a cool, dark place. Visit occasionally to relive sense of satisfaction.

Yield: Pure justice.
Unlimited servings.
Nutritional Value: None.

No guaranteed weight loss.

But somehow you feel a lot more positive about dating.

the
transition

fortune cookie wisdom

Sunday, June 9

Bonita, Valerie, and I stepped into the sunlight from the dimness of the movie theater and reached for our sunglasses. Bonita donned her frameless Gucci, and Valerie, a pair of tortoise shell, flea-market specials.

"I see you have new sunglasses," Bonita peered at Valerie.

"So how long did it take you to lose the last pair?" I took my Black Fly sunglasses off the top of my head and put them on.

"Three days."

Bonita and I laughed.

"Laugh all you want," Valerie said. "That's why I don't buy expensive sunglasses."

We walked down the aisle of shops and cafés. Valerie pushed through the door to a fast food Chinese place and we all stood looking at the trays of food behind the glass buffet. After making our selections, we perched on stools at a high table.

"So what did you think about the movie?" Bonita dipped her plastic spoon into her hot and sour soup.

I rubbed my chopsticks together to shave off the splinters. "I thought Diane Lane's performance was amazing."

"That French guy was hot," Valerie said.

"The movie made such a huge statement about choices. I liked the part when they flashed back to the taxi scene." Pinching a piece of spicy eggplant, I guided it to my mouth with the chopsticks and talked around it. "If she would've just gotten into the taxi instead of going up to that guy's apartment, none of it would have happened."

Bonita shook her head. "She had everything. A great husband. A family. And she sacrificed it all."

"For incredibly hot sex," Valerie added.

"I don't think it was worth it." I twisted the cap off my bottled water and took a sip.

"Euuuuwww." Bonita's face contorted as she pulled a straight, black hair out of her soup. The strand continued to unfold from the liquid until Bonita held a dripping hair about a foot long. "Sick. I think I'm going to vomit." She gingerly wiped her fingertips on a napkin.

"It's just protein." I laughed and took a bite of my tofu.

"Let's get out of here and go shopping." Valerie stabbed her fork into her chow mein and stood up.

On the way out the door, I grabbed a fortune cookie from the basket and unwrapped it. I snapped the crescent in half and pulled the thin rectangle of paper from between the crisp pieces. I read the words to my fortune: *In life, you will settle satisfactorily.*

What the hell does that mean? Settle? I have The List. I want what I want. *I don't settle.*

"What did it say?" Bonita asked.

"Nothing. It was stupid." I crumpled the paper between my fingertips and dropped the tiny wad into a trash bin.

After returning home, I flopped across the bed to take a nap before work.

My cell phone rang: "Ding Dong the Witch is Dead." The display on the screen showed the call coming from Valerie's cell.

"Miss me already?" I asked.

"Hey, do you want to go to a Wines Around the World party with me tonight?"

"I have to be ready to go on stage by nine and don't get off work until two."

"Call off work. I heard there'll be a ton of single guys," she said.

"There will be a ton of single guys at the club who are paying my bills." I rolled onto my back and balled the pillow under my head.

She sighed. "Try thinking long term. Are they all doctors and attorneys and rich corporate guys?" she asked, sarcasm lacing her tone.

"So, where is it and how did you get invited?"

"Kari, the chick who works at the Nordstrom makeup counter who is friends with that foot fetish guy I dated, well, she has a friend named Lana who's a real estate agent." Valerie tried valiantly to make the six degrees of separation make sense.

"That still doesn't explain how you got invited."

"I'm not finished. I guess Lana throws wine parties at her house in Laguna Niguel, so Kari invited me and said I could invite someone, so I'm inviting you and Bonita."

"I dunno, it's not really my scene. You know I don't drink, and even when I did, I hated wine. It's a waste of good grapes. So, what's the point?"

"The point is—I want you to go with me because it'll be fun."

Lana turned out to be a friendly Hungarian woman with tomato red hair and a thick accent. The guests were typical Orange County status mongers: rich guys and the gold-digging women trying to land them. The conversation revolved around wine, international travel, and poorly concealed bragging about luxury cars, investments, and expensive houses. I didn't have anything to contribute and didn't find the conversation interesting, so I sat quietly and looked around the room. Then the man sitting to my right turned to me and asked what I did for a living.

At that moment, I needed to decide exactly how interesting I wanted the conversation to become. I could say I was a freelance copywriter and also mention my unfinished book. Or I could play the shock card. Valerie and Bonita looked at each other and then looked at me. They knew my answer would depend on my mood.

I was bored.

"I'm a topless dancer," I deadpanned.

The reaction at the table was distinctly divided. The men leaned forward, brimming with curiosity. The women wore the same expression you would expect from cats that had been held down and drenched with a garden hose.

I fielded a few questions and that opened a discussion about women, men, and sexual expectations. A debate started about whether a woman owed a man anything if he bought her a drink in a nightclub. I sat back and listened as the conversation evolved.

The evening finally held some promise to be moderately entertaining.

the one that got away
Saturday, June 15

Josh and I maneuvered through the throng of people toward a little Mexican cantina to have lunch. The shops and cafés by the Rancho Santa Margarita Lake overflowed with brisk weekend business.

I saw a flash of blondeness when a tall guy in a white tank shirt broke through the crowd and wrapped me in a bear hug.

Startled, I stepped back from his embrace. "Ryan! Hi…how are you?" I noticed a tribal tattoo covering the inside of one forearm. A new addition since I saw him a year ago.

I turned to indicate my curious teen. "This is my son, Josh."

"Hey, nice to meet you." Ryan pulled off his sunglasses and extended his hand, pumping Josh's arm enthusiastically.

"So, what have you been up to? Did you ever end up marrying that golf guy?" Ryan asked.

His question pinpricked my heart. "No, he dumped me," I said with as much nonchalance as I could manage.

I looked to Josh's face to see if he seemed convinced that I was no longer affected by the break-up. It was a hard read; he was busy studying Ryan. I saw his eyes travel from Ryan's soul patch and small goatee, down to his lean-muscled arms.

"Does that mean I get another chance?" Ryan suddenly seemed so serious. He held me, unblinking, in his gaze. "My friends call you 'The One That Got Away,'" he said.

I looked at Josh and noticed his eyebrows raised, but I couldn't read his expression.

"You're the one who never showed up at traffic school." I couldn't resist the dig. "So, I guess I should call you 'The One That I Never Heard From Again.'" I smiled to let him know I was teasing.

"I know. It's a long story. It's stupid, really." He looked at Josh and then back a me. "Can I take you both to lunch?"

Ryan could be intense and I wasn't sure I was ready for it. Five years ago, when we flirted at the idea of starting a relationship, I was. Certainly not now. But Ryan *was* only offering lunch. "Okay," I said with a shrug. "When?"

"How about right now?" He smiled and put an arm around my shoulder.

Standing there, with his arm around me, it just seemed too soon. Lunch seemed too, I don't know, too—right now.

I pulled away from Ryan. "Actually, we just ate." I flashed Josh a look when his mouth dropped open in protest. "But I'll give you my number and you can call me."

I scrambled to find a pen at the bottom of my purse, scribbled my number on the back of a gas receipt, and handed it to Ryan.

He bent and planted a quick kiss on my cheek. "Okay, well, it was great seeing you again. I'll call you." He aimed a wave in Josh's direction. "It was nice to finally meet you."

After Ryan loped away, Josh turned to me. "Why did you say we already ate? I'm starving. And we coulda got free food."

"Maybe some other time," I said.

I saw Josh weigh my statement. He knew my "some other time" loosely translated meant: "It's not going to happen."

"He seemed nice. I think you should go out with him," Josh said.

"We'll see." That was as much of a commitment as I could make at the moment.

call the exterminator—this house has renters
Saturday, June 22

The display on the computer switched from 6:59 A.M. to 7:00 A.M. I had decided to get an early start. I scanned the classified section of the Pennysaver online and jotted the rental house information on a notepad. Nine days until the end of the lease and I still hadn't found a place.

I clicked the drop-down menu and changed the search area from Orange County to Los Angeles County. Maybe it was time to move up there. If I moved close to the golf course where Kevin worked, I could casually bump into him somewhere. Maybe at a stoplight. Or at the grocery store. Or if I found out where he lived and happened to jog by... Jog? I don't jog. I hate jogging. Oh, m'god. I'm a stalker. It's true. I'm an opera-loving bunny boiler exactly like Glenn Close in the movie *Fatal Attraction.*

Okay, so maybe following Kevin to Los Angeles wasn't exactly a good idea. Can you say *restraining order,* boys and girls? A manic laugh burst from my lips. Okay, that is sooo not an option.

I gathered my keys, purse, and the notepad. Time to go house hunting. What a pain in the ass. Finding the best rental was like finding a lump of cheese hidden in a suburban maze. I despised dealing with the Nazi home owner's associations that fine you for not having a saucer under a potted plant on your porch, and the gated Stepford communities full of soccer moms in pink velour tracksuits minding your business instead of their own.

After driving all over town, one after another, I crossed the rentals off my list.

"Oh, you have *two* dogs? No, I'm sorry, you can only have one."

"You're a writer *and* you work in a bar? Well, I'm not sure this is in your price range."

"It's just you and your teenage son? And you *homeschool?* Now, isn't that interesting."

I sat in my car and pulled at the bodice of my ridiculously conservative, ankle-length, floral dress. Halloween in June. This year, I'm dressed up like a woman you'd want to rent your house to.

I read the details of the last house on the list: Cozy two-bedroom. Tile floors. Fenced backyard. $1,550 a month.

When I pulled up in front, I felt a flutter of excitement. It was less than half a mile away from Valerie's house. Small, only 1100 square feet, but totally cute. Slate blue with white trim. It even had flowerbeds and window boxes.

A dour-looking lady walked across the lawn and introduced herself. How convenient. Erma is the landlord—and she lives next door. Quick tally time. Pro: save the cost of a stamp each month by not mailing the rent check. Con: live like a bug under a hot magnifying glass.

Erma unlocked the door and ushered me inside. Tile flooring throughout, except in the two carpeted bedrooms. Just the right size for Josh and me. Plenty of kitchen storage for my Tupperware. Perfect. A grassy backyard; the branches of a big tree on the other side of the block wall created a large pool of shade for the dogs. A two-car, detached garage with laundry hookups. Everything was absolutely perfect. I could barely contain myself from pulling that sour-faced woman into a spontaneous jitterbug.

"I love it! I can give you a deposit right now if you'd like." I unzipped my purse and reached for my wallet.

"Well…" she hedged, "I'd rather have you just fill out an application. I'd like to give everyone who is interested a chance to apply."

Nice. Translation: *I'd rather rent to anyone but you.*

I wanted to hide in the bushes on the side of the house and tell any other prospective tenants that it was already rented; thereby, increasing my odds of not having to check into a homeless shelter in a week and two days.

I filled out the application. All I had to do was wait for "the call."

It finally came at ten o'clock at night. First, Erma let me know that the couple she really wanted as tenants had changed their minds. She said it was my lucky day. And by the way, the pet and security deposits are doubled. It would cost $5,000 to move in. I could start tomorrow, but of course, I'd have to pay for the extra days, and if I decided to wait, she might change her mind and rent to someone else. So, naturally, I jumped on it. At least we finally had a place to live and it wasn't a cardboard box in the alley behind the YWCA.

the parting gift
Sunday, June 23

I sat cross-legged on the carpet. Tears blurred my vision. I knew the day would come. I thought I'd be ready to move out of our house. For eight months, it felt like I was in limbo, a thin chain of hope dangling from my neck like a secret locket. A little part of me hoped that still having Kevin's furniture and the house would somehow keep us tied together.

My cell phone rang. I looked at the incoming number. Ryan. Again. I thought about letting the call go to voicemail, but finally answered it.

"Hey, I've been trying to get a hold of you," Ryan said. "I left a couple messages. I really enjoyed our lunch date on Monday and wanted to see if you'd like to go out again."

I looked down at the pictures scattered around me in a semicircle on the floor. Kevin's beautiful face smiled back at me. I picked up a picture of him standing in front of Tobi's Shave Ice shop in Maui. Tan and bare-chested, he wore Hawaiian print board shorts, a Titleist baseball cap, and a big smile.

"So, what do you think? How about dinner tonight?"

More tears ran freely down my cheeks. "I don't think so. I have to pack up the last of my things to move tomorrow, so I'm gone when Kevin comes to pick up his furniture."

"Do you need some help? I could bring my truck and help you load up," Ryan said.

"No, that's okay. But thanks for offering." I wiped away the tears that were collecting along my jaw.

"Annette, I know this is hard for you, but like I said in those voicemail messages, if I can do anything for you, just let me know."

"Thanks, but maybe you should back off for a while. I need to get through this alone." I didn't want to sound harsh, but there just wasn't any room for Ryan when my heart and head were full of Kevin.

"I understand." He sounded like he really didn't. "I'll give you your space, but just know I still want to take you out sometime."

"Okay, thanks. I really have to go." I hung up and stretched out facedown on the carpet, my shoulders heaved with sobs.

Why couldn't he be Kevin?

"Mom?" Josh stood in the bedroom doorway. "I finished with the last of my packing. Can I spend the night at Adam's?"

I sat up and wiped the tears from my cheeks with the palms of my hands. "Take your toothbrush. I'll call you in the morning to help me load."

Josh eyed the pile of pictures on the floor. "You've been looking at those for two hours. Maybe you should pack them now."

I rose from the floor and gave him a hug and kissed his forehead. "I'll see you in the morning. I love you."

He hugged back. "I love you too." Josh walked out of the room, looking back once over his shoulder. "Don't cry anymore, Mom," he said quietly.

After I heard the front door close behind him, I bent to my task of sorting the pictures to compile a small album to leave for Kevin. I slid a picture into the opening of a clear sleeve.

My hand stopped when I reached for the next picture. I held it in my hand and the memories drew me into it. Bel Air. A small bed and breakfast tucked away on a quiet street. Kevin sat on the bed wearing a white T-shirt and jeans with his acoustic guitar slung across his body. He sang "Save Tonight" by Eagle-Eye Cherry.

Behind my eyelids, I could see his head bent over the guitar, his fingers strumming the chords. I quietly joined him and sang the words to my empty room. A new stream of tears rushed down my face and a sob choked my throat. Kevin played that song often as he practiced his guitar. I loved to listen to it over and over. Those lyrics he sang never held any meaning because never once did I think they would come true.

When I finished with the pictures, it was sometime after midnight. Time had passed unnoticed as I relived the events captured by each image.

I reached for the custom jewel case I'd made. The cover was an overlapped photographic image of my hand holding a red pill and a blue pill in my palm. It was a reference from a movie, *The Matrix*, and served as my statement about Kevin's choice to leave. I knew he'd understand.

I'd made a CD of songs for him. Ok, I admit the whole thing was a bit sophomoric, reminiscent of teen-angst mix tapes made back when the songs were recorded off the radio onto cassettes. But the lyrics of the songs I chose said everything to Kevin that I would never get a chance to say. Things I should have said on the last day I saw him.

I pushed the CD into the boom box beside me on the floor and pressed the play button. Savage Garden, Enya, Dido, Everything But The Girl, Craig David, Dirty Vegas, Laura Dawn, Vanessa Carlton, and Maren Ord played on a loop, again and again. I cried myself to sleep on the floor in the darkness.

In the morning with the U-haul truck loaded and waiting, I flipped through the photo album one last time. The chronology of our nearly two years together, smiled, hugged, and kissed in the images on each page. How could Kevin walk away from this? I set the photos next to the CD and left three red roses from our garden in a glass on the kitchen counter.

waves of introspection
Monday, July 1

The sun sank into the horizon and colored the ocean with a tangerine glow. A breeze swept in off the water, carrying a salty mist and blowing strands of my hair across my face. Life went on around me. A couple jogged in the dark, spongy sand. A family of tourists ran from the tide along the water's edge, their pant legs soaked to the knees. Laguna Main Beach looked the same as always, but with sharper edges today.

It was over. The lease expired. I had the final walk-through with the landlord and returned the keys. The house was empty when we arrived. Kevin had moved out the last of his furniture and left a note for me next to the glass of wilted roses.

Annette,
Here's the key and garage door opener. Thank you for the gift (although a little hard to take). We'll talk soon. Take care of yourself and Josh.

Kevin

Leaving the house severed the final tangible tie. That last moment should've ended my torment. But I felt hollow.

I sat staring at the endless loop of crashing and receding waves, and felt insignificant and lost. The evening chill moved me from my perch in the cool sand. I strayed into the Marine Room, a tavern across from the beach, and asked for a cranberry juice, light ice, with a splash of water, and a squeeze of lime. Funny. I can even complicate something so simple as ordering juice.

With the coldness of the glass pressed wetly against my palm, I wandered over to the jukebox and stood mesmerized in the glow. The flipping pages made a tinny clap as I browsed the long list of songs.

I liked the atmosphere in the small bar. It was dim, quiet, and warm. Only five or six people in the room: a few shooting pool, an old guy at the bar watching the game, a couple sipping martinis and leaning close together, the bartender. And me. I chose a table in the darkest corner. A place to listen to music picked to suit my whims. Classic jukebox—Journey, Elton John, Pat Benatar.

I stared across the room, but the scene faded along with the music, and images of Kevin pushed their way into view.

The relationship was really over. He was gone.

It was hard living in that tomb of a house surrounded by his furniture and other things he had no use for. But cutting the final ties felt like starting the break-up all over again. It was square one. The pain was raw and fresh.

I reached to drink from my glass but found it warm and empty. Somehow, the juice and the ice were gone after only a single sip. I thought about ordering another drink. But I knew that if I did, it wouldn't be cranberry juice. And I didn't want to go down that road, so I tucked two dollars under the glass and rose to leave. When I pushed open the door, the marine layer, like a low-slung cloud, rolled inland along Ocean Avenue. I turned my face to the sky and welcomed the salty mist that hung damply in the night air.

no fireworks like the real thing
Independence Day
July 4

I reclined on a lounge chair in Valerie's backyard. My cell phone rang again. The tone played the *Mission Impossible* theme. I pushed the button to send it to voicemail. The smell of barbeque smoke wafted from over the neighbor's fence. I heard Josh and Valerie's three teens shrieking in the front yard, embattled in a water balloon fight.

"He keeps calling. Are you going or not?" Valerie checked the line from the propane tank to the grill then wiped her hands on her jean shorts.

"I don't know. I told him the last time he called that I'd decide later."

"Later when? After the fireworks start?" Valerie grabbed a bag of chips and reached in up to her elbow.

"That's just crumbs. The kids finished it." I handed her a new bag. "Maybe I'll tell him I decided to stay here."

Valerie dug a chip into the mound of guacamole. "Bonita and the boys will be here in a while. We can do the fireworks thing with the kids. I think you should go hang out with Ryan."

"I don't want to leave you guys. We always do holidays." I hoisted myself off the deck chair and walked into the house.

I brought out a bowl of fat strawberries and tipped it in offering. Valerie waved it away and bit into another chip. I knew what was coming. We'd been friends for too long not to know each other inside and out.

"Don't think for a single minute," Valerie said, "that if either Bonita or I were in your shoes that we wouldn't go to a barbeque with a cute single guy."

Valerie always made it sound like my duty to all single mothers to lure a never-been-married, childless guy into a relationship, like it was some sort of test against the odds of it actually working out.

"Why don't you go?" I said.

"He doesn't like me, he likes you. Besides, it would never work. I have too many kids. And what is he, all of twenty-five?"

"He's twenty-nine. Almost thirty."

"Who's almost thirty?" Bonita breezed through the patio doorway wearing a sundress, her short dark hair tucked under a woven hat. She set a tray of her famous deviled eggs on the picnic table.

Bonita always decorated each egg half with a perfect swirl of yellow stuff, a little slice of Spanish olive on top, and a tiny parsley leaf tucked into the edge. It was almost an artistic crime to eat them. I once tried to copy her culinary flair and it just looked like a Dachshund with the runs crouched over the egg tray.

I leaned across the table and reached for one of Bonita's masterpieces.

"Ryan invited Annette to a barbeque and she's too chicken shit to go," Valerie said.

"Am not," I argued with a mouthful of egg.

"I'll go! I'll go!" Bonita waved her hand in the air and then let it drop. "But he wouldn't like me, I have too many kids."

Bonita looked me up and down. "You're not going to wear *that*, are you?"

I looked down at my tank top and the frayed, khaki, cargo shorts slung low on my hips—a pair I'd swiped from the Salvation Army box of clothes Josh had outgrown. "What's wrong with what I'm wearing?"

"The ponytail, the flip flops, and those long, baggy shorts—it's just not sexy," Bonita said.

"It's a barbeque and fireworks. I'm not changing clothes."

"So, you *are* going?" Valerie sounded pleased.

"Only so you'll shut up about it." I grabbed a mini gherkin from the relish tray and chucked it at her.

She ducked and the tiny pickle landed in the grass.

An hour later, I stood outside Ryan's screened door, nearly turning to leave without knocking.

"Hey, there you are." Ryan came around the corner of the condo carrying a case of Corona with a mesh bag of limes balanced on top. He smiled and nodded for me to follow. "Come meet my roommate. He's in the kitchen."

"Well, it's nice to finally meet The One That Got Away. I've heard a lot about you over the last five years. I was starting to think you weren't real." Mike smiled at me and turned to sprinkle sea salt on a foot-long slab of raw salmon.

Ryan rolled his eyes and smiled. "See, I told you he would call you that." He reached over and cut off a small chunk of salmon for me, and one for himself.

I didn't feel as uncomfortable meeting his roommate as I thought I would. I could tell Mike was like an older brother to Ryan, though they couldn't be more different with Mike's short, bear-like frame contrasting Ryan's tall, lean blondeness.

"So, Annette, Ryan said you've been a vegetarian for over ten years. How can you eat fish without getting sick?" Mike's dark brows furrowed.

I popped another piece of fresh fish into my mouth and savored the clean, delicate taste. "I'm not vegan, I'm actually a lacto-ovo pescatarian."

"A what?" Mike and Ryan said in unison.

"The only animal products I ate were eggs, cheese, and milk, then about three years ago, I got hooked on sushi. I usually say vegetarian because it's easier and I always feel stupid trying to explain."

"Well, I'm glad you still eat vegetables, I bought a ton. Now, why don't you two go somewhere and make-out while I finish in here." Mike pointed a bamboo skewer in the direction of the doorway.

Ryan took me by the hand and led me outside to a tall patio chair. He tilted the woven table umbrella to keep the sun out of my eyes and settled into the chair across from me. He looked down, absently tracing his fingertip around the tattoo on the inside of his forearm. "I was thinking of getting another tattoo and I wanted to know what you think."

"I don't care. Do whatever you want." I shrugged and took a sip from my glass of cranberry juice.

"I want it to be a mermaid with your face," he said.

My cough sent juice shooting out of my nose. The cold, red liquid burned my sinuses.

"Are you okay?" Ryan handed me a napkin.

When my coughing subsided, I tried to reason with him. "I really don't think that's a good idea," I said. "You can't just tattoo someone's face on your body."

"It's not just someone. It's you," he said.

What do you say to something like that? It was kind of flattering—in a weird, obsessive, stalker sort of way.

"I just think it's a bad idea," I said. "A tattoo is forever."

Ryan's expression turned serious. His blue eyes locked onto mine. "I know," he said.

Mike stepped out onto the patio, carrying a plate of vegetable kebobs and foil packets of fish.

Saved. Now I didn't have to find a way out of the tattoo madness.

"Mike. Here, take our picture." Ryan pulled a disposable camera from the pocket of his board shorts.

Mike set the plate on the sideboard of the grill and crouched like he was trying to fit the bulk of his body behind the little box camera. "Okay, smile and say sexxxx."

The smile on my face felt like a pose for a dental x-ray.

As Mike tended the grill, more people arrived. Soon the house and patio were filled with San Clemente surfers and their cherry-ChapStick girlfriends. The beer keg was flowing. Ryan introduced me around as his girlfriend. Each time, I winced inside. I was Kevin's girlfriend.

Was.

At nine, everyone walked across the street to the cliff-top to watch the fireworks launched from San Clemente Pier below. The night was clear and warm. Looking up the coast, I could see tiny pinpoints of colored light shooting into the darkness from Dana Point Harbor, Laguna Beach, and very faintly from Newport.

I leaned back against Ryan's chest and watched the reds and blues pop in the night sky above us, the greens and yellows bursting and falling in a shower of crackling light. Ryan's arms circled around me and pulled me close against him. I felt his kiss brush the top of my hair.

Kevin was gone and Ryan was here. And I guess that's what mattered: someone tangible.

reception slip
Friday, July 19

It must feel weird watching your father marry someone younger than you. Ryan wasn't dealing with it very well. He tried to be supportive, but I could see the strain in his face when he thought no one was looking.

"I feel like I'm betraying my Mom." Ryan fussed with the bowtie of his tux. "But when my dad asked me to be his best man, what was I supposed to say?"

Ryan had been battling his thoughts from the time we boarded the plane at John Wayne Airport. I sat quietly on the edge of the bed in a standard room, Luxor Hotel, Las Vegas. I wondered if Elvis would be at the ceremony, but I didn't want to upset Ryan by asking. So, I left my sarcasm packed neatly in my suitcase.

To me, the whole thing looked like the cliché of a mid-life crisis. If it were a newspaper story, the headline would say it all: Man Leaves Wife of 35 Years for 20 Year-Old Stripper, Starts Producing Techno Music Featuring Homosexual DJ from Miami.

The evening didn't get any less bizarre. By the time the skinny, Cuban transvestite in the cheerleading outfit, high-heeled pumps, and oversized rhinestone sunglasses, finished singing "I Will Survive" at the reception, I was pretty sure there wouldn't be anything to top that. Ever.

I moved around the hotel banquet room with a disposable camera, taking pictures of Ryan's relatives. It gave me something to do. Something normal. I looked across the room and caught Ryan's stare. He watched me from the bar and smiled. When I reached the last table at the edge of the dance floor, I turned the camera to Ryan's grandparents.

They looked sweet, frail, and ever so slightly shell-shocked. They leaned their heads together and grasped gently at each other's quavering hands. That beat in time overpowered all the craziness in life. Enduring love. That's what life was all about. That's what we all wanted.

I finished the roll in the camera and walked up an aisle between the tables, ratcheting the plastic dial to rewind the film.

Ryan came up behind me, wrapped his arms around me, and kissed my neck. "I love you," he said.

I turned around and wasn't sure whose face registered more shock: his or mine.

"I mean...thank you," he mumbled, trying to recover his composure.

I'm sure I still looked like I'd been clocked upside the head with a frying pan.

"I wanted to say thank you...for being here with me...and for taking the pictures of my family... Let's dance." Ryan pulled me by the hand toward the dance floor. Then he stopped abruptly and changed directions. "Nevermind. Let's talk." He pulled me at a half-run out into the hallway.

A hotel chandelier twinkled overhead. I noticed it when I looked up to see where Ryan was staring.

"I didn't mean to say that. I mean, not now. I mean, I feel it, but it just came out."

"It's okay. Just forget it," I said. The last thing I wanted was a conversation about love.

"No. I'm glad I said it, so now I don't have to worry about it anymore." Ryan leaned down and brushed his lips across mine. "I love you and now I can say it whenever I want."

He kissed me deeply and I returned his kiss. There was no way I could return his sentiment of love. The kiss was the best I could do. And it kept me from saying anything that would hurt his feelings.

i've got my saddle on my horse
Saturday, July 20

The Walgreen's on Las Vegas Boulevard was packed. Out-of-towners browsed aisles lined with tacky souvenirs and postcards. Ryan and I were on a different mission. Our cab idled in the parking lot as we stood in front of a wall of condoms.

Ryan hadn't brought condoms for the weekend and I certainly hadn't packed any. I hadn't planned to sleep with him. I wasn't sure I was ready.

The thought of having someone—someone other than Kevin—inside of me made me shudder. I didn't know if I could go through with it.

I looked around and was pretty sure that it was obvious to everyone. *I'm standing here staring at a buffet of rubbers. And yes, people, I'm preparing to get fucked.*

Ryan turned to me. He looked like he wanted to say something, but wasn't sure how.

I prompted him with a raised eyebrow. *God, I hope he doesn't expect me to choose a box.*

"I don't want you to think I'm bragging or anything, but these are the only kind that fit."

My eyes followed his hand as it plucked a green box of Trojans from the hanger. Size Large. A small smile tugged at the corner of my lips. Inside, I was doing the Snoopy dance in the end zone. Woo-hoo! Jackpot!

Finding a guy with a big dick was like twisting the cap off a soda bottle and checking to see if you're a winner. In my life, I'd always found the guys who should have *Thank You For Playing, Please Try Again* stamped on their underwear.

It had finally come down to it. Ten months had passed since Kevin turned my life upside down and erased our future. Ten months without sex—that's got to be some sort of world record for a thirty-five-year-old woman. Ten months and still I wanted only Kevin, but it was painfully clear he wasn't coming back.

I needed to let go. Really let go.

And if I was going to fuck to get over Kevin, it may as well be with a guy who has a big dick.

At the register, Ryan pulled out a fifty-dollar bill for the Trojans and tossed a pack of gum on the counter. I buried my face between the pages of a *People* magazine and tried not to make eye contact with the smirking male clerk. It wasn't until the cab ride back to the hotel that the reality of what I was about to do kicked in. The passing casinos were a blur.

In the elevator ride up to the room, I almost chickened out. The ascending floor numbers flashed on the display: a reverse countdown to sex launch. I felt a fluttering of anxiety in my chest. If I went through with it and Kevin ever found out, he'd never come back.

With the curtains drawn in the dim hotel room, I looked at Ryan between my parted legs. It was almost surreal. I watched as he practically strangled himself with a condom; it was like watching someone try to sausage a boa constrictor into a wetsuit. I didn't know whether to laugh or cry.

Ryan moved above me. His rubber erection skipped along the bare skin of my thigh and when he pressed himself inside, he groaned from the tight fit. It was a bad cliché of the born-again virgin, but I felt more like an impaled fish.

Even if I were wearing ruby slippers, with my ankles pinned behind my head, there wouldn't have been a way to click them together. Which was too bad, because all I really wanted to do was go home.

It was just sex and was as good as it can be, when you wish it was with someone else. Tears trickled from the corner of my eyes. Ryan didn't notice; he was too busy rocking in orgasm.

In the quiet of the darkness, Ryan stretched out beside me, trailing his fingertips along my bare stomach. "I do love you, you know." He propped himself on an elbow. "I've waited five years to be with you and it's everything I thought it would be." A pained, bitter laugh died in my throat. Clearly, we just had two completely different experiences.

Ryan was my symbolic step: my way of acknowledging Kevin would never come back, my attempt to move on. And it failed. I only succeeded in feeling like I betrayed the man who still owned my heart.

I pretended to doze off. Ryan spooned against my back and my last thought was of Kevin. If he hadn't left me, my life would never have come to this.

a life of beavis and butthead?

Saturday, August 10

Ryan set the styrofoam boxes of sushi on my kitchen table and pulled plates and bowls from the cupboard. Josh peeled the lid from his miso soup cup and took a sip.

I slid the DVD into the player. "*American Beauty* is such a great film," I said. "I love the symbolism. And Kevin Spacey does a phenomenal job. I think he's completely underrated as an actor." I pressed the remote key to start the movie.

"I heard about it, but never saw it." Ryan tore open a small foil packet of soy sauce and mixed it with a lump of wasabi.

Halfway into the movie, I glanced over at Ryan and saw his face hanging slack. "Don't you like it?" I asked.

He shrugged. "I don't get it."

Alan Ball was one of the best screenwriters in Hollywood and his script was so well crafted. How could Ryan not understand it?

"It's about how we try to keep up appearances and try to pretend that everything is perfect when we are really just masking the silent desperation of a soul that's dying inside."

Ryan stared at me blankly.

"I know a movie you'll like better." Josh ran to his room and returned with one of his DVDs. He popped it in and clicked past the set up. Ryan sat beside Josh on the couch.

The sophomoric antics of *Jay & Silent Bob Strike Back* filled the screen. Fart jokes. Boner jokes. Josh and Ryan doubled over with laughter.

I moved from the table to the kitchen and crunched the take-out boxes into the trash.

"Annette, quick, you have to see this." Ryan's laugh echoed in the room.

"You guys go ahead, I'll clean up." I turned on the faucet to rinse the plates.

Okay, so maybe we don't have the same taste in movies. We like the same music. The warm water turned my hands pink. He's great with Josh.

For the last three weeks, they'd devoured truck magazines, talked about engines and rims, went to a car show, built my Ikea pantry and shelves, and had quiet conversations about "boy stuff." Josh needed someone like that.

I switched the water to cold and let it run through my fingers. Ryan had been persistent. Completely attentive. And extremely affectionate. It felt good to be wanted. He would never leave like Kevin did. I turned off the water and dried my hands on a towel. Leaning against the doorway, I watched the guys together.

"Watch this part, watch this part." Josh's elbow nudged Ryan's side.

Ryan's arm slung across the back of the couch put his tattoos on display. A California edition of Billy Idol. I had to admit, he had a certain magnetism. After the false start, the sexual chemistry between us was definitely there.

Ryan's bad-boy toughness softened when he looked at me. He mouthed the words 'I love you' and turned his attention back to the television.

Maybe that was all that really mattered: someone who would love us.

grocery store pony sex
Sunday, August 11

The Summer Jam concert ended early, hours before sunset. The Crips and the Bloods, two rival black gangs, traveled from Los Angeles to Irvine to spent the day throwing their colors around, along with whatever else they could find. I saw someone two rows below us get pegged in the head with a flying Nike.

Ryan and I ducked to avoid the randomly launched food and full water bottles, and positioned ourselves near people wearing clothing colors other than blue or red. It was safer to just enjoy the hip-hop music and stay out of the conflicts.

I was glad we hadn't brought Josh along. He would've liked the music, but I didn't want him exposed to the environment. He'd groused about not going, until I offered to drive him over to our old neighborhood to spend the night with Adam.

LL Cool J was in the middle of his set, singing "Phenomenon," when the scuffles accelerated into a full riot. LL chastised the crowd for their behavior and for interrupting the show, but his protests were swallowed in the sounds of girls screaming and fists connecting with flesh. A police helicopter circled overhead and uniformed officers in protective gear entered the amphitheater, filing the people one at a time through the exit gate. The fighting continued, deep within the press of the crowd.

The anarchy of the day echoed in my head. I stared at the ceiling and tried to dissect the social motivations of such destructive behavior—it just didn't make sense. In the darkness of the bedroom, I could hear Ryan's rhythmic breath of deep sleep. The blue glow of the digital clock read: 1:57 A.M.

I slid my hand under the sheet to rub him up while he slept. When Ryan was fully erect, I climbed on top of him and rocked back and forth, my body weight pressing him inside of me. I could feel his thickness and pushed hard against it, forcing it deeper, trying to fill the void.

Ryan awoke just before he climaxed. "Hi..." his voice low and groggy, greeted me. His hands reached out to grasp my hips, stopping their motion as he shuddered in orgasm. In the faint light of the room, I could see a smile curving his lips.

"Go back to sleep," I whispered as I climbed off and moved under the covers.

I did it because he was there. And because I could. But I still felt hollow.

a south american rat fuck parable
Monday, August 12

The cursor on my computer blinked. The glaring white page felt like a black hole. No, not a black hole. It was more like an impenetrable wall that was blocking anything creative. I couldn't figure out how to fill the page with words. Not just any words, that was easy. The right words. Infinitely harder.

It was easier to avoid writing completely than to work through it, so I picked up the phone and called Valerie. "Let's do lunch today," I said.

"Okay. Meet me at the sandwich place by my office, I have something funny to tell you about."

I stepped down the short hall to Josh's room. With the loss of a homeschool zone, his bedroom became tight quarters. His computer desk sat wedged in the corner between his bed and the wall.

When I walked into the room, Buddy jumped off the bed, lowered his head, and left the room quickly.

Josh sat at his computer playing *Tomb Raider*. I moved behind him and pressed my palms on each side of his head, tilting it back so he could see me. "How many times have I told you dogs don't belong on the bed?"

Josh crossed his eyes. "At least a hundred million."

"Well, now it's a hundred and one million."

159

"Um, Mom…isn't that a hundred million and one?" he said, still looking at me upside down.

"Thanks for the math lesson, Mr. Smarty Pants." I let go of his head and sat on the edge of the bed. "I came to tell you I'm going to meet up with Valerie for lunch. And I'm swinging by the grocery store on my way back. Do you need anything?"

Josh thought for a moment. "Double A batteries and microwave popcorn." He turned back to his computer game. "Is Ryan coming over tonight?"

"I don't know. Do you want him to?" I said.

Maybe it was the tone of my voice that made Josh turn the question around on me. "Do *you* want him to?" He swiveled in his chair and studied my face.

Since the conversation felt like it was going in that direction, it was the perfect time to nudge it along. "We haven't really talked about it and I was just wondering, what do you think about me being in a relationship with Ryan?"

Josh seemed to consider how to respond. "He's nice. But I think he's just your get-away guy."

"What do you mean?" I felt a twitch in my stomach, like the feeling of being caught in a white lie.

"It's like you like him because he helps you get away from being sad."

Get-away guy? Talk about out of the mouths of babes. Was it really that transparent, even to a child?

Once I made it to lunch, I sat across from Valerie in a daze.

She bit into her sandwich, a piece of lettuce wiggled outside her mouth as she chewed. "So, check this out." She finished chewing and swallowed. "I was watching the Discovery Channel the other night. It was soooo funny."

My mind wandered, only half listening to another one of her endless TV stories. My sandwich sat untouched.

Am I just settling satisfactorily like my fortune cookie predicted? And like my son so clearly pointed out?

Valerie took a sip of her iced tea then pulled off the plastic lid. "The show was about this South American rat..." She plucked out an ice cube and popped it into her mouth, crunching noisily.

I always swore I'd never settle for less than exactly what I wanted. That was the whole purpose for The List. But is staying with Ryan only because he loves me the same thing as settling? Can I stay in the relationship even if I know I'll never be in-love with him? I pulled a limp slice of tomato out of my sandwich and abandoned it on the side of the wrapper.

Valerie punched the air with the straw. "And you're not going to believe what the rat does," she paused for effect. "During mating season, it literally fucks itself to death."

"What?" The absurdity of her statement snapped me back to attention.

"Yeah, can you believe that? I was watching it and thinking, what stupid animal fucks for no reason until it finally dies? And then I had this total epiphany. My ex-boyfriend was exactly like that rat."

I didn't say anything in response. As much as I didn't want to admit it, I could relate.

sexual stir-fry

1 hard man
1 open woman
2 lbs. dicey sexual attraction
16 oz. flavored body oil

Prepare cooking surface. Heat woman to sizzling. Coat with body oil.

Insert man. Toss with sexual attraction.

Serve with flat carnal abandon.

Yield: The illusive orgasm.
Unlimited servings.
Nutritional Value: None.

No guaranteed weight loss.

Unless you are on top.

twin towers reflection
Wednesday, September 11

First thing in the morning, I tied the wooden stick of a tiny American flag to a fat, ivory candle and pulled the white ribbon into a bow. Tilting the candle at an angle, I lit the wick. My plan was to tend the candle all day and through the night to honor the victims of 9/11 on the first anniversary of the tragedy.

I carried the candle from room to room as I tidied up. When I finished the morning chores, I decided to get out of the house for a while. I just wanted to go somewhere to quiet, close to nature.

When I climbed into the driver's seat of my car, I carefully held the candle between my legs as I drove; the heat of the flame rose to warm the space under my chin. I pulled into the parking lot of Mission Viejo Lake. Balancing the candle and a short-legged beach chair from my trunk, I walked to the end of the paddleboat dock.

An almost imperceptible sway gently rocked the solid structure. I sat in the chair and closed my eyes, listening to the creak of the old wood and the gentle lap of the water against the posts.

One year, and I could still remember every detail of that horrific day.

It was a Tuesday. Kevin's second day off work.

We were asleep in a borrowed vacation condo on a golf course in Palm Springs. The night before, we had planned to spend the next day by the pool, and maybe go into town in the afternoon to do some shopping.

Kevin's cell phone rang, startling him awake. He scrambled out of bed in his underwear and ran into the living room to answer it before the ringing woke up Josh. I shifted under the sheets and stretched out my feet, seeking a cool spot. I opened one eye and tried to focus on the bedside clock; it was a few minutes after six.

Kevin returned to the room in a rush and fumbled with the TV remote.

I sat up in bed. "Who was that? What's wrong?"

"It was Carson. He said there was an accident at the World Trade Center." Kevin sat on the end of the bed in front of the TV.

163

I crawled across the covers and leaned my bareness against his back.

We saw the images on the television screen unfold in chaos. Plumes of black smoke rose from the North Tower. Tiny bodies fell the length of the long, gray building. The camera captured papers fluttering and swirling. There were people screaming and running through the streets.

We sat clinging to each other and watching in horror. Sobs wracked our bodies. The explosion. The second plane. The collapse. Shaking, and wrapped in each other's arms, we cried out again and again.

"Oh my God, no..." became our litany as the hours passed. We sat in shock, awash in tears. The news reports revealed that it was a terrorist attack. The Pentagon was also hit. Another hijacked plane crashed.

We crawled back beneath the covers, still watching, crying, and holding each other. I felt a headache searing behind my eyes from the force of my tears. All those people. So many people.

When Josh finally awoke, he peeked into the room, saw Kevin and me crying, and quietly closed the door. I heard him restart the DVD he had fallen asleep watching the night before.

I called Mom to see if she had heard from our relatives in upstate New York.

Her voice was almost matter-of-fact. "I'm sure they're fine. Binghamton is a long way from New York City. You should turn off the TV and go about your day. You can't change anything by sitting glued to the news and crying over it."

Mom was always logical. But her reasoning just didn't make sense to me. Being three thousand miles away from the terrorists' target didn't mean we were safe and unaffected. Exactly the opposite. It meant none of us would ever be safe again.

The tragedy shook Kevin to the core.

A lot happened in my life after 9/11. Kevin left me a little over a month later. From that point on, my world had reduced in size to a microcosm that revolved around a broken heart. It was human nature. Our perception of the universe changes in relation to the random acts that directly affect us. My armchair philosophy. While the families who survived 9/11 mourned the loss of their loved ones, I mourned the loss of my own. On that day, every American lost something.

At the time, I didn't know that stories like mine had played out across the nation. The terrorist attack made Americans question what and who was most important to them in their lives. In that single, tragic day, wheels were set in motion: divorces, break-ups, and for the lucky ones, marriages.

I opened my eyes and looked out across the lake. Expensive homes drew a picket border along the horizon. I wondered if the people in those houses had everything they wanted in life. Was their home on the lake the expensive box where they stored their happily-ever-after?

I still wanted to find 'happily-ever' and work my way toward 'after.' Maybe it wasn't exactly a feminist ideal, but I was okay with that; I believed I could have love and an equal partnership. The hard part was finding someone who fit into my future and my present.

Watching a pristine sailboat in the distance, I thought about the last time I had come to the lake. Josh had paddled a kayak across the glassy surface, showing off his skill at keeping the craft upright. As each day went by, he became more independent. For the last thirteen years, it had been a delicate balance of my responsibilities as a mother and my needs as a woman. Both were equally strong. And equally important.

My cell phone rang *The Munster's* theme. Home. I pulled the phone from the pocket of my nylon jacket and pressed it to my ear.

"Mom, did you forget? Winter league practice starts tonight. We need to leave soon."

"I didn't forget. Pack your gear, I'm only a couple blocks away." I walked to the car, carrying the chair and the still flickering candle.

the list revisited
Monday, September 23

"How's the homework coming?" I leaned against the doorway to Josh's room.

He swiveled in his chair. "I need help with the new project in the life skills book. I have to make up a budget for the month and go grocery shopping. It says to use our real electric bill and stuff like that."

"It's almost noon, how 'bout you take a break for lunch. Make a sandwich or something, and I'll help you with that later."

Josh followed me out of his room. "Mom, can I have some money? I want to go to McDonald's and have lunch with my friends from the high school. I'll come home right when they go back to school. Can I?"

"I suppose. But stay out of trouble and make good choices." I ruffled the spikes of his hair.

The "good choices" comment was my standard mother mantra, but I wasn't worried about Josh. He was more mature than most of those high school kids I'd met.

After Josh left, I wandered around the tiny house. I felt restless and couldn't pinpoint exactly what it was. My cell phone rang the *Mission Impossible* theme. And then I knew. It was Ryan. And I didn't feel like answering the call.

On a rational level, it didn't make sense. Ryan behaved like the textbook, picture-perfect boyfriend, but even calling him my boyfriend made me wince. I should've basked in his attentions, but strangely, I often found them more irritating than comforting.

I needed to talk it out with someone. I tried to think of who would be the most logical, unemotional person I could call. I figured Spock was currently out of the galaxy, so I called my mother.

The phone rang once and she picked up. "Mom, I'm conflicted about Ryan. Can I bounce some thoughts off you?" I flopped across my bed to talk.

She informed me that she was on her way out the door to run errands. "Make it brief," she said.

I launched feet first. "All we ever do is have sex. I mean, that's not totally a bad thing, the sex is good—"

"That's probably more information than I need," she said.

"Sorry."

"Moving on..."

"We barbeque, watch Monday night football, listen to the same music. He's easy to be around and he loves me. Overall, he's got a lot of good traits that are on my list, but just not the education or the communication skills. I can't talk to him about anything." I ended with a sigh.

"So why are you staying with him?" She administered the Vulcan mind freeze.

Good question.

I rolled onto my back and stared at the ceiling. I figured maybe I could be average happy like most people. Average seemed safe. Not completely fulfilled, but not miserable either. I could hold out for Prince Charming, but what if he didn't exist? Or worse, what if I found him, but he didn't want me?

"Maybe I thought I could just feel intellectually fulfilled by talking with other writers and wouldn't need to have that with Ryan."

"Is that something you can live with for the rest of your life?" she asked.

I shifted the phone to my other ear and sat up against the pillows, "I think so. I mean...we have fun together just hanging out... He's good with Josh. He's kind to me." Even to my own ears, the reasons sounded weak.

Mom brought the discussion to an end. "If that is what you choose, then you must completely accept it from the minute you wake up every morning."

I hung up the phone and curled onto my side.

Why did that sound so much like a death sentence?

almost a dream come true
Thursday, September 26

I'm not sure why I went to the golf tournament. People milled around me and I felt like the stationary horse on a carousel. Then I saw him.

Kevin's eyes pierced right into me and gripped my heart. A wave of longing flowed over me and I wasn't sure how to react. It had been so long since I'd seen him. He came to me slowly, almost hesitantly.

"I've missed you," Kevin said.

That's when the tears fell. They raced down my cheeks, collected along my jaw, and spattered onto my dress. I searched his face. Afraid to say anything, I stood woodenly, daring not to breathe, soaked in tears.

"I still love you and I want to get back together. I can't stand to be away from you anymore," he said.

His words were enough to break the dam. "Oh Kevin, I love you so much. I've missed you so very much. I'll quit the club and move to Los Angeles with you. Nothing matters anymore. I just want to be with you." It all came pouring out in a rush.

He stepped forward and wrapped me in his arms. I melted into him and cried hard. Relief and joy flooded my entire body.

I was startled awake by Ryan's hand sliding up my bare thigh as he spooned against my back. The morning light pried between my damp eyelashes. I had carried my tears across the threshold of my dream. For just a second, I wanted to pretend it was Kevin curled against me, but reality shredded the thought. It wasn't Kevin; it would never be Kevin again.

Inside, I peeled away from myself, leaving Ryan holding only my shell. I curled around my bruised heart, hoping to stop the bleeding sorrow. Ryan's hand scalded my thigh and I couldn't stand to lie there a second longer. "I have a ton of stuff to do today," I mumbled as I pulled away.

Under the shower spray, I leaned against the tiles, my arms wrapped around my body. The heat of the water made my tears feel cold sliding down my cheeks. It was a long shower. Memories and daydreams swirled around me, mixing with the steam.

Drying off slowly, I agonized over reentering the bedroom and seeing Ryan's face haloed in my sheets. I loitered in the bathroom, trying to wish him away.

The rhythm of applying body lotion set my logical mind churning. Kevin was physically out of my life, but still such a presence in my heart and in my head that it was impossible to move on. God knows I tried.

Maybe I needed an exorcist.

Okay, mildly amusing thought, but my therapist said that a more suitable solution would be to determine if Kevin was still in my heart and in my head because I imprisoned him there.

Psychobabble mumbo-jumbo.

I was still in love with him. Yes, I conceded to that. My therapist said until I got over it, I was just wasting Ryan's time. And she said I should cut him loose. I let out a slow sigh—cleansing and steadying.

I opened the door to the bedroom. Ryan was dressed and the bed was neatly made. He stood awkwardly in the middle of the room.

"You seem kinda distant this morning, so I'm gonna take off and give you your space, but before I go, is something wrong? Did I do something to piss you off?"

"No." I brushed off the question, not wanting to go into the real reason for my mood. Something of disbelief in his expression made me tack on. "I just had a very disturbing dream."

"It was only a dream." He reached out to wrap me in his arms.

"I'm all too aware of that." I pulled away.

He took my hand and guided me to sit with him at the edge of the bed. "Was it about me?"

An involuntary laugh came out with my negative reply.

"Was I even in it?"

"No," I said. "You weren't."

"What was it about?"

I told him once when we began dating to never ask a question if he couldn't handle the answer.

"I dreamt Kevin and I got back together."

"Well, are you going to?" His voice tightened around each word.

A bitter laugh danced around my response that it would never happen.

"But you want to." It was half question, half statement.

Unwavering, my eyes locked with his. "I'd do it in a heartbeat."

He studied my face for a moment.

"Then what the FUCK am I doing here?" he yelled. "And why the FUCK are we even together?"

"I don't know," I said quietly.

Ryan launched off the bed, grabbed his keys, and was out the door in less than a minute. I heard him leave at least fifty feet of tread marks on the asphalt when he sped away.

There, it was done. I padded to the bathroom in my slippers and began blow-drying my hair. But I knew it wasn't totally over. There would have to be that uncomfortable exchange of personal property.

Bent at the waist, with my hair flipped over, the whir of the blow dryer masked Ryan's return. I saw his feet planted in the doorway—he had nice feet, for a guy—maybe he came back because he forgot his shoes. I continued to dry my hair upside down.

Ryan reached out and unplugged the cord. "We need to talk."

I followed him to the bedroom and sat cross-legged on the bed.

He paced along the end. "I just don't get it," he said. "Sometimes I don't fucking understand you!" He flung his hands in the air. "Most of the time, I don't fucking understand you!"

Motionless, emotionless, I let him go on.

"When are you going to figure it out? He left you! He doesn't want you anymore!"

My quiet litany of 'I know' didn't quell his storming. I could feel my eyes welling up, not from the anger in his harsh words, but because I knew what he said was true. And that hurt more than anything else could. I knew Ryan was only lashing out because he was hurt and frustrated. It wouldn't take a session with a therapist to figure that out.

"Why don't you open your eyes and see that you have someone right in front of you who loves you and wants to be with you, right here, right now. If you don't get over him and move on, you're going to be miserable and alone for the rest of your life."

The continuous mantra of 'I know' was still my only response. There was nothing to argue about. Everything Ryan said was true and I knew it.

My mind wandered into that warm place where I kept memories of Kevin wrapped in tissue and saved like precious artifacts. A spool of familiar scenes played over and over in my head like a *Twilight Zone* marathon.

How did I ever get to this point in my life? I'm living in this place where nothing makes sense except clinging to the strongest love I've ever felt.

I caught a glimpse of myself in the mirrored doors of the bedroom closet. The natural curl of my hair had crept back in from an incomplete blow-dry. Barefaced, tear-streaked, and frizz-headed, I looked like a witch.

Ryan sat on the bed and smoothed a wrinkled frown from my forehead with his thumb. "Don't give up on me. I want you to know I'm willing to take the risk that this relationship won't last because I love you and I want to be with you, no matter what."

"I'm just a waste of your time," I said.

"Let me be the judge of that." The intensity of his gaze bored into me. "And stop trying to spare me from getting hurt. I know what I'm getting myself into and it's my choice."

"Ryan…" I sighed, wanting to find a way to make him understand. "This has nowhere to go as long as I'm still in-love with Kevin. I have nothing to give you."

I wondered why he couldn't see the sign blinking over my head in blue neon: Emotionally Vacant.

"Well, I think you're worth waiting for and I just hope that someday you'll love me at least half as much as you love him."

The whole ordeal left me completely wrung out. I finally told Ryan I needed a nap and he had to leave.

"Don't call me. Don't come by. I just want to be alone," I said.

After he left, I crawled under the covers to nap away my persistent thoughts of Kevin.

Or maybe to catch up with him in another dream.

mars/venus in the kitchen
Friday, September 27

The doorbell rang. Ten in the morning, and I was still in flannel pajamas. I looked through the peephole.

Oh, shit. It's Ryan. And he brought flowers.

He rang the doorbell again.

I stood quietly, trying to will him away. Just go. I'm not here. Just go.

"Annette, open the door. I know you're in there, your car is in the driveway," Ryan called out.

"What if I'm really not here?" I said through the door.

"Open the door. I have something for you."

I wonder if this is the part in my pathetic life story where I open the door and Ryan shoots me right on my porch after saying something about how if he can't have me no one can, and then it's on the eleven o'clock news, and Kevin sees it and decides he was wrong, but it's too late because I'm dead, and he realizes we could've been happy together forever if he hadn't broken up with me and ruined everything, because then, none of this would have ever happened with Ryan, and I wouldn't be lying here dead.

"Annette, are you going to open the door or just leave me standing out here forever?"

I unlocked the deadbolt and let him inside.

He walked past me into the kitchen, pulled a vase out of my cabinet, filled it with water, and arranged the flowers. While I watched him, he avoided my gaze. Then he turned to me. "Before you say anything, I just want to tell you why I came by."

I leaned against the handle of the refrigerator with my arms crossed.

He set the flowers in the middle of the breakfast table and stepped close to me. I had to look up the length of his six-foot frame to reach his serious blue eyes.

Funny, I never seemed to venture far from type. They were always tall, always blonde, always blue-eyed.

172

"I want to thank you," he said.

His words brought me back from my objective analysis. You what? I'm sure my face showed my obvious puzzlement. "What are you talking about? Thank me for what?" I said.

Ryan reached into his pocket and withdrew a black velvet box.

Oh God, don't do it. Do *not* ask me to marry you! My instantaneous wish for the tile floor to open up and swallow me was unfortunately not granted. Where do you find a genie when you really need one?

"I want to thank you for being honest with me and I want you to have this." He held out his hand for me to take the box.

"I can't accept that." I stepped back. "I said what I said because it's how I feel, not because I'm playing some kind of game."

He stepped forward, the box still in his outstretched hand. "I want you to have this because I appreciate your total honesty. It was hard to hear what you told me yesterday, but I respect it."

I held up a hand to stop him. "I just—"

"Don't interrupt. Let me finish," he said. "I don't think I've ever met a woman who was so honest. That's one of the main things that makes you so special to me."

Ryan opened the box and turned it to show me a gold necklace with a pendant of a bold, trillion-shaped opal resting in a gold cradle setting.

"Don't say you can't take it. I want you to have it." He lifted the necklace from the box and unhooked the clasp. "Turn around, I want to put it on you."

As far as I could tell, the chain was too delicate for him to choke me with it.

I let Ryan step behind me and lift the open necklace above my head. His fingers fumbled a moment trying to secure the lobster claw clasp.

"I know this doesn't change anything. I just want you to know I love you and I'll always be here for you, no matter what." His heavy hands rested on my shoulders.

Ryan turned and walked to the door. Wordlessly, he kissed the tips of two fingers, lifted them in salute, and closed the door behind him.

Okay, so the Mars/Venus lesson to learn here is that to get a guy to buy you jewelry, you have to tell him you love someone else?

And men think we are hard to understand?

he's not heavy, he's my stalker
Sunday, October 6

I stepped out of the gym and climbed into my car. I checked the clock in the dash. Enough time to head home, shower, make dinner, and relax for a little while before going to work. I pulled my cell phone from the glove box. Five missed calls. I pressed the button to listen to my voicemail.

Ryan called to say hello. Next message—Ryan, asked me to call him back. Ryan again, called to ask where I am. Ryan—called to say he was going to drive by my house. Last message, Ryan said he was in my driveway waiting for me. Irritation made me squint behind my sunglasses.

When I arrived home, I expected to find his truck in front of the house. Instead, I saw a note tucked into the frame of the front door.

Annette,
Was in the area and thought I'd drop by to see you.

R~

I unlocked the door, went in, and set my purse on the kitchen counter. The answering machine flashed. I pushed the play button. Ryan. Ryan. Ryan. Ryan again. Ryan. Ryan. Ryan. Seven messages. And three hang-ups; I could only speculate who it was.

I snatched my cell phone out of my purse and autodialed his cell phone.

"Hi Baby," he answered, obviously checking the Caller ID.

"What are you doing?" I shouted into the phone. "Why did you call me fifteen times?"

There was a second of silence on the line.

"I thought maybe you were taking a nap and didn't hear the phone," he said.

"So, you drove by my house?" I couldn't fathom what he must've been thinking. "Don't you think that if I *were* taking a nap, I might not *want* to answer the phone because I was *sleeping*?"

"But I didn't see your car."

"That's not the point! I was at the gym!"

"Oh."

Exasperated, I switched gears. "What are you doing tonight?"

"Nothing," he said.

"Why don't you come over." It wasn't a question; it was a statement.

"Okay, I'll be—"

I hung up before he finished his sentence.

Starting in the kitchen, I collected things that belonged to Ryan. A box of lemon meringue pie mix he wanted me to bake for him, three tins of oysters, and a six-pack of Corona. From the bedroom closet, I pulled out his Quicksilver T-shirt and a black nightclub shirt with flaming dice on it. Off the nightstand: a Kodak envelope of pictures from his dad's wedding and a pack of gum. I stacked it all on the chair by the front door.

When Ryan arrived, I had already rehearsed what I was going to say. I answered the door and he aimed a kiss for my lips. I turned and he caught my cheek. He followed me into the kitchen and we sat at the table.

"So, did you want to watch a DVD or do you want me to take you out to dinner and a movie?" he asked.

"Actually, I just want to talk." My intro made him shift positions in the chair. I took a quick breath and launched into my mini speech. "I think you're a great guy. You're loving, and thoughtful, and easy to be around. I know you'll make someone a wonderful husband someday..."

Ryan's eyes searched my face.

"But, it won't be me," I finished softly.

"What do you mean by that? Are you breaking up with me?"

It came out in a near whisper. "Yeah." I nodded slightly and pressed my lips together.

Ryan's brows furrowed and he looked pained. "If I'm so great, then why do you want to break up with me?"

I knew he'd ask. I'd asked myself the same question since we started dating and it finally became so clear. It just wasn't something I could live without. I would've been settling. And not even satisfactorily.

"We never have anything to talk about. Have you ever noticed that? We go places. We hang out. We have sex. But we never *talk* about anything."

He shrugged and looked at the floor. "I'm a man of few words. I talk when I have something important to say."

"I need more." I rested my hand on his arm. "I just don't think we have an intellectual connection."

"Are you saying I'm stupid?" His anger flared and he jerked his arm away.

My voice rose in pitch to match my feelings. "No, I'm saying I need to be able to talk freely, share ideas and thoughts and concepts with the person I'm in a relationship with."

Ryan lifted his palms. "Okay, so what do you want to talk about?"

I shook my head. "It has to happen naturally because we both have something we want to share."

Ryan looked at me like I was speaking in a Mongolian dialect.

"Maybe I'm not explaining it well, but what I mean is—I don't think we should see each other anymore. At all."

"If that's the way you want it, fine." He pushed back his chair from the table and walked across the room. "Have a nice life." Ryan shut the front door firmly behind him.

dumpling

2 cups all-purpose resolve
1/2 tsp. disappointment
1/2 tsp. regret
3 Tbsp. short explanation
3/4 cup emotional concerns

Combine resolve, disappointment, and regret.
Cut in short explanation with two dull knives until consistency of
complete understanding.

Pour in emotional concerns, stirring until softened. Turn out
decision. No knead to reconsider.

Drop dumpling gently, but firmly. Serve warm.

Yield: Ability to move on.
Unlimited servings.
Nutritional Value: None.

No guaranteed weight loss.

You feel bad, but know it was the right thing to do.

booty challenge
Friday, October 11

I wove through the crowd and approached the bartender. I wanted to grab a quick glass of juice and continue trolling for private dances. The couches were busy—it was a good money night.

When I stepped around a tall guy in a football jersey, I saw Ryan leaning against the bar on one elbow. "What are you doing in here?" I asked. It had been almost a week since I'd broken up with him.

"Don't be mad at me. I just came in to get a beer and talk to you."

"I don't have time. I'm working." I couldn't keep him from coming in, but that didn't mean I had to stand around with him. I walked away and he followed me across the room.

I spun to face him. "Stop following me. I have to get back to work." The music beat like a pulse in my head.

He reached for his wallet. "Look. I'll pay you for a private dance so we can talk."

"I'm not going to take your money. Just tell me what you want to say."

Ryan set his beer on the railing and reached for my hand. "When I told the guys at work we broke up, they said if I really wanted to be with you, I had to fight to get you back, so that's what I'm doing," he said.

I shook my head, trying to make sense of that little nugget. When do a bunch of guys building concept cars have time to watch soap operas?

"Ryan…" I pulled my hand from his. "That's a nice idea, but it doesn't work that way." I stepped aside while a guy lined up his shot on the pool table.

"So, you don't still like me, even just a little?" He grabbed his beer and took a swig.

"You're a great guy," I began, wanting to be kind but also honest. "And I do like you…but all we really had was sex. You knew I was just coming out of a relationship, I never lied to you. I'm sorry I couldn't give you more than I did. I am. I'm really sorry."

Ryan looked across the room and was quiet for a moment. The music blared, filling in what would have been an uncomfortable silence.

He picked at the label on the beer bottle. "If you only wanted me for sex, then why don't we just have sex?" His voice held a note of challenge. When he looked at me, his eyes grazed over me in a naked hunger. "What are you doing after work?"

I shook my head. "You won't be able to handle it."

Ryan stepped close and leaned to whisper in my ear. "Try me." His voice was low and sexual; it promised raw, barnyard sex.

A little voice in my head harped that it was *not* a good idea, but it was immediately squashed by the physical sensations that responded to Ryan's closeness. The warm musk of his cologne filled my senses and I could almost feel the force of him pressing roughly between my thighs.

I stepped back and met his eyes directly. "I get off at two."

"I'll be there." He set his beer on the railing and walked out of the club.

On the drive home, I wondered if he would actually show up. I couldn't decide if I really wanted to have sex with him and chance falling back into that codependent relationship—at least, that's what my therapist called it.

As I turned the corner onto my street, I saw his lifted Chevy parked along the curb in front of the house. Ryan climbed out of the truck and wordlessly followed me inside. He walked ahead of me into my bedroom and I closed the door behind us—out of habit rather than necessity.

I was glad Josh went to a sleepover with Valerie's kids. If the encounter with Ryan turned out the way I hoped, we'd be lucky not to wake the dead.

The light above the backyard wall cast a soft illumination into the room through the sheers covering the sliding glass door. It was dim, but not dark. I studied Ryan in the half-light. Neither of us moved nor spoke.

Ryan closed the gap between us in two strides. He scooped me up with his hands cupped around the back of my thighs and crushed me against the door.

His body straddled between my legs, he kissed me full on the mouth. His tongue teased and probed. It was sexy as hell and I returned his kiss. I could feel his hardness pressing against me and my body automatically responded. He carried me over to the bed, my thighs wrapped around his waist.

Ryan pulled me off of him and threw me onto the bed. I stared up at him as he began un-belting his jeans.

He paused with his hand on his zipper. "Do you have any idea how much I love you?" he said.

Tires screeched to a halt inside my head. What a barnyard sex buzz kill.

I sat up and clicked on the nightstand lamp. "I knew you couldn't do this, this was a bad idea, I think you should go home."

"I'm sorry. I won't say anything." Ryan climbed onto the bed with me and reached to turn off the lamp.

I rolled off the other side of the bed and paced the room. "I'm serious. This was a totally stupid idea, I should've known it wouldn't work."

I could've kicked myself for being such an idiot.

"Okay, here's the deal. It's almost three o'clock, so you have two choices. You can leave now, or you can sleep for a few hours and leave before the sun comes up," I said, "But no sex."

I hoped he'd choose to go. I only offered the second option because it was so late and I knew he'd been drinking.

"I want to spend one last night with you." His eyes implored me to agree.

We climbed into the bed and Ryan moved close, wrapping his arm over my torso. He kissed my shoulder and spooned against my back. In a matter of minutes, I was asleep.

When I awoke in the morning, he was gone.

part four

finding

annette

the plan
Saturday, October 12

It's official: dating sucks. And I'm going to be single for the rest of my life. But I'm okay with that.

Now, it was time to plan my future around self-actualization, personal growth, enriching my life with exciting experiences, learning new skills and crafts, and taking up a hobby. My therapist said I should focus on something productive like that.

I could take a bellydancing class; I'd always wanted to try that. Handwriting analysis might be interesting. Or knitting.

I flipped through the community recreation brochure. The class title jumped off the page. Why didn't I think of it sooner? Golf lessons. Perfect.

Kevin always wanted me to learn to play. If I took golf lessons, I could turn pro. Join the LPGA Tour. And be in the perfect position to bump into Kevin at a tournament. Maybe he'd even see me on *ESPN* or the cover of *Sports Illustrated*. By then, enough time would have passed, we'd both be more settled, and it would be the perfect way to get back together.

It was all so absolutely and completely perfect. I could go on with my life without obsessing about Kevin and then sometime—maybe ten or fifteen years from now, our separate futures would merge again.

I tore the registration sheet out of the catalog and began filling in the paperwork. The class was scheduled to start in a month. That would give me plenty of time to buy all the clubs and accessory crap I'd need.

Golf lessons. What a great idea.

the rise of a matriarchal society
Tuesday, October 15

We were all flopped across floor pillows on Valerie's living room carpet while the kids played video games in the adjoining family room. Bonita and Valerie nursed their glasses of Merlot.

"I think I'm going to fire my therapist." I rattled the juice-tinted ice cubes in my glass. "Well, not really *fire* her. I just don't think I need to go there anymore."

Bonita winced, making an air sucking sound through her teeth. "Do you really think that's a good idea?"

I shrugged. "She never really told me anything I didn't already know. So, why spend money talking to a stranger about random shit I can figure out for myself?"

Valerie peered over her glass. "I kinda like the idea of paying someone to listen to me talk. Then they don't have any choice, they have to."

"If you're going to try dating again, don't you think it would be better to have a professional around to help you?" Bonita asked.

"I'm done dating—for a while anyway," I said.

Valerie snorted. "Yeah, we'll see how long that lasts."

"I'm serious," I said. "Dating is such a pain in the ass. I think I'll just stay single for the rest of my life."

"Then you can be queen of your own castle." Bonita was rapidly approaching a full kosher pickling. She wandered out of the room to uncork another bottle.

"Yeah, queen." I warmed to the idea. "If I were queen, I'd pass a law where every guy would have his penile dimensions tattooed on his forehead with ink that glows under the black lights in a nightclub." I poured more cranberry juice into my glass from the pitcher on the coffee table.

"Too small, throw him back," chimed Bonita from the kitchen.

"It would revolutionize the entire dating process." Valerie laughed and sucked the last of the Merlot from the bottom of the bottle. "They always check out the size of our boobs, we should be able to check out their packages."

"Wait, wait." Bonita poked her head back into the room and suppressed a small hiccup. "We should create a commune for suburban divorcees."

"Hellooo… That would actually require me to get married and divorced first," I said.

"And we can have male sex slaves like those tribes of Amazon women. And we won't have to shave our legs," Valerie said.

"Val, you never shave your legs anyway. You could braid the hair and put beads in it." I reached for her furry leg.

She quickly shifted to pull away. "What's the point? No one sees them but you two anyway."

Bonita returned to the room and lowered herself to the floor. She rolled onto her back, lifted her feet toward the ceiling, and contemplated her bare toes. "I need a pedicure. Let's all get one this weekend."

"Seriously," Valerie said, "we should just move in together. After the kids go off to college, we should buy some land and build three cottages on it."

"We can grow old together," Bonita said.

I lifted my glass in a toast. "To a celibate, man-free life of slumber parties, pedicures, and hairy legs."

It seemed as good a future plan as any other.

birth of the elect
The Break-Up One-Year Anniversary
Wednesday, October 23

A giant tent filled the expansion lot alongside the Orange County Performing Arts Center. We stepped through the wood shavings scattered on the ground and sat on one of the bales of straw set out like couches in the open area near the entrance.

I looked around while Mom read the program. Theatre Zingaro: a French equestrian performance troupe. I thought the tickets would make a good early birthday present for her.

"It says here," she turned the page, "that this is their third time in the United States. They flew twenty-three horses all the way from a Paris suburb called Aubervilliers." Mom sat engrossed in the information, her short, gray curls peeking above the edge of the brochure.

I may as well have been in France. I was at least a continent away in my mind. Mom and I were at the show to celebrate her sixty-first birthday, and I guess, unofficially, my one-year anniversary of The Break-Up.

After a year, it wasn't like I thought about Kevin every day. At least that torment had passed, though I didn't remember exactly when.

People began moving into the tent, so we rose and followed. The tickets were good. Our seats were in the row closest to the partition of the circular arena: an unobstructed view.

The performance of *Triptk* began to the strains of Stravinsky's "The Rite of Spring." Unfolding before us, there was the beginning of a new life, a struggle fraught with birth pangs. The symbolism was not lost on me when foals played out their capriciousness in a lost paradise.

After the intermission, a male and female struggled with each other in a dance between the ossified and the tender. In the end, a lone, cloaked rider sat motionless on a prancing steed as darkness descended. The final lingering wind of the clarinet haunted my thoughts.

While the audience filed out of the tent, Mom and I sat quietly in our seats.

"What's the weather like where you are?" she asked. "You weren't even paying attention."

"I was too," I said, still absorbed in the spell of the performance. "I felt like the story mirrored everything in my life. Ryan. Kevin. Where I'm going with my future."

The look on Mom's face said she clearly didn't see how I could make that connection to any symbolism in the show. Trying to express my thoughts about it made my heart feel heavy. "Today is the anniversary of The Break-Up and I can't believe it's been an entire year since he left."

"I wondered if that was bothering you," she said.

"I decided that I'm not going to date anymore. I need to do my own thing—alone. Ryan was a mistake. And if he hadn't been so persistent, it never would've gone as far as it did."

I studied Mom's face to read any unspoken thoughts. She seemed to be weighing her next words.

"You can't control what other people choose for their lives. Ryan wanted all of your love. It's very much like what you wanted Kevin to give you, but he couldn't."

Her logic was always delivered with brutal honesty. It had a certain clarity that came from wisdom and objectivity. But knowing that didn't make it any easier to hear.

She was right though. My relationship with Ryan was a mirror image of my relationship with Kevin. Kevin must've felt that being with me was settling for less than what he wanted. I didn't want to settle in my life and I couldn't blame him for feeling the same way.

dating dilemma
Friday, October 25

The music pulsed. It was a typical Friday night: groups of guys gathered to drink beer, watch the shows, and flirt with the dancers. A single three-minute set on stage could easily yield from $75 to $100 in tips, but with forty girls on the rotation list, a stage set only came around once every two hours. The big money was from the private dances. Five in a row brought in $100 in fifteen minutes.

I glanced across the crowded club, looking for my next meal ticket. My breath caught in my chest. The roar of blood coursing through my body drowned out the voice of the DJ announcing the drink specials and the next girl on stage. I walked hesitantly toward the bar.

His blonde hair, the shape of his face, the outline of his body—Kevin. It startled me to run into him like this. I never expected to see him again and couldn't imagine why he would show up at the club.

Should I say hello? A sinking feeling buckled my stomach.

He looked briefly in my direction, yet nothing registered on his face. He turned back to his drink.

As I got closer, I realized the guy had a fuller face and broader shoulders. Even sitting on the barstool, I could see he was taller. It wasn't Kevin. An involuntary exhale drained the tension from my body. I didn't need to worry about being friendly and thinking up something casual to say.

In that single, terror-stricken moment, I had discovered a new medical breakthrough: contact lenses would prevent heart attacks.

I walked past the blonde guy at the bar.

"Excuse me, are you okay?" He reached out to touch my arm. "You were looking at me as if you were frightened."

"Sorry. I thought you were someone I used to know."

"My name is Steven." He held out his hand and I shook it. "I'm sure I would have remembered you if we had met before," he said.

"I'm Beth. It's nice to meet you."

"Can I buy you a drink?" He flagged his hand to summon the bartender.

"No, thanks. I don't drink." I knew as soon as I said it that my response was a dead end, so I tried to rescue the moment. "I'm like a camel. I know I should drink more water, but I hate water, I know it's good for my organs and my skin, but it doesn't taste like anything—so, what do you like to do for fun?"

It was always so much easier to talk to cute guys in flirty stripper-speak. With Steven, there was something about him that made me stumble and feel like I was in a ridiculous struggle to create a normal conversation.

Steven looked mildly amused by my rambling. "I enjoy traveling. I just came back from a mountain biking trip in Utah, and I'm leaving for San Francisco tomorrow for a couple days."

I leaned against the bar railing. "I've never been to San Francisco. But I like sourdough bread."

Because clearly, my discerning palate more than makes up for my lack of worldliness and my inane comments. God, he must think I'm such a dork.

"Would you like to go with me?" His offer sounded genuine and friendly.

For some reason, I had an immediate urge to say, *Sure, why not!* Something about his gentle manner made me feel like I would be safe with him. It sure sounded like a great adventure: hop on a plane for a weekend in San Francisco with a perfect stranger. But then, again, it also sounded like a great way to end up with my body chunked in twelve different Ziploc freezer baggies.

"Are you sure you're not a serial killer?" I studied his face closely.

"Not that I know of." Steven chuckled and shook his head.

Would he actually tell me if he really was?

"Because that would be my luck."

"You can be most assured that I am definitely not a serial killer."

"I figured you probably weren't. I think I'm a bgood judge of character…" I smiled at him playfully. "…but I'm going to have to pass on the San Francisco trip."

"That's too bad. I think we would've had fun. May I have your number so I can take you out to lunch sometime?"

Hmmm…dilemma.

"Well, I'm not really dating right now," I said. "I'm just sort of focusing on… other things. But I guess you can call me and we can talk on the phone."

I wrote my number on a cocktail napkin and handed it to him. He folded it carefully and pressed it into his pocket.

delete key = weapon of mass destruction
Tuesday, October 29

"It's been two hours already. Is it supposed to take this long?" I rubbed the searing lump on the back of my neck.

"I'm not sure," Mom shrugged. "I've only done this once before."

It was the flat blind following the visually impaired.

"I thought computers were supposed to save time." I looked at the mess of disks, instruction manuals, and cables around the second monitor perched unstably on my bed. We both crouched on the carpet in sweats, hunched over the project like mad scientists.

Around four in the afternoon, Mom began transferring the data on my hard drive with a cable from my old computer to the new one. My Cro-Magnon version software and Stegosaurus bone hardware had finally become extinct. Okay, so I admit, I'm a complete technotard and when it comes to gadgets, I'm not exactly screwing at the top of the pile in a technology orgy.

For an early Christmas present, Mom bought me a new species of PC with tons of great features that I didn't even know how to use.

I looked up to see Josh leaning in the doorway with an amused look on his face. "Need some help?" he asked.

From the age of seven, Josh had loved to disembowel old computers he scavenged from neighbors. My garage still held casing carcasses and a treasure box full of motherboards.

"No thanks. I actually need it to work."

Josh rolled his eyes. "Yeah okay, whatever," he said and wandered away.

Mom smiled, her silver hair disheveled from running her hands through the curls. "I think I've got it. I finished transferring all your data for your banking, recipes, photo files, and address book."

"What about the rest?" I asked, peering over her rounded shoulder.

"Well, I just selected and highlighted all the files inside your 'Writing Stuff' folder. I wanted to do it separately because it's so big. Now, all I have to do is—"

The mouse pointer slipped from the copy key to the delete key under Mom's quavering touch.

Every little yellow folder instantly disappeared.

ALL FILES DELETED—popped to the center of the screen.

Mom's face crumpled and she burst into tears.

"Oh God!" The words choked past my heart, which had rocketed into my throat. My blood pressure shot up: full body flush, staggering dizziness. Fade to black was almost a physical reality. I grabbed the edge of the dresser for support and fought to keep the darkness from closing in.

Everything I'd written in the last six years.

My book. Scripts. Articles. Editorials. Essays. My thesis. Journal entries. The beginnings of a stage play. A 200-page grammar textbook project. Seminar and craft notes. All of my industry contacts and conversation logs. Gone.

"Tell me you have it backed up on a disk?" Mom's tears ran freely, her hands grasping at mine.

I think I'm going to throw up. "No," I whispered. "I don't."

Why didn't I have my files backed up? Blind faith in technology. Frugal, blue-collar sensibilities that balked at spending extra money for an external backup drive. The reason really didn't matter.

"It's okay, Mom. It'll be okay," I said, not sure if I was trying to convince her or myself. "There's got to be a way to get it back."

Her shoulders slumped, tears continued to zigzag down the lace of her parchment cheeks. "I'm so sorry."

The idea popped almost audibly. "Norton Utilities," she said, "I think it has a recovery wizard in the recycle bin." Her voice gained strength. "I think it might work to get your data back."

Mom launched the recovery function. One by one, each of my 467 files began to reappear on the screen.

I crossed my fingers: a clichéd, stupid superstition.

Finally, at ten o'clock, the recovery wizard prompted us to finish the last command. Then the screen froze. End task to black. No response. Warm reboot to blue screen.

CRASH.

It all went down.

The operating system crashed and now the files were unreachable, trapped inside a computer that could no longer be accessed.

Mom left an hour later, drained and feasting on self-reproach. I was still in shock. I didn't cry. Well, not sobbing anyway. Tears only filled and slid out of my right eye. Strange. I thought the left side of the brain controlled the right side of the body. And it was the right side of the brain that had everything to lose.

I slipped into a bubble bath scented with lavender oil, took a small fistful of Ibuprofen and washed them down with a cup of hot cocoa. A candle flame sent flickers of light dancing into the shadows while my muse curled in the far back corner of my mind. Crippled. Tight fetal position. Quaking in fear.

I'll never write again.

The bath water turned tepid. Chilled and shaking, I stared at the ceiling and continued my litany of unintelligible prayers.

crisis pilaf

2 computer end-users
467 pc. vital documents
1/4 tsp. computer knowledge
2 lbs. anxiety

Take 1 end-user. Collect vital documents in copy function bowl using small amount of computer knowledge.

Completely evaporate documents until nothing remains.

Simmer anxiety until last end-user goes totally limp and all tears are absorbed. Fluff with pitchfork from mental hell.

Yield: Complete breakdown.
Unlimited servings.

Nutritional Value: None.
Guaranteed 2 lb. weight loss.

All water weight from ceaseless crying.

8 miles of inspiration

Sunday, November 10

Josh and I sat in the dim theater listening to the music while the last of the movie credits rolled. For our mother/son date, Josh wanted to see *8 Mile*.

"So, where do you want to go for dinner?" I asked once we settled back into the car.

"Peppino's," he said after taking a minute to think. "Can I have spaghetti with meat sauce? The big one, not the kid's one. And a salad, and some hot bread, and that brown vinegar in the oil on a plate?"

"Peppino's, it is." I directed the car across town. "So, what did you think of the movie?"

"It was great." He turned in the seat to face me. "I liked the part where Cheddar shot himself in the nuts. That was funny. But I thought it was sad when Rabbit forgot what he was going to rap. That's embarrassing." He studied my face. "Did you like it?"

"I liked how hard he worked to make a better life for himself. I liked that he had a dream he pursued and a passion for his music," I said.

There was more to it than I could explain to Josh. The movie resonated with me. I wasn't exactly the target demographic, but Eminem's song, "Lose Yourself," could've been my personal theme when I decided to leave Fontana and move us to South Orange County.

It was a big step and I wasn't sure I could afford it, but he deserved to grow up safe. With plenty of opportunities. No meth labs. No trailer parks. No predators. The OC was like paradise—and culture shock. Maslow's theory executed. Our hierarchy of needs had moved from basic survival to success— with the help of a U-haul truck.

My thoughts kept me silent for the short drive. Josh sat hunched over his Gameboy, his thumbs tapping quickly on the buttons.

The hostess at the restaurant seated us at a table for two in the middle of the room. After we ordered, Josh's face turned serious. "Mom, what do you want me to be when I grow up?"

"Happy," I answered without hesitation.

"No, that's not the right answer." He shook his head. "I mean, what do you want me to *be?* A doctor? A lawyer? What?"

I dipped a crust of bread into the circle of balsamic vinegar on the small plate between us. "I want you to be whatever you want to be, as long as you're happy."

"What if I want to be a rapper?" he said.

"Well, if that's your passion, then you better start practicing." I covered my mouth with a cupped hand and began breaking down a beat with my lips.

Josh's eyes widened. He reached across the table and snatched my hand away from my mouth. "Mom! What are you doing?" His shoulders hunched, he glanced around the room to see if anyone heard my poorly rendered beatboxing.

"If rapping is really your passion, I'll help you pursue it any way I can," I said.

The waitress brought our food and the conversation stopped while we ate. I twirled my fettuccini around my fork using a large spoon as a base.

Josh paused mid-shovel with noodles hanging from his fork only inches from his mouth. "But what if I don't have a passion?" His voice lowered in defeat.

I wanted to go around to his chair and hug him, but that would have embarrassed him too. "You're only thirteen. Don't be in such a hurry to grow up. You only have seventeen years to be a kid. You'll have more than seventy years to be an adult. You'll figure it out when you're ready."

three's a crowd

Saturday, November 16

My cell phone rang. With my eyes still sealed shut with sleep, I fumbled in the dark to find it.

"Hullo?" I said.

"Hey buuuddy, what'r ya doin'?" a male voice asked.

I peeled one eye open and squinted at the clock. "Bryce? It's four in the morning and I'm sleeping! What the hell did you think I'd be doing?"

His laugh was half snort, half hiccup. "I got a verry serus queston fer you," he said.

I sighed and braced myself for a long conversation. "What is it this time?"

"Could you do me a fayver?"

"Only if you promise to stop drunken dialing me. I swear, there should be some sort of public service campaign to keep you off the phone when you get like this."

I'd met Bryce at the club just before summer. He was pickling his sorrows in imported beer and shots of Jack Daniel's. I spent the evening trying to talk him out of killing his liver over a girl. From there, we somehow formed a quirky lonely-hearts bond of phone support and text messages. Whenever either of us began drowning in self-pity, we called. Sometimes we'd talk for hours, sorting through our feelings. My emotional recovery was finally solid. Bryce still had a long way to go.

"I met a new grill at a bar t'night. I think she likes grills too. Would you have sex with us?"

"WHAT?"

"No, no. Shhhh. No. Wait. It'sssokay," he said in hushed tones. "I don' think yer attractive. But I think my new grill might like you..."

I sputtered and choked on a laugh. "Good night, Bryce." I hung up the phone.

It rang a few seconds later. "Don' say no right now, jes think 'bout it," he urged.

"Good night, Bryce. I'm hanging up now." I hung up, turned off my cell phone, and went back to sleep.

Consciousness finally arrived around eight o'clock. I rolled over and turned on my phone. Five missed calls. I listened to the messages. Each call featured Bryce trying a different tactic to persuade me to sleep with him and his most recent feminine acquaintance. I laughed out loud. All the calls had come in at approximately thirty-minute intervals, almost as if it took him that long to think up another reason for me to do it. It was sad, but it was funny.

A pathetic kind of funny.

The phone rang in my hands. I answered it without bothering to check the incoming number. "Listen closely." I formed my words carefully, "I am *not* going to have a ménage à trois with you and some bar bimbo. So, don't even think that you can convince me to do it."

There was a pause on the line. Then I heard Steven's smooth, mellow voice. "Actually, I was only planning to ask if you'd like to join me for lunch."

I felt like I could've roasted marshmallows on the glowing embers of my face. I stumbled over a disjointed explanation about Bryce that sounded more like the plot to a kinky Japanese soap opera.

Steven finally suggested I tell him all about it on our date.

"Okay, but if I go out with you, you can't call it a date."

the mominator
Monday, November 18

Josh came through the front door with a stormy expression on his face.

"Hey, Wonderboy, what's up?" I looked over the top of the *Writer's Digest* magazine I was reading.

"If I tell you, you have to promise you won't get mad." Josh bargained like a game show host.

I straightened in the chair. "Just tell me."

"Don't get mad, but I think I might have to get in a fight tomorrow."

"With who? Why? What happened?"

Josh sat on the floor beside my chair with his head bowed. He picked at the rubber sole of his shoe. "A kid over at the McDonald's parking lot by the high school was doing burn-outs and screeching his tires and I told him he doesn't look cool, he just looks like a dumbass who has to buy tires a lot."

A smile tugged at my lips. Scientific proof. Candor is hereditary. But the question remains, is it nature or nurture?

"I just wanted to tell you, so when I go over to visit my friends at lunch tomorrow and come home all beat up, you'll know why."

I set the magazine on the side table. "First of all, you need to know when and where you can shoot off your mouth. I suggest you don't do it with boys who are bigger and older than you." I stood up and patted the spikes of his hair. "Second, you're not going to get beat up."

I grabbed my car keys off the wall hook behind the front door and picked up my purse. "Go clean your room. I'll be back in about an hour."

A little over forty-five minutes later, I pulled back into our driveway, opened the garage, and began unloading the car. I'd had to put the top down to transport the largest item home.

I met Josh in the hall between our rooms. I had pulled my hair into a ponytail, changed into old gray sweats, a wife-beater tank top, and cross-trainers. "Come into the garage, I want to show you something."

As soon as we entered the garage, his eyes bugged out. "Whoa! No way! What's that?"

"That's BOB," I said. "A Body Opponent Bag." I slipped my hands into a brand new pair of purple sparring gloves and secured the elastic bands around my wrists. I took my stance in front of the training dummy and rained a series of blows on the pink rubberized flesh, finishing with a jab to the well-defined solar plexus and a right cross to Bob's chiseled polymer jaw.

There were certain benefits of growing up fist fighting in parking lots. A year of Shotokan didn't hurt either.

"Mom, you look like the lady in *Terminator 2*," Josh shouted over the sound of my punches connecting with the dummy.

"Now it's your turn." I took off my gloves and tossed a larger black pair to Josh.

He took a few awkward swings.

I coached him through the dynamics of punching power. Elbow thrusts, blocks, and back-knuckle strikes. I demonstrated how to crush a windpipe and how to break a knee. Then I told him the rules.

"Don't ever pick a fight with someone. If I find out you did, I'll kick your ass myself." I paused long enough for Josh to realize I was serious. "But if a guy comes at you, knock him down. Hard. And tell him you don't want to fight," I said. "If he gets up and comes after you again, knock him down harder. Just know that he wants to hurt you, and he will, if you give him the chance." I stepped close to Josh, right up in his face. "Don't give him the chance."

I popped *The Matrix* soundtrack CD into my old boom box and set it on top of the washing machine. "Now, practice everything I showed you." I left Josh in the garage pounding on B.O.B. to the manic shrieks of Marilyn Manson.

One of Josh's friends called later that night. He said the boy from McDonald's drove by our house and saw Josh pummeling the dummy in the open garage.

Josh never did have to fight him.

gentlemen only ladies forbidden
Tuesday, November 19

The rattle of the golf ball dropping into the plastic cup was the best sound I think I'd ever heard. At least, on the golf course. I sank a twenty-foot putt that made my golf partner gasp.

I already had myself convinced that the LPGA tour was within my grasp. And it was only my second class of golf lessons.

Everything about golf reminded me of Kevin, but it was a different feeling now. No longer a searing grip on my heart; it had faded to a soft nostalgia for something that felt like it existed in another lifetime.

I abandoned the golf plan to get back with Kevin even before the classes began, but decided to continue with the lessons for recreation. After two days, I felt like I had a natural talent for golf that could really go somewhere. How ironic.

The class moved to the chipping practice area. I swung the club to catch the bottom of the ball and bounce it onto the green, but it was more of a chop than a chip. My club dug into the grass and never made it to the ball. The reverberation quaked up my arm from the impact with the earth. I tried again and a clump of grass peeled back like a scab. I moved the ball and tried again. I connected with the ball and it sliced to the right, directly into the instructor's ankle.

"Fore?" I winced when he looked at me sharply.

Jamming my 9-iron back into my golf bag, I wheeled it away from the chipping green and decided to salve my ego with another world-class run of putting.

Back on the putting green, I found I couldn't have knocked a donut into the Grand Canyon with a croquet mallet. It didn't make sense. Just twenty minutes ago, I was sinking putts like Tiger Woods with tits.

I hate golf. Stupid game.

Why did I ever want to learn this crap anyway?

I quit.

FOR SALE: Callaway ladies golf clubs—starter set. With rolling bag included. 10 boxes of Titleist balls. Foot Joy golf shoes, size 7. Liz Claiborne golf apparel, size 2. Make me an offer. I'm not in-love with the golf pro anymore.

outlook turnovers

~

1 lb. fresh perspective
16 oz. self-satisfaction
1/2 tsp. pure delight

Roll perspective until sunny and fluffy.

Fill with self-satisfaction. Sprinkle with pure delight. Fold lengthwise.

Cut into individual pockets of freedom. Pinch open ends with giddy realization.

Bake until golden and luscious.

Serve with warm glass of high spirits.

Yield: Total fulfillment.
Unlimited servings.
Nutritional Value: None.

No guaranteed weight loss.

You know you're hot, no matter what else is going on in your life.

part five

the
real
thing

seven-hour splash

Wednesday, November 20

The valet at the Surf & Sand Hotel opened my car door. "Checking in?" he asked.

"I'm just here for lunch." I took the parking stub and tucked it into my purse, making a mental note to have it validated in the restaurant.

My sandals made a clicking sound on the flagstones as I hurried down the steps toward the seaside bar, already an hour and a half late. Not the best way to start a first date. Okay, I know it wasn't technically a date, but that was only because I told myself it shouldn't be.

A gritty sprinkling of sand crunched under my footfalls. I stopped for a deep breath, then stepped through the doorway. Steven's back was to the entrance. I could see his blonde head tilted to cradle his cell phone against his shoulder.

I slid onto the stool beside him. A children's book lay open on the bar; his work-worn hand reached out and carefully turned the last page. He finished reading the story in Danish into the phone. I was so late that I missed hearing the dental adventures of *Karjus and Baktus*, not that I would've understood a single word.

"I'm sorry I'm late. Did you get my message?" I asked when he ended his call.

"I was already here." Steven held my gaze.

"I really am sorry. I hoped I'd catch you before—"

"It's okay." He eased the moment with a slight smile. "I took the time to flip through my magazine and read a bedtime story to my nieces in Denmark." Steven tucked the book into the backpack at his feet.

While he retied his tennis shoe, I noticed the current issue of *The Economist* rolled and tucked into the mesh side pocket of his bag.

"You look nice," he said.

"Thank you." I smoothed my gauzy skirt, suddenly aware of how over-dressed I was. My beige, soft lace top was supposed to be a nice romantic complement to the skirt, but I only succeeded in looking like the bride at a bohemian wedding.

We ordered drinks and moved to a table facing the windows. Steven pulled out the table so I could slide onto the cushioned bench. The row of windows opened wide to a gentle breeze. Sunlight glinted off the wave caps while seagulls dipped and called in the clear sky. The day was more May than November.

Lunch passed with easy conversation and only one awkward moment. When I attempted to spear it with my fork, a grape tomato from my Niçoisé salad shot across the table, left a messy trail of dressing, and bounced onto the floor. Steven pretended not to notice.

After lunch, Steven stood and offered his hand. "Would you like to take a walk on the beach?"

I couldn't think of anything I'd rather do. I just wanted the date to go on and on.

"That would be great," I said.

Steven threw his backpack over his shoulder and I followed him down the narrow stairs toward the sand. My eyes passed from his broad shoulders encased in a white T-shirt down to his—YIKES. Hideous shorts. Navy blue corduroy OP shorts resurrected from the early 1980s.

But I suppose I can overlook the shorts. A smile pulled the corners of my lips. Steven's hips were narrow like his waist. From the back, he looked like a Calvin Klein underwear model. His thighs were shapely and strong and he had amazing calves—rounded and well muscled. I was glad he couldn't see the appraising look on my face.

We stepped into the sand and Steven held my purse while I removed my sandals.

When I finished, I reached out and said, "I can take it now."

He adjusted the strap over his left shoulder. "It's okay. I'll carry it for you," he said, taking my hand in his.

Funny. If I had asked an American guy to hold my purse in public, he would've acted like I handed him a flaming tampon. I almost laughed out loud at the thought. I liked that Steven was different.

We walked in the dark, spongy sand at the water's edge. One stream of conversation flowed into another and Steven's pockets filled with the shells I collected along the way. Sandpipers skittered up and down the shoreline with the ebb and flow of the tide, their little legs an animated blur of motion.

It was the most perfect day on Earth.

My hand felt warm, cradled in the slightly rough cushions of his hand. It was comforting, the feeling of strength and tenderness in the way his wrapped around mine. From one end of the beach to the other, and back again, the rhythm of our conversation matched our languid pace.

Steven told me how he fell in love with the United States when he came for a year as an exchange student in high school. Then he returned to Denmark, but promised himself he'd be back. He applied for a student visa and came to attend Northeastern University. After college, he started a business cleaning houses, and twelve years later, had become a general contractor who built and remodeled custom homes. Word of mouth as his only advertisement.

"I love being here, love what I do, and my boss allows me to take long lunches," he said, adding a smile to go with his joke.

I couldn't help but admire someone so solid, so self-made—with such quiet confidence. No silver spoon. No self-importance. So real.

I bent and picked up a milky-colored stone. Turning it in my palm, I found it was a smooth piece of glass tumbled and fogged by the sand. I rubbed it between my fingers as we walked.

"What about you?" He swung my arm gently, our fingers laced together.

"There's not much to tell. Grew up on an Arabian horse ranch, but always wanted to live near the ocean. My dad was a sergeant for the L.A. County Sheriff's department. I was a daddy's girl and he was my Superman. He died at forty-six of congestive heart failure when Josh was only four months old."

I could've spent all day talking about what it was like to lose my Dad, but it was always easier to gloss over it than relive the darkness. I didn't want to drag down the mood of the date, so I continued on. "I have a little sister who is nine years younger. We've never been very close. She's in Afghanistan right now, in the Army. My mother moved to the high desert, and still has a few horses." I wrapped up my less-than-interesting autobiography. "And some day, I'm going to be a rich and famous writer." I nudged my shoulder against him.

"Well, maybe I should ask for your autograph now," he said.

"Maybe you should," I teased.

Steven stopped and looked across the horizon. "I know we've spent the entire day together," he said, turning to face me, "but would you like to stay and watch the sunset?"

"With you? Definitely." I gathered my skirt against my legs and lowered myself onto the sloping hill of sand.

He moved to sit close beside me, our shoulders touching.

The sun sank slowly, spreading a red-violet banner across the sparse clouds. The sand shifted under me as I leaned against him. He wrapped his warm arms around me and I wanted so much to turn and kiss him, but I wanted him to kiss me first. Everything about the day felt so absolutely perfect; I didn't want to do anything to ruin it.

The sun disappeared into the ocean and faint stars appeared, dotting the twilight sky.

"We know they had good food for lunch. Maybe we should stay to have dinner." His tone sounded like he was joking about the time, but the look on his face said it was a real invitation.

"I can't believe how late it is. I have to get home." I felt like my carriage would turn into a pumpkin if I didn't leave while everything was still perfect.

We collected my car from the valet and I drove him to where he had parked, pulling up behind his Suburban at the curb. I watched him walk to his SUV and, for the second time, marveled at his fitness.

"I have something for you," he called out over his shoulder.

I saw him lift a parking ticket from the windshield and flip it onto his dash. I crossed my arms on the frame of my open window and watched him as he pulled a box from behind the driver's seat. Steven walked back to my car and folded himself into the small passenger seat of my Celica.

He handed the box to me. "I hope it's the right thing. You mentioned that you lost your contact database on your old computer when it crashed, so I thought you could use this on your new computer."

"Wow, thank you. You didn't have to do this." I turned the software box in my hands. It was the latest version and brand-new.

I had a crazy, giggling urge to kiss him. But instead, I reached across the seat and hugged him. "Thank you. That was so thoughtful."

The illumination from the streetlight cast shadows under his high cheek-bones when he smiled.

"May I kiss you?" He looked at me like he expected I might say no.

His question surprised me. I was more familiar with a guy driving his tongue down my throat like a derailed train. It seemed sweet and enchanting that Steven asked for a kiss.

"Of course," I said, but I couldn't help smiling.

Our noses bumped. We turned our heads slightly in the same direction and bumped again. I giggled. Steven touched my cheek softly with his hand and guided our lips together. When we pulled slowly apart, we shared a gently curving smile.

I reached out and touched the dimple in his chin. "I love this."

He leaned over and we kissed again.

"You have to go," he whispered against my lips.

"I know," I whispered back.

Our lips pressed together in a final goodbye. Steven climbed out of my car and walked around to the driver's side. He leaned in to kiss me through the window.

"Goodnight," he said at the end of the kiss.

"Wait." I opened the door and stood to give him a hug.

It was a full body hug; his arms wrapped around my upper back, holding me tightly against him. The top of my head came to just under his chin.

"I had a great day," he said.

"Me too. I don't want to leave."

"I don't want you to leave." He kissed the top of my head.

We stood quietly, gently rocking in our embrace.

"Okay, I'm really leaving now." I climbed into my car and closed the door.

"Roll up your window and drive away. Fast." He waved, walking backward toward his Suburban.

As I drove down the street, I watched him in my rearview mirror until he was out of sight.

What an amazing day. What an amazing guy.

sushi & a basket of issues
Sunday, November 24

The sushi bar owner walked us to the door, nodding and smiling, right up until he locked it behind us. Steven took my hand as we stepped off the curb.

"Maybe we should've taken the hint and left when they started wrapping the fish," I said.

Steven looked around the old strip mall from the coin-op laundromat to the tiny thrift store. "I'm glad you brought me here. The sushi was excellent. I never would hvve guessed this door in the wall would have such good food."

I looked at Steven and replayed his comment over again in my head. Door in the wall? Then I realized what he meant and laughed at the way he had mangled the colloquialism. "I think you mean 'hole in the wall.'"

"Does it embarrass you if I make mistakes?" he asked.

"Absolutely not. I think it's cute." I squeezed his hand.

We walked to Steven's SUV and he opened my door. Once we climbed inside, I made up my mind. I'd been contemplating the timing of the big reveal all through dinner. I almost didn't want to do it.

"Steven, I want to tell you a few things."

"Okay." He looked perplexed by my lead-in, or maybe it was my gallows tone.

I took a deep breath and fired the facts like a machine gun. "As you know, I'm a single mother of a teenage boy. But what you don't know is that I also had my tubes tied, and I filed bankruptcy three years ago, and I don't own my house, I rent, and I don't even have a savings account. I also never finished my university degree—I dropped out eight units short of my Bachelor's because I refused to rewrite my thesis. I'm trying to become a published writer, but I pay my bills by dancing at the club, and I'm desperately nearsighted, and I have rotten time management; I'm always late everywhere I go. I'm not a very good cook. I'm horribly sarcastic and Obsessive Compulsive." I exhaled a final breath. "And I went to a therapist because I was obsessed over my ex-boyfriend."

Steven was quiet while he mentally reviewed the contents of my Pandora's Box. After an awkward silence, he said, "Are you trying to talk me out of wanting to date you?"

I shifted in the seat to face him. "No. Not exactly." When I dumped my basket of issues into his lap, I stared out the front windshield. Now, I looked at him and tried to gauge his reaction.

"Then why did you tell me all that?" he asked.

"Because I figured it was better to tell you up front every bad thing I could think of about myself so, if you wanted to leave, you would do it before I got too attached." I looked solidly into his eyes and lifted my chin slightly.

I waited for the axe to fall. No guy wants to sign up for a relationship with someone who has such obvious baggage and issues. The complete tally: all liabilities, no assets.

The light over the parking space illuminated the interior with an indirect glow. I could see Steven weighing my words.

Finally, he spoke. "I don't care about any of that. It doesn't mean anything. I feel good when I'm with you, you're smart, you make me laugh, and I feel like I could talk to you forever. That's more important to me."

I let out the breath I didn't realize I was holding. He didn't seem bothered by everything I had disclosed. He said he wasn't. I could only hope he was being honest and that it was really true.

With my relationship disclaimer out of the way, our conversation moved seamlessly from one topic to another. Politics. Religion. Social psychology. Travel. It was amazing. Just like our first date, the hours flew by. My head began to buzz and my eyelids suddenly felt very heavy. I looked at the digital clock on the dash: 4:17 A.M.

"You're not allowed to take me out on any more dinner dates," I said. "Look at what time it is! I'm surprised I haven't fallen flat on my face already."

Steven smiled and leaned over the center console for a kiss and said, "Is it over already? I just can't get enough of you."

landscaping and other acts of foreplay

Tuesday, November 26

The house phone rang. I picked it up in the kitchen and peeked out the slider to the backyard.

"Hey, let's meet for lunch." I could hear Valerie shuffling papers in the background.

"I can't. I have company," I said.

"Who?"

"A new guy. You don't know him." Through the glass, I watched Steven re-pot my rubber tree, his bare hands tamping down the soil around the base.

"And you didn't even tell me?" Valerie's irritation was clear. "I thought you weren't dating anymore."

"This one's different. He's sweet, he's funny, and he even brought me grass," I whispered.

"Marijuana? He bought you mara-wanna? You've never done drugs in your life! Who *is* he?" Her curiosity spiked the volume of her voice.

"His name is Steven. He's thirty-six, he's Danish, he speaks four languages, he's got an MBA, he owns a construction company, and he's beautiful."

Val didn't miss a beat. "Bring him to Thanksgiving." Her statement was less an invitation than a demand. I knew she would spend the evening dissecting him like a lab frog. It was always like that with any new guy.

"I don't know if he has other plans, but I'll ask. I gotta go. I'll call you later." I hung up.

The day was unseasonably warm. I carried two glasses of lemonade into the backyard and stopped to watch Steven show Josh how to fit the strips of sod against each other so the grass would grow together.

I lingered near the doorway behind them. Their first meeting was going well. Josh had always been so easy-going. And it was obvious Steven liked kids. They laughed and talked without any sign of awkwardness.

I overheard them planning Josh's fourteenth birthday—laser tag, go-carts, batting cages, and rock climbing at Boomers, a local fun center. I liked seeing them together; Josh needed this. I needed this.

After taking a quick shower, Steven leaned against my bedroom doorway. I stood, sorting clean clothes from the basket. He glanced around the room and his eyes came to rest on the neat stacks of papers on my desk.

"Do you mind if I read this?" He lifted a clear report binder from the top of my inbox. The title, in seventy-two-point font and all caps, read: MY FIVE-YEAR PLAN.

"Go ahead. But you have to promise not to laugh at my lists. It's my OCD thing," I said, continuing to fold the pile of laundry on my bed.

"I won't laugh," he said as he peeled back the cover. His eyebrows rose when he saw the interior. "Wow, each page in a sheet protector too?"

"You promised." I flashed him a mock scolding look.

"I'm not laughing," he said with a huge smile stretched across his face. He sat in my desk chair and began to read. Steven turned the pages slowly.

I peeked up from the clothes to study his expression. I saw him turn back a few pages to reread something.

When he finished, he set the folder on my desk. "I have two questions for you." Steven leaned back in the chair and looked at me intently. "Why don't you have anything listed that includes having a relationship? And are you really planning to move to Fiji in five years?"

"When I wrote that, I planned to be single for the rest of my life." I didn't mention that until I met him, the only person who I thought could change my plan was Kevin.

"I don't see how you could possibly think that way, but now what about Fiji?" he asked.

"Fiji? Fiji was a symbol more than an actual place. I planned to escape to an island somewhere if I failed at everything else in those five years."

"I see." He rose from the chair and stepped close to me. "What are you going to do if you find someone who wants to change your five-year plan?"

"I don't have a plan for that." I looked down at my bare toes curling in the plush carpet.

Steven gently turned my face up to his. "Good. Don't make one."

the wishbone is connected to the guy bone

Thanksgiving
Thursday, November 28

"Knock knock…" I pushed open the door of Valerie's house, juggling a plate of pumpkin bread and my purse. Josh squeezed past me and ran up the stairs to find the rest of the kids.

"In here!" Valerie called out.

Steven paused to balance the bowl of salad in the crook of his arm and close the door. I walked into the kitchen and watched Valerie hoist the turkey pan from the oven.

She looked up just as Steven entered and set the salad on the counter. "Oh m'god!" she said under her breath. She lifted the turkey onto a serving platter. When I moved across the kitchen, Valerie leaned over and hissed in my ear, "You're sick! He looks just like Kevin!"

True, there was some resemblance at first glance; I had made the same mistake myself. But the more time I spent with Steven, the more I realized they were like night and day.

"Woo-hoooo…helloooo…" Bonita's heels clicked on the slate entryway. She entered the kitchen with an ever-present bottle of Merlot and a tray of cheeses. Her sons made an appearance to drop off plates of deviled eggs, then slipped away to find the rest of the kids.

After the table prep was completed, everyone formed an assembly line, and soon the plates were filled for a Thanksgiving feast. My plate was the only one conspicuously missing turkey. Valerie, Bonita, Steven, and I sat in the formal dining room. The six teens went out and settled at a big table in the sunroom, squabbling like true siblings. Twelve years of being raised together made them feel like family.

I knew it wouldn't be long before the inquisition began. The girls were noticeably curious about why I'd been hiding him. They both studied Steven intently and hung on every word from the first moment he spoke. I felt both proud and a little wary of showing him off. I think I felt more uncomfortable about him being judged than he did.

Steven was engaging, kind, and funny. He carried the conversation, which was mostly one-sided from all the personal questions he fielded.

Yes, he loved doing custom construction. The best part was watching the reaction of his clients when he made their vague ideas come together in something solid and functional.

Traveling. Traveling was definitely his hobby, more of a passion really. He couldn't watch a plane fly overhead without wondering where it was going and wishing he were on it.

Denmark was a great place to grow up, but no, he would never go back, except to visit. The business opportunities were much greater in the U.S.

I watched Steven with the same admiration I always felt. He looked so relaxed, leaning slightly to rest his elbow on the arm of the chair while he talked, an occasional sip from his glass of wine.

"So have you ever been married?" Valerie knew the answer. I'd already told her, but she asked anyway.

"I was for ten years. We met at university in Boston."

Without missing a beat, "What happened?" Bonita hunched forward like she was poised to dive into a pool of gory details.

"The divorce was mutual. We sat down one night and decided it wasn't the type of relationship we wanted anymore."

Steven had so much class. I never heard him trash his ex-wife, but I knew he was the one who prompted the split. Her hyper-focus on her career and lack of effort to fit him into her schedule had turned them into strangers that were sharing a living space.

"So, how long have you been divorced?" Another question Valerie knew, but asked him directly.

"Two years. I just started dating again a few months ago. It surprised me to find someone I really liked so quickly." He reached over and covered my hand with his.

"What about Angela?" I teased, pulling my hand from beneath his. I turned to Valerie and Bonita, "She was a twenty-three-year-old he dated right before me."

Steven laughed, a joyous noise with an unusual tone that always prompted people to turn and look. "That girl would have killed me. All she wanted to do was go dancing at raves until the sun came up."

"So, of course, he traded her in for a rickety old cow like me," I said.

Steven smiled at my sarcasm and then became serious. "Actually, I had already sold my house in Laguna Niguel and shipped my car to a new condo I bought on the beach in Fort Lauderdale. It was supposed to be my last weekend in California when I met you."

That was something I didn't know. It was weird finding that out in front of my friends. It felt like a private disclosure and a public declaration all at once.

Valerie and Bonita caught the exchange, looking from Steven to me, and back again.

He filled in the answer to everyone's unspoken question. "So, for now, I'm renting a room from a friend of mine. Until I see how things go."

Steven smiled at me, and a warm feeling spread through my chest.

I guess we'd just have to see where things went.

real family fun

Saturday, December 14

I poked my head into Josh's room. "Wake up, belated-birthday boy."

"Hey Mom." Josh wiped at the corners of his eyes and arched his back in a waking stretch.

I hooked my thumb in the direction of the bathroom. "Hop in the shower and I'll start breakfast. Steven is on his way over for your Boomers day."

Josh's birthday had fallen on Thursday, so we did the roll cake tradition that night after dinner, Josh ooh'd and ahh'd over his gift—a full weight bench and dumbbell set—and we planned the celebration for the weekend.

Once we reached the family fun center, we started with a round of mini golf. Josh launched a teasing competition, marked with verbal sparring and serious putting. Somewhere along the way, we accidentally switched courses and were playing on a different trail of colored flags.

As soon as we turned in our putters, Josh took off at a run toward the laser tag building, glancing behind to make sure Steven and I still followed.

Steven reached to capture my hand in his as we walked. "It's nice to see he's having a good time."

"Thanks for taking us out for his birthday." I pulled him to a stop and stood on tiptoe to deliver a quick kiss.

"Hurry! Come get in line," Josh called out to us.

We had to wait until a group of ten gathered before being allowed to suit up. The activity coordinator, a freckled older teen with a shock of red hair, handed us each a vest with a hard plastic sensor on the chest, and our mock futuristic weapons.

We entered the multilevel maze and saw the room was illuminated by black light. Everyone scattered, ducking behind partitions, awaiting the signal to engage in laser combat. This was my kind of game. I hunted like a predator, low and stealth, until I rushed my target with what probably sounded like an absurdly PMS-driven battle cry. I saw Steven once in the fray. He nodded to me, smiled, and then ambushed a group of teens we didn't know.

The game ended with Josh protesting, "I got you first!" Which clearly wasn't the case, but I laughingly agreed with the birthday boy anyway.

I was still in commando mode, so when Josh pointed to the rock climbing wall, I was ready.

Steven, Josh, and I strapped into the diaper style harnesses. Josh chose the most difficult face and climbed it like an Olympic monkey. Steven started up the intermediate face, and since I'd never climbed before, I positioned myself at the bottom of the beginner side. I stepped one foot after the other, reaching with the opposing hand for the next grasp. It was harder than it looked.

I glanced up and over at Steven as he reached to ring the bell at the top. Josh had already been to the top, rappelled down, and was working his way up again.

I was stuck in the middle of the wall. I looked up to the bell, and it seemed so steep and far away. Then I looked down. Big mistake. Clinging more tightly to the artificial rock handles, I pressed myself against the face of the fiberglass mountain; I couldn't move. I'd always had trouble with heights, but didn't expect climbing an amusement park toy would be a problem.

On his way rappelling down, Steven stopped beside me. "Going up? Or going down?" he asked.

"Neither." I stuck to the wall like a smashed spider. "I think I'll just stay right here for a little while."

Steven looked at me curiously. "Are you okay?"

"Yeah, I'm fine. Just thought I'd hang out here."

He must have figured out my problem because his tone changed from playful to soothing. "Just let go with your hands and push away from the wall with your feet."

Let go? Funny guy. I wasn't letting go of shit.

"Hey Mom!" Josh yelled from the ground. "Hurry up so we can ride the race cars."

It was clear I couldn't exactly spend the day where I was. My fingers were already getting sore from hanging on so tightly.

I looked over at Steven and managed a weak smile. He smiled back and stayed beside me while I slowly backed down. I stretched each foot and hand to reach the next lowest rock until finally I stood on terra firma, my legs quivering slightly. Okay, note to self: No more feet-off-the-ground stuff.

Racing go-carts was a totally different story. Heart like a wheel, I channeled the spirit of Shirley Muldowney. "Catch me if you can," I called out to Steven and Josh as I pulled out of the starting area.

We whipped around the small track. I cut in close at the corners, squeezing the boys out of the turns and pressed the throttle open through the entire race, using the body of the small cart to maneuver to keep the lead, not allowing anyone to pass. Wild laughter bubbled up from my chest and I let out a shriek of victory at the end.

"Mom, you're nuts. I could've beat you if you weren't driving so crazy mean." Josh looked surprised and a little amused.

Steven pulled me against his side and kissed the top of my head. "Wow. You're a little terror behind the wheel."

Something about the speed and the competition made my pulse quicken. "Someday I want to try the real thing on a NASCAR track," I said.

"That would be scary," Steven said.

The day passed with laughter and all the giddy excitement of adolescent fun. Bumper cars. Batting cages. Air hockey. Video games. After a while, we collapsed into a booth to refuel with greasy pizza and chocolate milkshakes.

On the drive home, Josh fell asleep on the backseat of the Suburban. Steven held the wheel with one hand so he could hold my hand with the other while he drove.

I had a sense of peace I hadn't felt for a long time. Steven seemed to fit so well into our lives; it was as if he belonged there all along.

a date with hedonism
Tuesday, December 17

Steven called The Four Seasons in Carlsbad to schedule a massage and facial for us. Then we'd have the private room to ourselves for another four hours.

When we walked in, flute music whispered in the background and a gas log fire flickered, casting shadows on the walls of the warm room. Twin chaise lounges curved around a small table set with wine, fruit, and cheeses.

Once settled in the couple's spa room, we waited for the massage and skin therapists to arrive.

"Try this." Steven held a cracker supporting a thick slice of brie.

I took a bite. The cheese stuck to the roof of my mouth and a piece of the cracker dove between the folds of my robe.

My first brie. I giggled a puff of cracker dust. "It's good," I mumbled around the cheese.

Steven held the top of a crimson strawberry, offering me a bite. He leaned over, and with the tip of his tongue, licked a drop of juice from the corner of my lips. We kissed the sweetness between us.

When the therapists arrived, we settled ourselves on each of the tables under the soft, warmed sheets.

I started with the facial; Steven with the massage.

It was my first facial, so I wasn't sure what to expect. I thought for sure I was going to smother when Skin Lady steamed me and wrapped the hot towel around my face like a swirled cone. Hoping I wouldn't die from asphyxiation, I took little breaths and concentrated on trying not to hyperventilate.

I heard Steven groan. I tried to peek through the cloth covering my face, and wondered if guys ever got an erection during a professional massage. Rub—rub—BOING. Instant pup tent with no campfire or marshmallows in sight. A giggle slipped out.

"So, you're enjoying your facial over there?" Steven's voice was slightly muffled in the cushioned face rest on the massage table.

"This is great. And by the sounds of it, I'm going to really enjoy my first massage too."

"We should do this at least once a month." Steven groaned again.

How could I argue with that? And why would I?

Steven and I switched tables and my massage began.

I tried to will my muscles to feel firm and less jiggly. Massage Lady seemed to spend far too long squeezing and kneading my lower back fat. It was like she was trying ever so unsubtly to tell me I needed to go to the gym more often. I just knew she thought my body felt like soggy Playdoh.

Concentrating harder, I sucked it in, but it didn't seem to be helping. I finally decided that since she'd never see me again, it was okay if I was a little squishy. As I relaxed, my body sank into the cushioned table, and I gave in to the kneading motions of her hands.

I awoke just as the therapists left the room and closed the door quietly behind them.

When I climbed off the table, my muscles felt like they hung loosely from my bones. I wrapped myself in the warmed robe and felt it cling to my lightly oiled skin.

"How was that?" Steven opened his arms and pulled me into an embrace.

I rested my head against his robe and circled my arms around his waist. "Absolutely wonderful," I said.

"Would you like to go into the heated pool?" Steven pushed open the French doors to the private patio.

It was chilly and the dark clouds threatened rain. We ran barefoot across the flagstones, tossed our robes onto a table, and plunged into the steaming water. When we surfaced, the sky opened to shower us with cold rain.

We moved to the far end where a patio umbrella near the edge of the pool sheltered us from the sky. Steven sat on the bench seat and floated me onto his lap. My cheek rested on Steven's damp shoulder and his arms wrapped around my body underwater. Raindrops splashed into the pool and bounced, creating hundreds of tiny rippling circles on the surface. The steam cast a low fog around us and we kissed while the rain beat a soft rhythm on the umbrella overhead.

All of it had been so magical. It was something I could only imagine in a scene from a movie. Every minute I spent with Steven was better than the last.

"I'm getting pruney," I whispered against his lips.

"Let's get out. My head is getting cold too."

We ran for our robes and ducked back into the room. Steven pulled a chaise lounge close to the flickering fire and we cuddled together on it.

"In case I forget to tell you later, this has been an amazing day. I love being with you," I whispered in his ear.

Steven turned to face me, capturing my gaze. "I think you're an amazing woman."

He slowly pulled one end of the sash on my robe until the bow untied. Then reached to part the folds, exposing my bareness to the warm glow of the fireplace. He began at my neck, kissing and tasting down the length of my body. I closed my eyes, reveling in the feel of his hands and mouth touching and exploring. I looked down to run my fingers through the damp waves of his hair.

Steven lifted his body and poised above me, our gaze shared the intimacy and desire we both felt. He entered slowly and our lips met in a deep kiss.

Hedonism at its best.

the grinch who skipped christmas
Monday, December 23

It was two days before Christmas and I wandered from room to room— irritated.

I always enjoyed the bustle of mall shopping during the holidays, often stopping to sit on a bench to people-watch. I loved spending the entire day trying to find exactly the right gift for someone.

Last year, Christmas was a disaster. Between Buddy's destruction of the tree and the tow truck incident, I knew this year's celebration would have to be exponentially better. I looked forward to sharing our Christmas with

Steven. When the starting gun for Black Friday went off, I had called him to chatter about my grand plans.

Steven sounded less than thrilled. He admitted Christmas had always been a huge disappointment when he was growing up. I could feel his discomfort; it was so strong it was tangible. He had a certain cynicism toward the huge commercial ritual and said it never lived up to the expectations it promised.

I had approached Josh about it while he was watching a DVD. "Hey Wonderboy, can we talk?"

He pressed the pause button on the remote. "Did I do something wrong?"

"No, I just wanted to talk to you about Christmas. Steven's not really a big holiday guy, so I was wondering if you'd mind if we skip it this year?"

Josh considered my question a minute before speaking. "Can we buy a few things on my list?"

"Of course. We'll still exchange a few presents, we just won't do that whole traditional decorating thing."

"Okay, that's fine with me," he said, clicking the play button to continue watching his movie.

So, it made sense. We would avoid the chaos and the hype. Not bother hanging lights on the house, or buying a tree, or decorating. We would just skip Christmas.

The weeks had passed with holiday images plastered everywhere. Even after ten years, I still marveled at the fact that in South Orange County, all the block walls around the gated communities were decorated with bulbs and garlands, the trees in the beltways laced with blinking lights. In my old hometown, the decorations would've been stripped bare as soon as the city's seasonal maintenance truck reached the end of the block.

Everywhere I looked, it was festive. But in our house, it looked like any other day.

I just couldn't shake my ratty mood. In the last few days, it had amplified. By the time Steven came over after work, I was hanging on to the brittle edge of reason.

"Hello, Beautiful." Steven wrapped me in a greeting embrace. He pulled back and searched my eyes. "Are you okay?"

"Yes. No. I don't know." I pressed my face against his white T-shirt. A wave of sorrow washed over me and my shoulders shook with silent sobs.

He led me to the couch and pulled me onto his lap. "What's wrong?"

"Nothing. I don't know why I'm crying." I kept my eyes lowered, staring at the floor.

"Are you PMSing?" It was that tentatively asked question, the one with the potential to provoke an instant masticating decapitation.

I shook my head. No period, just an overwhelming, unexplained sadness.

The memory caught me by surprise: I was ten, maybe eleven. Dad crouched in the corner of the living room, screwing two wooden poles together, fitting them into an iron stand. He smiled over his shoulder. "Nettie, sort the branches in piles by the color of paint on the end of the wires," he said.

Of course I knew what I was doing. I'd helped put up the artificial tree for as long as I could tell my colors. I reached into the huge, tattered, cardboard box with the yellowed tape on the corners and pulled out the next limb.

I truly loved that ugly, plastic Christmas tree with the storage-mashed branches.

"I think I do want to have Christmas," I whispered to Steven while tears flowed freely down my cheeks.

"Is that why you're crying?" Steven's tone carried the full weight of his confusion.

Why? There were so many little reasons why.

"I had to run around the tree to fluff the nylon needles because they were always flat," I said. As a girl, my tiny arms only reached halfway up the tree, so Dad ruffled the rest before he put the lights on.

"Mom stuck the hooks in all the ornaments and I would hang them. And it was my job to watch Tiki, our Siamese cat, and chase her away if she tried to eat the tinsel."

I struggled to answer his question. "Every morning I used to wake up early and lie on the couch in the dark, watching the tree we decorated blink colors across the wall. It was a magical, quiet time when everyone was happy." Another tear rolled down my cheek.

Steven's XY problem-solver gene kicked in. "What can I do?" he said. "Do you want me to buy you a tree?"

I wanted to share every detail of our family Christmas traditions. Each memory came back so vividly that I could almost feel Dad's presence in the room. "He used to tease me by opening his presents so slowly that I had to run over and tear off the paper for him. Then after we were done, he'd bake blueberry muffins for breakfast."

Steven guided me off his lap, and pulled me by the hand toward the door. "Let's go get you a tree," he said.

I thought I could skip Christmas and it wouldn't matter, but there was so much more beyond the chaos and hype. A love of family sharing decorated the tree and my soul every year. I realized having that again was more than a want; it was a need.

starbucks & the lottery
Friday, December 27

Steven looked at me across the small table. His hand curled around his cup of espresso. "I don't understand why guys you've been with in the past have never invested in your dreams."

I stirred the whipped cream into my hot cocoa. "I don't know. After I helped them, I guess they just left before it was my turn."

But how was it that I never saw it coming? Bonita said it was the Florence Nightingale Complex: I found broken men and tried to make them whole. Maybe, but it still didn't explain why they always left.

Steven reached across the table and covered my hand with his. "I don't understand how anyone could ever let you go."

I shrugged. What could I say? Kevin had insisted, 'It's not you, it's me.' That cliché sounded like an easy way out. But I guess any break-up line sounds lame when you are on the receiving end whether the reason is true or not.

A serious expression crossed Steven's face. "I've been thinking about some-thing important and I want to hear your thoughts about it. I don't want you to answer right away. I want you to think about it," he said.

"Okay, so what is it?"

"Would you ever consider quitting your job at the club to pursue your writing fulltime?" He studied my face closely for the answer.

I laughed. What was there to consider? "I don't need to think about it. Of course, I would," I said. "But I don't exactly have that luxury."

"What if you did?" He stared at me unblinking.

"Well, if I won the lottery tomorrow," I smiled and continued with the fantasy, "I'd find a way to invest it, so I could live off the interest. I'd quit the club, and work on finishing my book."

"So, money is your only obstacle?" he asked.

"I can't afford not to work. The bills won't pay for themselves while I'm playing the starving writer. If it were just me, it'd be okay, but I have Josh."

"How long do you think it would take you to finish?" he asked.

That was a good question. I couldn't even fathom what it would be like to have one day melding into the next with nothing to do but write. "Maybe three or four months." It was the best guess I could make for a hypothetical daydream.

Steven nodded slowly and took another sip of his espresso.

in-n-out double-double means i love you
New Year's Eve
Tuesday, December 31

Steven guided his Suburban into a shopping center parking lot toward an In-N-Out Burger drive-thru. "Did you want something?" he asked, scanning the menu marquee.

I checked the clock on the dash. We still had three hours before we were due at Valerie's for her first annual New Year's Eve Pajama Party. Josh rode his bike over early to help set up the decorations, so all we needed to do was shower, change, and show up.

"Is this all right, or did you want something else?" Steven hesitated before pulling forward to order.

"No, this is great. I'll have a grilled cheese, no onions, and a chocolate shake." I unclipped the seatbelt and shifted to tuck my legs under me.

The lot was nearly full and a long line stretched out behind us. After we collected our food, Steven pulled around to a parking spot.

He lifted his double meat, double cheese hamburger out of the cardboard car box and took a bite. I pulled the wrapper off the top of my straw and lifted the chocolate shake to my lips. I took a long, hard draw on the straw and thought my head would cave in.

Steven laughed when he saw the way my eyes bugged out. "Thick shake, huh?"

"Very." I pinched the collapsed straw to reshape it.

We ate intently, people-watching through the windshield. I followed Steven's gaze and saw a family with children eating at the stone patio benches. One little boy stuffed his mouth full of french fries. His sister swiped a fry from his cardboard box and before she could eat it, he snatched it back.

I watched Steven watch the children. There was no way I could mistake his expression for anything other than longing.

He noticed me studying him and turned his attention to his vanilla shake. "Kids are great," he said, shifting position in the seat.

Steven pulled the lid off his cup and stirred the fluffy whiteness with the straw before lifting it to his lips. He looked at me over the top of the cup. "Do you ever think you might want more?"

My eyes lingered on the family. If I had another child, this time, it would be different; I wouldn't be doing it alone. From everything I had learned about Steven, and seeing the way he interacted with Josh, I knew he would make a loving and devoted father. I looked across the interior of the SUV.

Steven's eyes were so blue and so warm; I could've swum in them forever.

"With you I would," I said quietly.

Steven leaned across the console between our seats and cupped my face, pulling me into a deep kiss. He whispered against my lips, "I'm in-love with you and I would love to have a child with you someday."

After a lingering kiss, I looked into his eyes. "I love you too." A smile pulled at my lips. "I was planning to tell you at midnight tonight, but you beat me to it."

"At midnight on New Year's Eve?" he asked with a smile.

"Well, it's better than doing it at a fast-food burger place. How cheesy is that?" I said.

love me s'mores

1 lovIng man
1 loving woman
16 oz. soft-focus ideals
2 exchanges of the ultimate endearment

Take one man and one woman. Warm soft-focus ideals of life together, spread evenly.

Insert mutual exchanges of the ultimate endearment.

Press lips of man and woman together firmly until sweetness overflows the edges.

Consume with frothy cup of every heart's desire.

Yield: Ecstatic happiness.
Unlimited servings.
Nutritional Value: None.

No guaranteed weight loss.

But you feel light as a cloud.

hindsight is 20/20
New Year's Day
Wednesday, January 1

"Oh m'god! You'll never guess who's on TV right now!" Valerie emitted a ten-decibel squeal.

I pulled my cell phone away from my ear and thumbed the volume button all the way down.

"Turn on Channel 13. I'm watching *EX-treme Dating* and you're never going to guess—oh shit, you don't have regular TV do you?" Valerie snorted into the phone, an incredulous laugh gone wrong.

"Remember that guy, Tyler, the musician-singer guy? He's on TeeeeVeeee! And he's on a date with this total slut."

I set down the umpteenth box I had moved from one side of the garage to the other. Brushing my hair out of my face, I cradled the phone on my shoulder and surveyed the mess.

Josh tried to help, but succeeded in making more of a mess by opening all the boxes to see what was inside. I finally sent him off to dig through the treasures hidden in the back of his closet.

It always gets messier before it gets cleaner. I repeated it a few times in my head, trying to keep from getting too overwhelmed by the project.

"Didn't you hear me?" Valerie practically screamed. "That guy you dated last summer is on this dating show I'm watching right now. You've got to come over and check this out. It's hilarious. He's making an ass out of himself."

"He is an ass," I said.

I took a break from my New Year's cleaning frenzy and parked myself on an old, tottering kitchen stool in the middle of the garage. "So, what does she look like?"

"You wouldn't believe it. First, they were in a hot tub and she wore a thong. And I didn't know Tyler had a tattoo on his back."

"It's amazing what you can learn from Reality TV," I said.

"No way! Now she's wearing a little schoolgirl skirt with her ass hanging out. You've got to get over here."

"Oh m'god! You're not going to believe what he said." Valerie choked on her laughter and coughed in my ear for nearly a full minute.

When she finally recovered, Valerie told me that at the end of the show, the girl said Tyler was boring and he quipped that her wrapper was better than her candy.

Okay, so maybe he was witty, but he had toenails that looked like peeling tree bark, he stood me up on my birthday, and I'm really glad he never saw me naked.

scooby snacks
Saturday, January 11

> **Hors d'oeuvre** (or durv': French.) n., American translation: I have no idea what's smeared on this cracker.

High Tea at the Ritz?

When Bonita organized the event to celebrate her friend Susan's birthday, I thought she was kidding.

"Are you sure they'll let us in without a pocket Chihuahua, pearls, and a stuck-up attitude?"

"It's not like that. It'll be fun," Bonita said.

When we met in the hotel lobby, we shared hugs all around. Susan tossed her long dark hair over her shoulder and whispered, "I've never been here before, it's beautiful."

Valerie, Bonita, Susan, and I sat down at our table to a panoramic view of the ocean. Set up on craggy cliffs, the Ritz Carlton Laguna Niguel occupied some prime real estate. There weren't any pampered, blue-haired crones like I expected, so I relaxed into my brocade chair.

The server set delicate teacups and saucers for each of us. I ordered the cinnamon spice tea.

Bonita sipped her tea. "You should try the black currant, it's delicious."

We played musical teacups as we taste tested each other's selections. Nothing like a little backwash among friends.

When the server brought the silver tray tower of finger sandwiches with smoked salmon, caviar, cream cheese, cucumber and completely unidentifiable lumps of mushy stuff, we descended on it like attorneys at a car wreck.

Within minutes, the silver reflected our hungry faces.

"If this is all we get, I'm going to starve to death." Valerie licked her finger and dabbed at a stray crumb.

"Yeah," I said. "Just add some flies around your mouth and I'll call Sally Struthers to set up a telethon."

Bonita slid back her chair and tiptoed to the waiter's station. "You don't mind if we just borrow this…" She smiled at a barely post-pubescent busboy and trailed her hand down the length of his arm as she reached for another tray. She returned to the table with the tower of munchies and a satisfied smirk.

After the feeding frenzy subsided, a waiter approached the table. He placed a small dessert plate in front of Susan, tucking a card under the edge.

Four forks dove into the gooey chocolate and caramel torte.

Susan pulled the card from the envelope, read it, and looked across the table at me. She held up the card. "Steven picked up the tab for our High Tea." She turned the card to read the script aloud, "It says, 'Happy Birthday, Susan. I hope you ladies have a wonderful lunch. The check has been taken care of. Enjoy your day together.'"

Valerie snorted. "Can you believe him? I'm sorry Annette, but Steven is just not normal. He's too nice." She leaned forward on the table with her elbows. "There's got to be something wrong with him that he's trying to hide."

"Why can't it be that he's just a thoughtful and sincere guy?" I said.

"Nobody is that perfect," Bonita said, shaking her head.

Susan sipped her tea. "If there are guys like that out there, I've never met one."

"He's the type of guy that the neighbors say to the reporters, 'He seemed so nice, I never would've expected he had forty-three dismembered bodies buried under his house.'" Valerie's look dared me to disagree.

"That's ridiculous. You just can't handle the fact that I found a true prince," I said. "You don't want to admit that the possibility even exists."

"I'm a realist. I'm just saying that there's probably something major about him that you don't know. For all you know, he could be a Danish spy," Valerie said.

My laugh came out as half cough, half choke. "Give me a break. There's nothing wrong with him. He's just a great guy."

"If he's so great, then why would he want to go out with you?" Valerie ticked the tip of each finger. "You don't own anything. You don't have a career. You already have a kid. And you have a ton of issues." She let her hand drop. "If he's so great, he could have anyone. Why choose you?"

Valerie stated all the points I was sure the others were thinking. Hell, I'd wondered the same thing myself.

"It must be for the blowjobs," I said.

Bonita and Susan laughed.

"It couldn't be anything else," Valerie said.

my pumpkin turns into a carriage
Saturday, January 18

The marine layer swirled a soft mist around us as we walked. Buddy and Nina ran ahead with Josh. They dodged the incoming tide and stirred the damp sand in the wake of their race. Soon we were alone on the empty stretch of beach.

Steven reached for me and gently squeezed my cold fingers between the warm cushions of his hand. He pulled me into an embrace and looked up into the sky.

"Too bad we can't see the stars tonight," he said.

I closed my eyes, rested my cheek against his chest, and listened to the rhythm of the churning waves.

"That's okay, I love the beach at night. And I love you. On the beach. At night." I stood on tiptoe to kiss him.

"I've been thinking." Steven pulled back to look into my eyes. "Remember when I asked you if you'd ever quit the club to write fulltime?"

"Yeah..."

"Well, if you're serious about becoming a writer, I think you should quit."

A heavy sigh pressed from my chest. "That's a nice idea, but I thought we already went over all that." I squirmed in his embrace.

He just didn't get it. It wasn't as easy as he made it sound. I couldn't just quit. The magazine guy had folded when he couldn't attract any advertising. And freelance writing was so muse-killing, I'd only half-heartedly pursued new contracts. The club was my main source of income.

I pulled away and took his hand. The tide crept farther up the beach and we moved to avoid soaking our shoes.

The momentary distraction didn't stray his course. Steven stopped and turned to face me. "I think you should have a chance to do what you really want to do. I want to be able to see you living your dream."

Tears of frustration welled in my eyes. I wanted it too and I was doing the best I could. Why did he keep pressing me about it? I wrapped my arms around his waist and buried my face in the front of his sweatshirt. I just wanted to listen to the waves and not have to think about how slowly things were going with my book. I still didn't even have an ending.

Steven leaned down to whisper in my ear, "I love you. I want to take care of you and Josh, so you can write fulltime."

"Are you sure?" I looked up into his eyes and tears spilled down my cheeks. I couldn't believe Steven had offered me the chance to focus on pursuing my dream. "You've never even read anything I've written. What if it sucks?"

"I believe in *you*," he said.

fat and happy remix
Wednesday, January 29

I heard him coughing in the bedroom. The sound traveled all the way into the kitchen. I stared down at the whole chicken carcass lying naked on the cutting board. The skin was covered with little bumps and it just looked miserably cold and pale. Lifting it gingerly by one knobby ankle or elbow or whatever it was, I let it sink into the pot of boiling water seasoned with bouillon.

My Danish prince was sick, so he definitely needed some chicken noodle soup. I hadn't cooked meat in over a decade, but how hard could it be?

I turned to see Josh watching me from the kitchen table. "I can't believe you're actually touching a dead chicken. You must be in-love with him."

After that odd comment, I paused to study Josh's expression. "I am," I said. "But what do you think about Steven?"

He pushed his homework aside and rested his elbows on the table. "I think he's nice. He's like a make-things-get-done guy. And you always look happy when you're with him." He shrugged. "So, I like him."

I turned and poked a fork into the lump of yard bird, pushing it around inside the pot. While the chicken enjoyed its spa bath, I moved to the cutting board to chop the celery, carrots, parsnips, and leeks. Then I backtracked to set a teapot of water on to boil.

"What do you think about me trying to be in a serious relationship again?" I said.

Josh considered my question for a minute before speaking. "I just hope he stays."

There it was. Hills like white elephants. The unspoken thought, finally brought up for scrutiny. I certainly couldn't blame Josh for his concerns. Every man who should have been important in his life had left him. And me. His father disappeared. My father died. And the few guys I tried to build a serious relationship with over the last fourteen years never made it past year number two. It would take a leap of faith for us both to believe Steven would be different.

I dumped the chopped vegetables into the pot, followed by a bag of egg noodles and put the lid on the pot.

I pulled up a chair next to Josh at the table. "I hope he stays too." I covered one of his hands with both of mine. "You know, not everyone leaves..."

When the teapot began a soft whistle, I rose and lifted it from the stovetop, pouring the steaming water into a thick ceramic mug. The bag of green tea floated and then slowly sank to the bottom, releasing the first golden swirl.

"Be back in a minute." I paused a second to rest my hand on his shoulder as I passed. "Finish up that essay and we'll watch a movie."

I carried the cup into the bedroom and sat on the edge of my bed. Steven's eyelids flickered and opened. A slow smile spread across his face.

"I'm a mess, huh?" His voice sounded raspy and parched. "Thank you for taking care of me."

"You're welcome." I lifted the damp washcloth from the bowl on the nightstand and patted it across his forehead.

"I must have a high fever. I'm transpiring all over."

A small giggle squeaked from between my lips. "*Per*spiring," I corrected gently.

"What did I say?"

"Transpiring."

"Oh. That isn't quite right."

"That's okay, I'll just give you the Danish discount." I loved his occasional language slips; they always made me laugh. "I'll just add 'transpiring' to my notebook of Stevonics."

I kissed the top of his head and Steven closed his eyes. "Rest for now and when you wake up later you can have something to eat," I said.

On the way out of the room, I walked past the mirrored closet door and did a double-take. My torso looked a bit thick. I swiveled and looked at my ass.

Plump.

Not the best word to describe a woman's butt—unless the butt belonged to someone else.

I unhooked the clasps on the straps of my jean overalls. They fell to the floor, pausing just slightly as they passed my hips. Maybe it's just the mirror.

I waddled into the bathroom with the overalls in a jumble around my ankles. Maybe that mirror would be better. A skinny mirror.

The skylight filled the bathroom with bright, natural light. I turned and presented my bottom to the mirror. Somehow my ass had morphed into a giant Georgia peach rolled in cottage cheese. I spun away from the sight and scrambled for the scale, nearly tripping as I stumbled out of my overalls.

I stripped off the rest of my clothes and stepped onto the scale. Eight pounds? When did I gain eight pounds? *How* did I gain eight pounds?

Okay, so it's winter. Steven's an amazing cook. We go out to dinner a lot. And maybe I have been wearing mostly overalls and sweats, but eight pounds?

I redressed and shuffled back to the kitchen, contemplating my girth. Happy fat. That had to be it. The antithesis of the break-up diet. I'm officially fat and happy. I think I'd prefer skinny and happy. Is that even possible? I wondered if Steven had noticed he's dating a tree trunk with legs. The waist-less wonder.

A heavy rattling sound drew my attention to the stove. I turned to Josh. "Why didn't you tell me it was boiling?"

"You didn't tell me I had to watch it," he said.

Boys. A short sigh pushed through my nose. I lifted the lid and looked into the soup pot. A cloud of steam fogged my lashes. The package of large egg noodles I had added formed a thick bubbling paste.

Oops. The beige colored mush didn't even look edible much less resemble soup. The water had almost completely absorbed.

Josh peered over my shoulder into the pot. "It looks like something the dogs barfed up."

"Should I throw it away?" I wondered briefly if take-out Chinese was good for a cold.

"No, I think it smells okay." Josh picked up the wooden spoon and poked at the bubbling mass.

"Will you taste it for me to see if it tastes all right?" I asked.

"Do I have to?" Josh looked from my face to the fork I held out to him. "If he's sick, then he won't really be able to taste it anyway."

I plied him with an exasperated look.

"Okaaaay. I'll try it," he said.

Josh took a small bite, tentatively scraping the food off the fork with his front teeth. His face contorted in a disgusted grimace, then he smiled. "I'm just kidding. It tastes fine, but it feels like mush."

I took a swat at his butt and he jumped away from my hand. "Hey, at least I'm being honest."

Well, it might not look very good, but it seemed to be edible. And I had already warned Steven that I wasn't exactly Betty Crocker. I could pretend it was *supposed* to be a big, gloppy mess.

Goulash—there's an idea. That's what I'd tell Steven I made for him: Chicken Noodle Goulash. Good, hardy sustenance. I could say I heard that it's better than soup for a cold.

once upon a time there was a princess...
Sunday, February 2

Select All. Copy. Paste. I harvested another diary entry from my journal and began massaging the record of my daily life into the next descriptive narrative for my book. I was lucky if I completed a single page in an hour. Sometimes several hours would pass as I mentally relived the moments of every account.

Steven stepped behind me and leaned down to kiss the top of my head. "How's the writing coming?" he asked.

I tilted my head back and we shared an upside-down French kiss. "Much better, now that you're here." I lifted my arms above me to stretch out the tight muscles in my shoulders and receive a hug.

"Actually, I've been here for a while. I was out mowing your lawn." He sat on the edge of the bed beside my desk.

"I thought that was Josh." Then I realized the absurdity of my statement. Josh hated mowing and wouldn't do it unless I offered money or threatened great bodily harm.

"I've got him out there now," he said, "doing the edging."

Steven stole a glance at my open document on the computer.

"Did you want to read it?" I motioned to the page view filling the monitor screen. I'd never thought to offer it to him before.

Steven looked at me with a mix of curiosity and hesitation. "Do you mind?"

"No, go ahead." I scrolled back to the beginning of the story and switched places with him.

Once Steven settled into my chair, I felt the disclaimers bubble to my lips. "It's just a first draft, so it's really rough. I know it needs a lot more work…"

He waved away my anxiety. "I only want to see what you do. I'm not reading to judge it."

I stretched out on the bed, tucked a pillow under my chin, and watched him read.

Steven stopped at the bottom of the first page.

"He broke up with you over the phone?" The contempt in his tone was tangible. "You never told me that. What kind of coward breaks up with a woman over the phone?" His brows pulled together. "Did that really happen or did you make that up?"

"It's true," I said, and wondered how he'd react when he reached the part about Ryan. "Are you sure you want to read it? It's everything that's happened since Kevin left, right up until I met you."

I could see him weighing the pros and cons in his mind until he finally decided. "I'd like to read it all. I think it would be a good way to learn more about you."

I immediately wanted to snatch back my offer. Maybe there were some things he'd be better off not knowing. But it was too late to change my mind without looking like I had something to hide.

"Knock yourself out. My life is an open book." I shrugged, surrendering to the inevitable—whatever that might be.

I rested my cheek against the pillow and listened to the rhythmic click of the mouse as he scrolled. Then I closed my eyes, just for a minute.

When I awoke, I saw night curtained the windows. A halo of incandescent light stretched from above the desk to where I lay across the bed. I lifted my head to find Steven watching me, still sitting in my chair.

"Hey." I offered a sleepy smile. "I wasn't snoring, or drooling, or doing anything gross like that was I?"

He shook his head. "Not that I noticed."

"What time is it? How long did I sleep?" I sat up and squinted to check the clock.

"About three hours. Are you hungry? Josh and I had pizza. I ordered a medium veggie with jalapenos for you. Do you want me to warm up a couple slices?"

"I can't believe you left me sleeping for three hours. It wasted our time together." The irritation in my voice was obvious.

The brightness of the computer screen highlighted the side of his face and his slight frown. "You seemed tired so I let you sleep. I read what you wrote, and we ate some pizza. No big deal."

I hated how tired I always felt in the winter, just about as much as I hated feeling like I'd missed out on something. But both of those sentiments were eclipsed by my curiosity.

"So..." I started the awkward segue, nodding toward the monitor. "What did you think?"

He leaned back in the chair and crossed his arms. Bad body language: distance and a closed position. He hated it.

"Come over by me." I smoothed the quilt with a few short brushes of my palm.

Steven moved beside me on the bed. He stretched out on his side and propped his elbow up to cradle his head in his hand. "Well, there is something I want to talk to you about."

I rolled onto my back, closer to him, and looked up into his face. "Okaay." My stomach sank and my heart thumped heavily in my chest. What if he thought my writing totally sucked? And what if he regrets his blind decision to support it?

Steven ran his fingers in my hair, stroking it back from my forehead. "Before we get started, I want you to know I'm not a jealous man."

Ryan. Of course that had to bother him. How can any normal guy read all the graphic details about his girlfriend having wild, monkey sex with a guy who has a giant dick?

He continued in the same tone, oblivious to my wincing apprehension of his next comment. "I wanted to ask you some questions about Kevin."

"Who?"

Steven looked puzzled. "Your ex-boyfriend?"

It took me a minute to switch gears. I was as astonished as he was by my response. I was just surprised that Steven considered Kevin a topic of concern.

"Okay, yeah." I stumbled over the awkward moment. "What do you want to know?"

Steven looked directly into my eyes and held my gaze. "Are you sure you're really over him?"

"Completely." The word came out without the slightest pause.

He still looked skeptical. "After everything I read about your feelings for him, I wanted to hear what you have to say."

I tried not to laugh. It certainly wasn't the right moment for it, but he looked so serious and I felt like his concern about Kevin couldn't be any less necessary.

I looked directly into his eyes. "I have such a greater connection with you on every level. Being with you just feels right. Yes, I was deeply in-love with Kevin, but there was a weakness in him that you don't have."

Steven considered my statement before responding. "In what way?" he asked.

"Kevin worried so much about what people thought of him. But you have this quiet self-assurance. I love everything about you." I rolled onto my stomach and I faced Steven, balancing on my forearms. "You have such a strong grasp on how you fit in with the world and where you're going. Kevin always seemed so uncertain and lost. I tried so hard to overlook it and be driven enough for both of us. In the end, he was the one who realized that our relationship wouldn't work."

Verbalizing my thoughts to Steven made them so much clearer to me. I'd never really know if I had uncovered the real reason from Kevin's point of view as to why the relationship failed. But to me, it felt like the final puzzle piece snapping perfectly into place.

"How can you be sure you're ready for a serious relationship with me?" he asked.

"Because I have absolutely no feelings of anxiety or any hesitation about committing myself to you. And I don't have any sense of unease about your ability to commit to me," I said.

It felt strange to spell it out, but somehow freeing at the same time.

Steven seemed satisfied by my answers.

We curled together on the bed, wrapped in an embrace. I snuggled the top of my head under Steven's chin and tucked my forehead against his chest.

His questions had challenged me to consider my intimate beliefs. In my everyday life, I thought of myself as a realist, grounded by rational thought. Hereditary. Thanks, Mom. But in romance, I felt more like I channeled the rosy spirit of Pollyanna. Complete idealism. That sensibility came straight from Dad.

I'd always entered into relationships with one-hundred percent trust. Trust in the guy's honesty, fidelity, and good intentions. No matter how many times I experienced the rug-pull of disillusionment, it never changed my nature. I wanted to believe I'd find happily-ever-after.

I knew women who, after being thrown from a relationship, would spend years in fear, feeding their bitterness, before they'd make another attempt to get back on the horse. Even when they did, they'd continue to pick at their festering emotions, never really moving on and letting them heal.

No matter where this relationship led, I knew I never wanted to be that kind of person.

bye-bye bump and grind
Friday, February 7

Music pounded through the speakers and filled the club with a rhythm heavy with bass.

Congratulations!

Happy Retirement!

You Go, Girl!

The three Mylar balloons bumped together at the top of a rainbow balloon bouquet. Tracer lights and canisters with multi-colored gels blinked patterns onto the main stage and occasionally swiveled, casting on the floor around our table.

I slid a fingernail under the flap of the greeting card and read the scrawled messages of well wishes from Heather, Bonita, and Valerie.

"Thank you, girlies," I said.

Heather was closest, so I leaned to hug her first. "I'm so glad you're finally out of here," she said, hugging me tightly and rocking back and forth.

Over Heather's shoulder, I noticed a group of guys sitting at the next table, eyeing us. I couldn't help but read their expressions. If the guys were writing the stage directions, we'd be on the floor naked, wrestling in cherry Jell-O.

Bonita was next to embrace me. "Now that you found your prince, you can live happily-ever-after," she said.

"I think you got lucky. What are the chances of actually meeting a decent guy in a strip club?" Valerie raised her hand to wave at a passing waitress.

"We need some shots over here!" she called out.

Sunshine balanced a round tray full of empty Budweiser 40s, her elbow wedged into the hip of her black vinyl pants. "What can I get for you ladies?" she asked.

"Lemon Drop."

"Lemon Drop."

"Lemon Drop."

Valerie, Bonita, and Heather called out like a canyon echo.

"Not me, I'll have—"

Sunshine lifted her free hand and shook her head, sending her long, red hair swinging against her shoulders. "Don't even say it. I know, the usual. I'll tell Rick to make the Beth Special."

"You are so Jack Nicholson in that movie *As Good As It Gets,*" Heather laughed.

"We're going to miss you, Beth." Sunshine's arm snaked around my neck for a quick hug. "I'll be right back with the drinks."

When Sunshine left, Jaimee approached the table. Her tiny, black, boy shorts and bikini top showed off her toned body. I could feel the tension from the other girls checking her out. But she ignored them completely. "Hey Beth, congrats on escaping this dump. I guess that means you'll be writing a lot now, huh?"

"That's my plan anyway." I smiled and stood to hug her. "I'm going to miss working with you though. Let's still get together and do stuff."

She moved out of the embrace. "Yeah, okay," she said, shrugging. "I need to go make some money."

After Jaimee walked away, the other girls were quiet until Valerie spoke. "Did you see her implants? You could drive a truck between them."

Before anyone else joined the shred session, I stepped in. "She's really nice. And she just doesn't have any body fat, that's why they look a little different."

Valerie, Bonita, and Heather all had implants and fuller figures. They'd never be described as athletic looking like Jaimee often was.

Heather changed the subject to relieve the awkward standoff between Valerie and me. "So, Steven must be pretty serious if he's offering to take care of you and Josh."

Sunshine returned and moved around the table, setting down each of the drinks.

Bonita leaned forward in her chair. "When do you think he's going to ask you to marry him?"

"I don't know," I shrugged and reached for my glass.

"I can't believe you don't have to work anymore." Valerie reached to pick up her shot. "Must be nice." She tossed it back and clunked the glass onto the tabletop.

I looked around the club. It pulsed with its own sexual energy. The red lights over the tables cast a flattering glow and the mirrored walls made the room look bigger than it really was. Guys and girls sat in black padded chairs around low cocktail tables, drinking and chatting.

I could almost see the curtain coming down and the credits rolling on this part of my life. Six years. I never planned to work in a strip club that long, but the money was good and somehow the years flew by. It felt strange to look around at everything that had become so familiar and know that I wasn't coming back. Ever.

lions and tigers and bearer bonds, oh my!
Wednesday, February 12

Josh and I finished the tram ride around the San Diego Wild Animal Park and set off to explore the rest of the exhibits on foot. I designed our mother/son date to incorporate a science field trip and a photography lesson to teach him how to use my Canon 35mm camera.

"Let's go see the big cats first," I suggested, glancing at the colorful map in my hand.

Josh was too busy looking at everything we passed to care where I led the tour. Right up until he saw the sign.

"Gorillas! Let's go see those. The sign says it's right over here." He pointed down a path in the opposite direction.

"Fine with me." I followed him as he raced ahead.

After the mock jungle trek, I leaned against the rail to read the placard of information aloud, while Josh mugged and aped the motions of the giant primates. Then I recalled an unusual fact I had heard about gorillas: the males had a two-inch penis when fully erect. No wonder they were always beating their chests. It must be to distract the females from the disappointment. I wasn't sure where I had picked up that little zoological gem, but I decided against sharing that bit of trivia with Josh.

Once he was done snapping pictures and the novelty of the gorillas wore off, Josh turned to me with an urgent look. "Mom, I am soooo starving right now. Can we eat before we do anything else?"

I consulted the map for directions, and soon we sat at tables in the Mombasa Island Cooker area. I handed Josh twenty dollars to buy me a salad, and a burger and drink for himself.

It wasn't my twenty. It was Steven's. He'd left a stack of bills on my desk after we returned from dinner the night before.

"You and Josh have a date tomorrow, don't you?" He had opened his wallet. "How much do you think you'll need?"

I felt weird, like I was some sort of charity case. I wasn't used to being financially dependent on anyone, especially not a man. Funny, it was usually the other way around. I had no problem offering monetary help to guys in the past, without so much as a second thought, but accepting it... That was a completely different story.

"How about a hundred? Is that enough for tickets, parking and food? What do you think?" Steven had peeled off the bills.

"Yeah, that's fine. That's more than enough," I'd said.

Josh returned with the food and handed me the change. It was only a few coins. I stared at it in my hand and felt like maybe we should have brought a backpack with sandwiches and drinks from home.

"This was too expensive," I said, staring at my salad.

Josh looked at me like I'd uttered something totally absurd. "Well, that's how much it always costs," he said.

What a completely bizarre feeling. When it was my money, it just didn't matter. I'd spend it like I had a printing press in the garage. But now that it belonged to someone else...

I decided I needed to tell Josh about the financial decision Steven and I had made. He needed to know our spending habits were going to change.

I watched him bite into his burger and tried to think of a good way to start the conversation. But I couldn't come up with one.

"I quit my job," I said.

Josh's eyes grew wide. "Are you going to get another one? What are we going to do for money?"

"Steven offered to take financial responsibility for us while I focus on finishing my book."

"Oh." Josh seemed relieved there wasn't a problem. "So, what does that mean?"

"That means he's going to pay for the bills and the things we need until I sell my book." Then I'm going to pay him back, I thought to myself. "Until then, I don't want you to ask him for anything. Come to me and I'll decide if we need it. Okay?"

"Okay." He shrugged and took another bite of his burger. "Can we see the lions and tigers next?"

a quiet change of heart
Sunday, February 23

A lazy Sunday. Steven and I watched Josh's little league baseball practice and then spent the day lounged on the couch with a marathon of my favorite Bob Hope and Bing Crosby DVDs. *Road to Morocco. Road to Zanzibar. Road to Bali.*

I wasn't up for much. My period had arrived like a freight train. By the evening, my Ibuprofen intake reached 3000 milligrams and I was retaining more water than a Sparkletts truck.

I noticed Steven staring at me.

"What?" I asked with listless irritation.

"I don't think you're happy." He looked at me seriously, unblinking.

A sick, sinking feeling landed in the pit of my stomach. A knot pinched the back of my throat and tears tingled behind my eyes. Kevin had said the exact same thing a week before he broke up with me.

My head began to throb. No. This can't be happening again. I could feel the tension in my forehead drawing my eyebrows together.

Steven continued. "It just doesn't seem like you're happy with your life," he said. "I think we're spending too much time together."

Kevin had tried to blame me for his desire to leave too. Why did they always do that? Why couldn't they just say *they* weren't happy?

I closed my eyes and tears spilled down my cheeks. I couldn't say anything then; I couldn't say anything now.

"Why are you crying?" Steven brushed his fingertips across the path of my tears.

"If you're going to break up with me, just do it and get it over with, don't try to make it sound like I'm the one who's not happy."

"What are you talking about?" Steven looked completely puzzled.

"You're doing it the same way Kevin did. Before he broke up with me, he tried to tell me I wasn't happy."

"Is that what you think I'm doing?" Steven shook his head and looked directly into my face.

"Well, aren't you?" My tears ran freely.

He gathered my hands together and held them cupped between his.

"My intention," he began slowly, "was to see if you'd like to take a few days alone at a hotel so you could write uninterrupted by me or Josh."

I exhaled a deep, shaky breath. Oh. I guess I win the Olympic gold medal for the long jump to conclusions.

"Don't be such a head basket. I wasn't planning to break up with you." Steven pulled me into a hug.

"Head case or basket case, not head basket." I started to laugh through my tears. "A head basket is what they use with a guillotine." I hugged him back tightly, still laughing. "I love you. God, I love you so much."

Steven pulled away from the embrace and held my shoulders to look into my eyes. "Someday I'll tell you to look up and then you'll know exactly how much I love you."

escape from the oc matrix
Saturday, March 15

As I packed my bags, I smiled at how it had all come about.

"I have a surprise for you." Steven led me to the couch and sat me down. He reached around to his jeans back pocket, removed a long envelope, and handed it to me.

I pulled out two folded sheets of paper and noticed the word eTicket at the top of the pages. It was better than the best ride at Disneyland: it was two tickets to St. Barthelemy. I had no idea where that was, but it meant we were flying somewhere.

Steven must've seen my perplexed expression. "It's in the French West Indies," he said.

I didn't have the heart to tell him I didn't really like Indian food.

"St. Bart. The Caribbean," he continued until he saw my light of recognition. When he said, 'Caribbean,' I smiled broadly. "Okay, so geography wasn't my best subject." I shrugged, a little embarrassed.

Now, I knew exactly where it was. I had spent the week on the Internet looking up anything I could find about the tiny island paradise, and I couldn't wait to get there. It would be the first real vacation I'd ever had.

Josh was far less excited. "Noooo. I don't want to go to Grandma's. It's boring as dirt out there. We never do anything or go anywhere."

"C'mon buddy, give me a break. At least you could be happy for me."

"I am happy for you," he said. "I'd just be happier if I was going too."

I gave him a quick hug. "I need you to help me out and take care of the dogs for me."

Josh paced the living room. "Then why can't I stay home and do it? I can stay by myself, I'm four-teen! It's not like I'm gonna burn the house down."

"Are you nuts? I can't leave you alone for a week." I stepped in front of him to stop his restless striding. "I trust you completely, but if Child Protective Services found out, they'd haul you away to a foster home so fast your socks would fly off. And I'd be arrested for abandoning you."

"That's just stupid. They don't need to find out."

I looked at him and shook my head.

"Okaaay. I'll go to Grandma's. I just wish I could go on vacation with you guys."

"Next time." I gave him a big hug then kissed his forehead.

Once Josh and the dogs were settled at Mom's, I let out a sigh of relief. I couldn't believe I was actually going on a vacation. When the Lincoln town car dropped us at the airport, I practically ran to the terminal.

Steven laughed at my excitement. "Hey, slow down or you'll arrive on the island before the plane."

dreadlocks and coconut oil
Sunday, March 16

I rolled onto my back and stretched, looking for a cool spot under the sheets. I looked up through the filmy mosquito netting draped around the bed and squinted until my eyes adjusted to the morning light. The ceiling fan beat a slow rhythm in the moist air. Faint lyrics of "Jamming" by Bob Marley drifted into the bedroom.

Steven peeked through the doorway. "Hey, sleepy girl, you're finally awake. Come outside, I made breakfast and put on a little island music for you."

I wrapped a bright pink sarong around my body and pulled my hair into a ponytail. I padded barefoot out to the patio and saw Steven had set the table with glasses of orange juice, a plate of sliced watermelon, a fresh baguette, and brie. Tropical blooms in a water pitcher sat in the center of the table. I settled myself into a patio chair and Steven carried out the rest of our breakfast: scrambled eggs and sun-dried tomatoes wrapped in flour tortillas.

When I looked up from the table, the turquoise ocean looked like a liquid jewel stretched all the way to the horizon. Gentle, rolling wave caps reflected the sunlight. It was all so beautiful. I could barely speak. I felt if I could choose my own heaven, I would want it to be here.

"Think you can handle this for a whole week?" Steven said with a grin.

Steven had rented a two-bedroom villa on St. Jean Beach. He arranged to have the refrigerator stocked and a maid come in daily.

"This is amazing. You're amazing." I leaned across the table and gave him a nibbling kiss.

"When we finish breakfast, let's go for a swim. The water is great. I went in while you were still sleeping." I saw tiny droplets of water still clung to his chest.

I lingered over breakfast, soaking up the view from the patio. It seemed so surreal. The entire week stretched out in front of us with absolutely nothing we had to do. We could sleep all day. Stay up all night. Walk up the beach. Play in the surf. Lie on the sand. Six lazy days and seven quiet nights. It was an eternity. It was paradise.

When I stepped off the patio, the sand pressed between my bare toes like powder. Steven and I ran across the beach and into the water. Steven struck out into the gentle swells with a strong crawl stroke. I waded in up to my waist and looked down through the water at my toes; I could see the frost-colored polish glittering like pearls emerging from the sandy bottom. I turned and floated onto my back, blinking in the bright sunlight.

"You can take your top off if you want," Steven called out as he swam back in my direction.

I looked from one end of the beach to the other; it was deserted.

"It doesn't matter if anyone comes around. It's a French and Swedish held island, and the women go topless on beaches in Europe all the time." He smiled his encouragement.

Well, it would keep me from getting tan lines... But with my luck, I'd end up with a tropical fish chomping on my little pink sinkers. Oh, what the hell, I'm on vacation.

I reached behind my back and pulled the strings to free my top. The bright floral triangles of material floated for a moment and began to sink. I scooped the top into a ball and chucked it far up onto the beach while I held one arm across my chest. I ducked back into the water up to my chin and looked around again.

It felt strange being topless in public. It was different at the club. That was a stage show, and in there, I was someone else.

Steven swam up behind me and turned me around with his hands on my hips. "Look at you, island girl," he said.

I moved into his embrace and we shared a salty kiss.

cheeseburger in paradise
Monday, March 17

"Let's take a walk to the marketplace and rent some scooters so we can explore the island," Steven suggested. "How does that sound?"

I rolled over in bed and snuggled against his bare shoulder. I didn't care what we did as long as we did it together.

After breakfast, we prepared for the day's adventure.

"If you could go anywhere in the world, where would it be?" Steven asked as he bent to buckle his basket-weave Mephisto sandals.

I lifted the bottom of my long, gauzy skirt and stepped down the steep stairs of the patio. "Sicily. I'd love to go to Palermo where my grandparents lived. Just find a bench in the middle of town and sit with you, watching people go by."

We walked in the dirt along the narrow, rough-paved road toward town. Our hands swung slightly, matching our stride, fingers interlaced together.

"So, you're not a sight-seer, tour bus type of girl?" Steven moved to my other side, separating me from the passing cars.

"Nope. I would just want to find a little family restaurant, eat there at every meal, and try everything on the menu. I'd want to vacation there the same way I'd live there."

Steven smiled and brought my hand to his lips to kiss my fingertips.

I was hot and sticky by the time we reached town. The sun beat down on our shoulders during the walk and it seemed that steam came right up out of the ground.

I wandered between the rows of brightly painted motor scooters while the lanky shop owner and Steven laughed and chatted in Swedish.

I didn't feel confident about riding one of the small-wheeled machines. Ten years ago, I often rode my Kawasaki Ninja, lane-straddling in Newport Beach along Pacific Coast Highway at seventy-five miles an hour, wearing L.A. Gear high-tops and a thong, but that was a long time ago. A very long time ago. And these just didn't seem as stable. I grasped a handlebar and gave it a shake, making it rattle all the way down to the kickstand.

"Are you ready to go?" Steven handed me the key to a sky blue scooter.

"Sure. Let's do this." I offered a big smile of false bravado. I started the engine and gave it a little gas—a little too much gas. It made a sound like an angry sewing machine and nearly shot right out from under me. I lifted the thumbs-up signal to Steven then death-gripped the handlebars.

Pulling out of the driveway, I wobbled like a foal on new legs. Steven rode ahead and led the way over the hill into Gustavia.

My tires bounced on the uneven pavement. Thirty-five miles an hour seemed far too fast for the rickety little machine. I hoped I wasn't going to

251

end up looking like a pink skid mark on the pocked asphalt.

We rode through the small town along the harbor.

The hull of an enormous, pristine white yacht gaped open, exposing racks of wave runners and a smaller boat inside. *Kingston, South Africa* was painted on the stern. I tried not to gawk at the opulence as I putted by, engulfed in belching puffs of exhaust. Each yacht was grander than the last. The small harbor looked like a yard sale for lifestyles of the rich and famous.

We finally stopped off for lunch in a bright yellow café across from the original Cheeseburger in Paradise, the legendary burger joint in the Jimmy Buffet lyrics.

The entire week passed and it was like listening to a new favorite song; it could play on the same loop over and over and I'd never get tired of it.

When we returned to Orange County, Steven and I waited for our suitcases at the baggage carousel in the John Wayne Airport. I leaned against his side and thought about the paradise we'd left behind. Just being with Steven, wherever we were, I felt more at peace with my life than I ever had.

contentment cookies

1 amazing man
1 woman in-love
1 island paradise
16 oz. quiet intimacy
2 lbs. brie

Pour man and woman into island paradise.
Mix in quiet intimacy.

Add brie and stir at languid pace. Drop into rounded spoonfuls onto a white sand beach.

Bake under tropical sun until golden and rested.

Serve with glass of fresh tranquility.

Yield: Incredible sense of peace.
Unlimited servings.
Nutritional Value: None.

Guaranteed 5 lb. weight GAIN.

It's either the bliss or the cheese; I'm really not sure.

sex toys r us
Saturday, March 29

I walked up the apartment steps carrying two trays of fruit. The invitation to Tawny's lingerie party had come as a surprise, but I decided to go anyway.

I rang the bell and waited.

Tawny threw open the door. "Hey, long time no see! Come in."

I noticed she'd gained weight, one or two dress sizes since I saw her last. Her long, dark hair had a new reddish tint in the thick curls.

I set the fruit on her bar counter and removed the foil covers. Steven had cut and assembled the platters while I was in the shower.

The fruit was perfectly sliced and arranged on banana leaves and set in a herringbone pattern with the fruit fanned into color wheel designs on top: watermelon, cantaloupe, honeydew, strawberries, grapes, and bananas.

"Wow! Did you do this?" Tawny looked at the platters with her mouth agape.

"Are you kidding? If I made it, the fruit would be chunked and thrown into a bowl. My boyfriend, Steven, did it."

"Are you sure he's not gay? I can't believe a straight guy put this together," she said.

The women at the party gathered around the trays, murmuring their surprise.

"Okay, ladies, I finally made it." A chubby blonde with a Southern accent bustled into the room carrying a large suitcase. "Ladies, have a seat and we'll get started."

She cracked open the case and passed around clipboards laminated with cutouts of nude men. "Gather 'round and all y'all take one."

It was like preschool paper dolls, porn edition. One clipboard made the rounds and brought nothing but giggles as it passed from one woman to the next. It finally ended up in my hands. The naked man de jour was dressed in a fireman's hat, jacket, and boots. He was gorgeous, but sadly, the poor man was sans pants. I say sadly, because his hose wouldn't put out the flame on a campfire marshmallow. I clipped my order sheet so it covered his tragic little flaw.

Ready to get the party started, Tawny dove her hand into the woman's suitcase and pulled out an enormous purple dildo.

"I named mine Barney." She held it up like the Olympic torch and then wiggled it to show its flexibility.

Tawny was always ahead of her time. When it came to sexuality, she was a new millennium woman back in the 1980s.

"This one's a top seller," Sex Toy Lady said, lifting a neon blue phallic item out of her case and setting it on the coffee table. She stretched the electric cord to an outlet. Suddenly the mock penis swung into action and began hula dancing on the table. Ball bearings rotated under the surface of the blue rubber skin.

I couldn't imagine how that could possibly be comfortable. It looked more like something Martha Stewart would use to mix cake batter than something I'd want to use for sex.

The Lady held up another item—a dildo with a suction cup attached at the base. "This one's perfect if y'all ever wanna fuck Brad Pitt." She licked the suction cup and stuck it wetly onto the television screen.

Although I can't say I never thought about the prospect, a dildo stuck to the TV wouldn't exactly be my preferred method.

The next item was a bottle of silicon lubricant. "It's amazin'," Sex Lady said. "You can even screw in a hot tub and it won't warsh away."

"Oh, this is my favorite!" Tawny reached into the grab bag and withdrew a hot pink, rubber cylinder the size of a Twinkie.

"It's perfect for giving guys hand jobs in movie theaters. If you grab it real tight on the end and pull it real fast, they blow their load instantly," she said.

I peeled my eyebrows out of my hairline. There are just some things I'd rather not know about my friends and their sex lives.

Except maybe which theater seats *not* to sit in.

After nearly two hours of sex toy show and tell, I turned to the lady and said, "When do we get to see the lingerie?"

The roomful of women burst into laughter.

Personally, I didn't think it was particularly funny. I actually wanted to buy something cute to wear for Steven and was pretty sure he'd prefer it wasn't a glow-in-the-dark strap-on.

I guess the joke was on me. I realized the fact that "Lingerie Party" looks more acceptable on an invitation than writing: You're invited to my Wacky Dildo Party—where B.Y.O.B. means Bring Your Own Batteries.

sunflower in a bucket of snow

Easter
Sunday, April 20

The Easter Bunny was very good to me this year.

He hopped into the bedroom of our rented mountainside condo with a tray of croissants, fresh berries, orange juice, and a little blue Tiffany & Co. box. I pounced on the box and pulled a tail of the white bow. It opened to a silver *Return to Tiffany* tag bracelet.

A family snowboarding trip to Mammoth completed Steven's Easter present.

We sat at the thick oak table in our room and watched the passing chairs of the ski lift from the window while we finished breakfast. After dressing for the day, Josh, Steven, and I stepped out of the lodge into the crisp morning air.

"Mom, you look like a sleeping bag with arms and legs." Josh laughed and shouldered his rented snowboard.

"Anything less than seventy-five degrees is too cold." Spring skiing, my ass. I'd rather be in St. Bart.

"Are you sure you don't want to try it?" Josh teased, stepping into the bindings.

"No. I'm fine. I'll just wait here and take pictures when you guys come down," I said.

"Are you sure, honey?" Steven held my shoulders and looked into my eyes. "If you want, I'll hang out with you in the lodge."

"No, of course not. You guys go up and try not to kill yourselves. I'll just watch."

The ski lift scooped Josh and Steven onto the bench seat. I followed the cables with my eyes until their seat was a speck against the blue sky.

I trudged carefully in the slush to the end of the run where they would eventually descend. Skiers and snowboarders whizzed by. I watched their movements as the skiers toed in to slow down and the snowboarders plowed their boards. It looked easy enough.

A small boy, not possibly older than seven, carved down the hill on a board the size of a Popsicle stick.

If that little guy could master it, I wouldn't have any problems; I'm pretty coordinated.

Soon an older lady followed; the unruly curls of her gray hair sprung from underneath a knitted hat as she slid to a stop in the icy trenches of muddy snow leading to the lift.

Okay, that did it. If a ninety-year-old woman could snowboard, I sure as hell could.

I tromped to the ski shop and rented a snowboard and boots. It wasn't long before Steven and Josh came zipping down the hill. Josh's experience on his skateboard made it a quick and easy transition to the snow. Steven skied for years in Switzerland, so Mammoth was little effort once he adjusted to the snowboard.

I stood holding the board and shuffled my boots in the slushy snow.

"You're going to snowboard?" Josh laughed and covered his mouth with a gloved hand.

"Are you sure you don't want to practice first?" Steven asked.

"No, I got it. I can do this, let's just go."

Steven sat beside me on the lift bench. I linked my arm through his and curled it tightly. With my other hand, I death-gripped the metal frame of the seat.

The biting wind from the ascending lift chapped my cheeks and I shivered.

"Look at how beautiful everything is." Steven nudged my side.

"That's okay. I'll take your word for it." I kept my eyes squinched closed. The board dangled from my right leg and felt heavy enough to pull me off the seat.

I could just see it. Me, free-falling hundreds of feet directly into a pine tree and being carted away on a stretcher to a waiting medevac helicopter. Now, that's my idea of a great winter vacation.

"Get ready to step off," Steven said as the ski lift reached the top. "Hold out the leg with the board first and step into it with your other foot as you come off the seat."

WHOMP.

I tripped over the snowboard and found myself facedown under the lift.

The next bench was empty and narrowly missed hitting me in the head. I stood up quickly before another seat arrived and hobbled off the angled mat, one leg free, the other still snapped into the binding.

Steven held out his hand to help me step into the snow. "Are you all right?" he asked.

A cute, young blonde with a bright pink scarf tucked into her resort staff vest lifted a camera in my direction. "Would you like a picture?"

I brushed the dirty slush from the front of my jacket. "No," I smiled with gritted teeth. "I would *not* like a picture."

Steven helped steady me as I snapped into my bindings. I swiveled my hips toward the run and nudged my board forward. I skied ten feet and promptly fell over.

My bottom buried in the snow, it was like dropping anchor. I couldn't move until Steven came over and hoisted my anvil of an ass off the ground.

I stood unstably until he snapped back into his own bindings a few feet away. And then I fell over again.

"See if you can get up on your own," he said.

It was the most absurd exercise further proving Newton's first law of physics. Forget the apple, just use my ass. There seemed to be some sort of magnetic field in the snow pulling me down. I fell every six feet, sometimes less. Once my butt landed in the snow, there was little I could do to lift myself. I struggled like an upended turtle.

On another three-foot distance ski, I fell forward onto my hands and knees. I pulled to a crouched position and clawed at the edge of the snowboard until the weight of my bottom pulled me over backward into the snow again.

It took forty-five minutes just to get far enough away from the lift so I couldn't see it anymore. It felt, only slightly, like progress.

"When you want to turn, point your arms in the direction you want to go," Steven called out.

The grade of the hill changed and I started to pick up speed. My snowboard was headed straight for a large, rough-barked tree trunk along the side of the run.

"Turn! Turn!" Steven yelled.

By then, I was flapping my arms like Super Chicken. I knew I needed to stop, but wasn't sure how. I kicked my legs out from under myself and the board spun in the snow. I landed hard. When my ass hit the ground, I bounced. My beanie and sunglasses flew off, and I slid thirty feet headfirst down the hill.

Yard Sale. Snow accessories. Finders-keepers.

I lay still in the snow, staring up at the clear blue sky. Hot tears filled my eyes.

"Are you okay?" Steven plowed to a stop beside me.

Quickly, I reached to wipe away the tears. I didn't want him to see me cry. When I pulled my gloved hand up to dry my eyes, it dropped a dusting of snow across my face.

Steven unclipped his boots from his board and crouched beside me. "Ready to try again?" He took off one glove, brushed the snow off my cheek, and leaned to kiss my forehead. "I love you," he said.

"I love you too." It came out in a whisper. I couldn't trust my voice wouldn't break.

I felt like such a failure. All I wanted to do was be perfect for him. I wanted so much for him to love me because everything about me was right. And exactly what he wanted.

This beautiful, wonderful man loved me and had so much patience. But all I wanted to do was scream down an avalanche by kicking my feet and pounding my fists into the snow.

Josh slid to a stop a short distance away. "Geez Mom, this is the second time I've passed you. And you still haven't made it down the hill once yet?"

Steven shot Josh a warning look, shaking his head slightly, and waving a hand low to signal Josh to shut up.

That's when Josh became the target for a motherly iron-melting glare.

He caught the look. "Well, I'm gonna go." He waved. "See you in a few minutes." Josh maneuvered his board and shot down the hill.

Steven reached under my arms and lifted me to my feet, turning me around like a propeller until I faced the right direction.

Again, I skied ten feet and fell. I sat in the snow and unclipped my boots from the bindings.

Steven looked into my eyes for a long moment. Without a word, he stepped out of his bindings and shouldered both snowboards. He leaned to kiss my cheek and we walked the rest of the way down the hill holding hands.

There was just too much of a gap between my sheer force of will and my technical abilities. Maybe there are just some things that I really can't do.

golden girls take the scenic route to hollywood
Thursday, May 8

Yesterday, I called Valerie on the phone. "You're old!" I cackled like a witch and then hung up.

The annual pre-birthday telephone assault.

Today, I gifted her with my traditional birthday song. It was "Happy Birthday to You"—with a twist that included comments about her living environment, as well as, her odor and facial resemblance to a small primate. I crooned the song off-key at the top of my lungs, dragging out all of the vowels in yooou, zoooo, and monkeeey. She laughed, as did her partners at the firm and the rest of the staff that were apparently standing in the room while I was singing.

You've got to love speakerphones.

We planned to meet at Bonita's condo in Costa Mesa. Slated for Valerie's thirty-seventh birthday: a drive up to the City of Angels, dinner at a Mexican restaurant, and then over to see *The Producers* at the Hollywood Pantages Theater.

We arrived at Bonita's—all wearing the same suede boots.

Isn't there a proverb: birds of a feather shop together, or something like that?

"No one will notice." I waved off the minor social disaster.

We climbed into Valerie's SUV for the road trip. Bonita hopped in the back. I rode in the shotgun slash navigator position—the perks of getting carsick like a dog.

"Which way should we go?" Valerie asked.

She rarely ventured north of the Orange County line.

"Take the 405 Freeway North to the 605 North to the 5 North to the 101 Freeway," I said. "It's the fastest way with the least traffic."

For the first thirty-five minutes, we drove in silence, definitely some sort of Guinness Book world record.

"How about some music?" I hoisted my bulging, leather CD case, opened it in the middle and flipped the pages. Bob Marley, John Mayer, Natalie Merchant, Nelly, Next, Nine Inch Nails, Pet Shop Boys, The Police, Puddle of Mudd...

Eclectic, yes. Alphabetically OCD, absolutely.

"Do you have any jazz?" Bonita asked, leaning between the seats.

I faked a cough. Excuse me whilst I remove this bone from my throat. "Um...noooo," I said. "My CD collection would rise up in mutiny and shrink-wrap me in my sleep."

"How about something Top 40 that we can all sing to?" Valerie said.

I slid a blood red CD into the player and advanced to the third track so we could all sing along to my favorite codependency theme song. In unison, we belted out the lyrics, earnestly promising we would be there to save some guy and take him away from his life.

"We should go to a karaoke club some night," Valerie said, "but first we should stop off to pick up a case of ear plugs and pass them out before we start singing."

I ran with the idea. "Let's just buy a karaoke machine, hook it up to my big screen and we can have singing slumber parties."

"And we can bring a few bottles of wine," Bonita said.

Can you get evicted for singing like a drunken dog with its tail caught in a door?

"Exit Santa Monica Boulevard and turn right," I said to Valerie.

"What's the name of the restaurant?" Bonita asked.

"El something-or-other. I ate there once with a friend's family."

"Is it open for dinner this early?" Valerie looked at me. "You called to make a reservation, right?"

"I called, but it was hard to understand the guy who answered the phone. I think he said they changed owners and now they serve Mexican seafood. When I asked, he said we don't need a reservation."

"Mexican seafood sounds good," Valerie said. "For lunch, I had grilled Ono brushed with a rosemary marinade. Fish is on my diet. I didn't eat the rice pilaf though, too many carbs."

"How long ago did you say you were here?" Bonita asked, looking out the window at the passing shops and pedestrians.

"About fifteen years ago," I said.

I took a second look at the neighborhood we were driving through. Bubbled and stick letter graffiti decorated the walls. Gray wrought iron bars covered the murky store windows.

"Are you sure it's safe for us to be driving around here?" Bonita asked.

"Of course it is." I giggled. "We can use you as our cultural liaison."

"Very funny, pinche pendeja," Bonita shot back.

"Just keep driving east, I'm sure the neighborhood will get better," I said to Valerie.

We passed Los Angeles City College.

"Oh m'god, we're in East L.A.!" Valerie shrieked.

"I think that's it." Bonita pointed from between the seats.

Valerie pulled to the curb.

There it was. El something-or-other Coyote. A boxy cement hut that was surrounded by a wire fence in the middle of a parking lot of broken asphalt. The squat gray building was flanked by brightly painted metal picnic tables chained together with rusty links.

A window sign read: *Two For One Fish Taco Tuesdays*.

We burst out laughing.

"I am *not* getting out of this car," Valerie said.

"Are you sure we don't need reservations?" Bonita asked, trying hard to appear serious.

"Well, a fish taco *is* Mexican seafood," Valerie chimed in, picking up Bonita's game.

"This is not what I remember," I offered in defense. "The information operator gave me two listings. This is just the wrong one."

Valerie accelerated, leaving the taco stand behind. "Why isn't there a single u-turn lane in this horrible city?" she asked, after driving a few blocks.

"Just make a right here at the corner, then go around the block to the next light. We can make a big circle and go back the way we came," I said.

Halfway around the block, we found ourselves on a cramped residential street flanked by rundown apartments. A used car graveyard packed the curbs on both sides.

"Odelaaayyy." A carload of gangbangers in a blue Chevy Impala whistled and yelled out the window, gesturing as our cars passed closely on the small street.

"Don't look, don't look," Bonita hissed. "Just keep driving."

"Another great idea, Annette," Valerie whispered tightly.

"Don't be such a chicken shit." I laughed at their melodrama. "Just think of it as an adventure."

Back on the main street, we stopped at a red light. "I'm driving the nicest car around here and we obviously look like we should be somewhere else," Valerie said. "The last thing I want is to be shot and car jacked."

BAM!

We all jumped when the delivery truck in the next lane released its air brakes. Then we looked at each other and laughed.

I dialed the second number. "The other El what-ever-it's-called is on Melrose a half block from Beverly Hills," I said.

"At least that's in a decent area," Bonita said.

The funky shops on Melrose rolled past the window like a silent movie. Tragic looking youth lounged in iron chairs outside coffee shops. Traffic crawled from one short cycle stoplight to the next.

We pulled up in front of the restaurant. "This is cute," Bonita said, peeking out the window.

"Much better." Valerie switched off the ignition.

We breezed through the entrance like formidable, slightly aging, but well-preserved Charlie's Angels. All we needed was a wind machine, 70s style pant-suits, and the right theme music.

The restaurant was completely empty: too late for lunch, too early for dinner. The staff of waitresses loitered by the bar, chatting with the cute bartender.

The hostess settled us into our seats and we perused the menu. Bonita and Valerie ordered two margaritas apiece. Each glass was the size of a ten-gallon fish tank. By the time the food arrived, the conversation had become an exercise in man bashing.

"Men suck," Valerie said.

"They're all stupid," Bonita added. She took another sip through her straw.

I sat silently with nothing to contribute, and picked at my cheese enchilada with the edge of my fork.

"They all cheat," Valerie said. "Every one of them."

Her thoughts obviously still dwelled on her ex-boyfriend and it fouled her birthday mood.

"Worse than that, they promise they'll commit and they never do. I hate that." Bonita's face contorted in disgust.

I took a sip of my cranberry juice, moving the ice around in the glass with the straw. "Maybe you shouldn't date men who aren't available. Every time it ends, you're miserable."

"Well, not everyone is perfect like you," Bonita said, taking another drink of her margarita.

Valerie fixed me with a hard stare and then looked away.

Ok, so maybe it was a little blunt to come out and say it, but it was hard to hear Bonita cry about getting her heart broken on a regular basis when it wouldn't happen as much if she dated available men.

Valerie turned back to me. "So. How are things in your little world?" Her tone was sharp and aggressive.

It was then that I realized I had stopped talking to them about Steven, but I couldn't remember exactly when. I'd discovered that anytime I mentioned something wonderful, it was met with disdain. And there are only so many times a person will reach out to touch a hot stove.

"Fine," I said. "We have to get going or we'll be late." I pushed back my chair.

Sobriety dictated the car seating assignments. On autopilot, I navigated the SUV through the city traffic.

While I waited for a stoplight to turn green, a guy on the corner caught my attention, and I couldn't stop staring. He was wearing rub-faded jeans, and stood bare-chested. My eyes traveled up his frame. Washboard abs, square pecs, ripped biceps, chiseled jaw, high cheekbones, piercingly beautiful eyes, with hair tousled across his forehead. I really love men. Fascinating creatures. So very—

A car horn honked.

I pulled forward and almost rear-ended the car stopped in front of us.

"Stop staring at that stupid billboard," Valerie said, "or you'll end up crashing my car and we'll never get to the theater on time."

I heard Bonita mumble from the backseat, "That's okay, he's probably gay anyway."

A man with a gray flag waved us into the parking lot a half block from the theater. I walked away from the car, briskly stepping over the gold-outlined stars embedded in the sidewalk along Vine Avenue. Audrey Hepburn. Jackie Coogan. We crossed Hollywood Boulevard toward the Pantages; Bonita and

Valerie trailed slightly behind me. None of us spoke.

I handed my ticket to the usher at the door. In a mocking tone, he lisped and gestured to our boots. "Oh now isn't that so cute. Did you call each other and decide to wear them together?"

"Real fashion police make more than minimum wage," I snapped at him in response. "Just stick to tearing tickets."

I wasn't sure if I was more irritated by his attempt to ridicule us or by my feeling that he was implying that we were all the same.

more than a foreign accent
Sunday, May 18

"Thank you guys so much for coming all the way up here." Bryce's tall, wiry frame pulled me into a bony embrace. He continued to mug for the flashing cameras, the diploma case held tightly in his hand.

"Congratulations." Steven shook Bryce's free hand.

Bryce continued to pump his arm exuberantly. "Thanks, man. I never thought I'd finish."

I gave him another hug. "I knew you could do it."

We joined the rest of Bryce's friends, navigating through the pedestrian traffic surrounding the Loyola Law School. Steven and I climbed into his Suburban to follow the celebration caravan to a trendy Japanese restaurant in Huntington Beach.

When we walked through the front door, "What I Like About You" by The Ramones blasted through the speakers. Everyone headed for the back room toward the teppan grills.

While we waited for the hostess to seat us, Steven and I stood at the bar next to Bryce's college buddy, Neil. With one sweeping glance, I could see Neil was a typical nightclub hound with a freshly minted law degree. Once he ditched the cap and gown, he sported a swing-era bowling style shirt of black satin, a pair of zebra-print creepers, and an attitude.

Neil pulled a tall bar chair away from a woman who was about to sit on it. Then he settled himself onto the seat. His beer bottle dangled from his hand as he rested his arm on the edge of the bar.

He responded to our stunned looks, "The way I see it, if women want all this feminism stuff and equal opportunity, then they have to deal with the consequences." He shrugged and swigged his beer. His motioning with the bottle made the contents slosh out.

He continued defending his moronic wisdom. "See, if my girlfriend is mad at me and expects me to sleep on the couch, I tell her if she's mad, she can go sleep on the couch because I'm not getting out of my bed for her." He punctuated his statement with another splash of beer.

"So, where is your girlfriend tonight?" Steven asked, angling for the inevitable answer.

"Well, we kinda broke up," Neil said.

I smiled into my glass of cranberry juice.

"So, how long have you guys been together?" Neil asked, using his beer bottle like a pointer.

"Almost six months." Steven leaned to kiss the top of my head and snaked his arm around my waist.

Neil directed his attention to me. "So, I bet when you met him, you were really turned on by his accent. I bet that's why it was easy for him to hook up with you. Chicks dig guys with accents."

A flat, humorless smile pressed my lips together. "No, that wasn't it," I said. "I could just tell by the way he was sitting that he had a big dick."

Steven coughed on his sip of beer.

"Wow, okay, hey, that's cool." Neil gave Steven an awkward elbow nudge of approval.

"It was nice meeting you," Steven said. "It looks like our table is ready now." He guided me away from Neil and leaned to whisper in my ear, "Do you have any idea how much I love you?"

"No," I said playfully.

"That guy was being an idiot. Too bad he's too drunk and too stupid to know it." Steven stopped in the aisle and turned me to face him. "You are so amazing to me. I love the fact that I never know what you'll say next."

Steven pulled out my chair and we seated ourselves at the far end of a U-shaped table ringing one of the teppan grills. Bryce and his girlfriend, Sheila, sat along the curve, flanked by two of her girlfriends and their dates.

Our Asian chef arrived and sprinkled water on the hot iron grill. It sizzled and popped as he tapped an elaborate symphony using the side of his knives against the metal. He concluded by flipping the blades in the air and catching them. "Order, please," he said.

Clockwise around the table, we called out our food selections.

Soon sautéed shrimp flew through the air and the naughty games began. Sheila pulled out the front of her shirt and a plump shrimp dropped between her bare breasts. Bryce dove face first after it. One of the girls next to Sheila one-upped her by leaning back in the chair and lifting the edge of her mini-skirt. It was clear she had either forgotten or misplaced her panties when she dressed for the evening. The teppan chef, without pause, flipped a chunk of beef between her legs.

"What about you, Annette?" Bryce motioned to the shrimp bouncing like a paddleball on the end of the chef's metal spatula.

I laughed, waving my hands to ward off the suggestion. "No thanks. I always make a point of avoiding the possibility that any part of my body will ever smell like seafood."

Steven and I shared a large square tray loaded with sushi. While we ate, we watched the sexy food fest like spectators of a foreign sport. At a nearby grill, another chef incorporated a cucumber carved like a giant phallus topped with sour cream. One of the guys in the group placed it protruding from the zipper of his pants. His girlfriend made a show of devouring the vegetable.

The room was loud with laughter and the pulse of chanting obscenities. Various couples started doing alcohol body shots and there wasn't a single person in the room who needed more alcohol.

I leaned my head on Steven's shoulder. He pulled my chair closer to his and slung his arm around my back. I nestled against him and watched the scene playing out in front of us. I felt old. Or maybe just older. And settled.

A few years back, it could have been Valerie, Bonita, Heather, and me wearing sizzling food like a hot chick buffet, but somehow it seemed like another lifetime, a time I could look back on with a wicked little smile, but not one I was ready to revisit.

I felt comfortable and content in my life with Steven. Whenever I was with him, my heart beat like a cat's purr. And I knew I was right where I wanted to be.

I lifted my lips close to Steven's ear. "Are you ready to leave?"

"Definitely," he whispered back.

the choo-choo song for satan

My Birthday
Sunday, May 25

I heard Steven rustling around in the kitchen. The morning light seeped between my lashes. I snuggled deeper under the covers, pulling the down-filled comforter over my head.

Steven and Josh entered the bedroom singing the birthday song. I pushed myself up in bed as they came in. Steven carried a breakfast tray of croissants and berries. Josh held a glass brimming with orange juice in one hand, and a pink and green striped gift bag in the other.

"Good morning, Mom. Happy birthday," Josh said, climbing onto the bed beside me.

"Happy birthday, honey." Steven set the tray across my lap and kissed the top of my head.

Josh lifted his gift above the food. "Open my present first."

I reached into the bag and withdrew an object wrapped in wrinkled yellow tissue paper, crisscrossed with scotch tape. I peeled at the reinforced wrapping and finally freed the present: a neon blue, light-up shift knob for my car.

"Now your car will look cool like *The Fast and the Furious*," Josh said, his excitement bubbling over. "I can put it on for you if you want."

I leaned to give him a hug. "Thanks, sweetie. It's a great gift." I looked over in Steven's direction and he returned my smile.

Josh hopped off the bed. "Come in the other room. There's an even better present in there."

I scuffed into the living room in pajamas and my Eeyore slippers.

On the table, I saw a red bow wrapped around a remote control with JVC printed along the top edge of the small black rectangle.

"Is it a new stereo?" I asked.

I looked over to the entertainment center and saw a black electronic unit hooked up and set under the DVD player.

"No," Steven said. "Go see."

I walked over and squinted at the printing on the unit.

"A karaoke machine!" I closed the space between us in a half stride and threw myself into an embrace with him.

"Now all you have to do is read the instruction manual." Steven smiled and pulled the book from behind his back.

"Noooo," I whined. "You know I hate that." I was famous for fiddling with electronics just enough to figure out how to work the basic functions. That was why every gadget I owned showed a different time of day. I never bothered to read how to set the clock.

Josh waved the song CD case in front of me, playing keep-away. "If you can take this from me, I'll show you how to use it," he said.

Before he could blink, I had Josh in a headlock. "Never forget, I brought you into this world and I can take you out of it." I noogied the top of his head with the knuckles of my fist.

After his quick surrender, I decided to use the automatic disk changer function for the karaoke machine: Josh. He sat next to the unit, switching out the CDs for me.

I crooned the "Chattanooga Choo Choo" song like a tone-deaf 1940s big band singer. I sang it five times in a row with the volume turned up loud.

Steven snapped a digital picture of me belting out the last line of the song. My mouth formed a gaping O, with my head thrown back, I warbled the final word. I ended with a huge smile directed at Steven.

"You look so happy. I love seeing you like that." He leaned down and kissed my forehead. "I'm glad you're enjoying your present."

I sang for three hours straight—through every track on the ten CDs that came with the machine, until finally, my voice was nearly gone. I had a blast, even if it was unjust torture for the neighbors on a quiet Sunday morning.

The phone rang. I thought it might be the verbal equivalent of a neighbor pitching a shoe at an alley cat on the back fence, but it was Heather calling to wish me a happy birthday and confirm our knitting date. I told her I was on the way.

When I pulled into the parking lot at Tall Mouse Crafts, I saw the sign on the glass doors announcing the free knitting lessons and another sign that was advertising a thirty-percent-off sale on yarn. My absolute favorite word: FREE. My next favorite word: SALE.

I met up with Heather and we settled ourselves side-by-side at one of the long folding tables. I was surprised there weren't more people in the class. How can anyone pass up free knitting lessons?

Our instructor, her shoulders hunched into the shape of a *C,* smiled and introduced herself as Ethel. She held up a set of knitting needles, showing the proper way to hold them, how to drape the yarn between our fingers and cast on.

Three women, about our age, sat across the table from Heather and me, laughing at their own fumbling. They chatted lightly about current events.

Heather and I focused on our knitting. I tucked the end of one needle into a loop of yarn on the other, crossed the strand wrapped around my finger and pulled it through. I felt slow and awkward but was starting to get the hang of it. With any luck, I'd have an entire scarf by next winter.

"Guess what Steven gave me for my birthday," I switched the needles in my hand to start another row. "A karaoke machine," I said without giving her time to actually guess. "I didn't even ask for it, he just knew I loved singing so he picked it out because of that."

I thought she muttered, "Isn't that special." But I knew I must've heard wrong. "So, how are things with you and Derek?" I said, still concentrating on moving the yarn along my row.

"Fine," she said tightly.

I glanced at Heather. Her stabbing movements sent one needle flipping from her hand. It clinked onto the floor and bounced under the table. She scowled and bent to retrieve it.

"Here, let me help see if you dropped a stitch," I said.

Heather jerked away, her face stormy. "Oh, so now you're perfect at this?" She yanked and pulled at the yarn, her hands fisted around the needles. The knitted line she had created drew taunt.

I noticed the women across the table eyeing Heather's violent flailing. I leaned over and whispered, "Relaaaaax. It's only knitting. This is supposed to be fun."

Heather huffed and fussed with her yarn. "Don't tell me to relax!" she hissed through her teeth. She threw the knitting needles and knotted yarn onto the table. "I can't do this." Heather pushed back her chair and reached for her purse.

I gathered my materials and followed her into the parking lot. "I'm sorry this didn't turn out to be fun for you," I said. I didn't know what else to say.

Heather looked at her watch. "Now I'm late to meet up with Derek and my whole day is wasted." She jammed her key into the lock to open her car door.

"Look, I don't know what your deal is, but you need to mellow out before you drive anywhere," I said.

"Whatever." She got into her car and slammed the door. She drove out of the parking lot and left me standing there.

I climbed into my car and called her on the cell phone as I headed home.

She seemed to be a little calmer. I avoided talking about knitting or Steven, not knowing exactly what had set her off, so I picked a current event topic I overheard the women at our table talking about. A young surfer who had her arm bitten off by a shark was apparently going around the country giving inspirational talks about how the accident had been God's will.

"Don't you think that's odd?" I asked. "I mean, it's great that she's getting on with her life and doing something positive and good after the accident, but the shark was probably hungry and thought she was a seal. I hardly think God is up there playing *The Sims* with a sea creature expansion pack."

Heather was quiet on the line.

When she finally spoke, the malice in her voice was unmistakable. "Ever since you met Steven, you've changed."

"What do you mean? I have not," I said.

"Yes, you have! You used to be conservative." Her voice twisted in disgust. "Now, all of a sudden, you've turned into a Democrat."

Hardly a crime, but maybe a certifiable sin to a woman with an autographed 8x10 picture of President George W. Bush on her refrigerator door.

"Now you don't believe in anything. You've turned into a fucking atheist!" she shouted.

Stunned, I opened my mouth to protest the out-of-right-field attack, but her tirade gained momentum. "You have! You're a fucking atheist! A FUCKING ATHEIST!" she shrieked into the phone.

I waited to hear if Heather's head would spin around and I listened for the gagging sound that accompanies projectile vomiting. Where do you find an exorcist when you really need one?

Even through the phone, I could hear her chest heaving with emotional exertion. I wondered, at what point, had I morphed into a mortal enemy? It was like a bad *Twilight Zone* episode—like when you think you recognize your world until you realize nothing is the way it was and nothing will never be the same again.

Heather's voice quaked in indignation. "After twelve years of friendship, I don't even know who you are," she said. Then she hung up.

the baby and the bath water
Memorial Day
Monday, May 26

My cell phone rang: "Ding Dong the Witch is Dead." The Caller ID showed Bonita calling from her cell phone.

I hadn't talked with her or Valerie since the Hollywood trip. I didn't call them and they didn't call me. Three weeks without a single word was like a lifetime compared with years of daily chatter. It seemed a distance continued to grow between us as my relationship with Steven developed. And I wasn't sure how to mend the gap.

"Hi," I answered the phone, trying to sound casual, as if I'd just spoken with her earlier that day.

"Hi…how are you?" Bonita's tone sounded a little strained, almost like she, too, wasn't sure what to say.

"I'm fine. What's up?" I said, still a little guarded.

"We hadn't heard from you, so I thought I'd call to see how you've been."

She didn't mention Valerie's name, but I knew who "we" was. I had stopped calling Valerie because of her repeated backhanded comments about Steven. I could only imagine it came from a place of jealousy, but it was hard to ignore the negative feeling it gave me.

"Things are pretty much the same." I said. "We celebrated my birthday yesterday and we're getting ready right now to leave so we can launch the Seadoos in Dana Point Harbor."

"That's right…happy birthday." Bonita seemed a little embarrassed to have missed it.

"Thanks," I said.

The conversation died on the line.

Me not calling Bonita was like throwing the baby out with the bath water. Whatever tension there was between Valerie and me, Bonita was caught in the middle. I considered her more Valerie's friend than mine, since Valerie had introduced us.

"Well, we were just wondering if you were coming over for the Memorial Day Barbeque," Bonita said.

It seemed a strange question since I hadn't been invited. Although it had been a tradition for years, considering the current strain in the friendship, I never would've just assumed and shown up at Valerie's house.

"I'm sorry. I have plans with Steven."

The conversation lagged again and I wasn't sure how to revive it. I didn't know if Bonita was extending an olive branch or whether it was a fishing expedition on Valerie's behalf. I didn't feel like sticking my neck up on the chopping block to find out.

Valerie wasn't the one calling, so that sent a message all its own. I didn't think we were going to be friends anymore. There would never be those little cottages on the communal property so we could all grow old together.

It was sad to think I was losing friends I'd had for over a decade. But when I thought about the basis for our friendship, aside from all being single moms, it seemed the only thing Valerie, Bonita, and I really had in common was a bond of shared bitterness about past failed relationships.

I had let go of that and was finally happy. So maybe I did change.

da plane! da plane!
Monday, June 2

Steven and I stretched the blanket across the sand near the waterline. The gentle lap of the water accompanied the soft breeze of early evening. We sat beside each other and watched the sailboats tack across Mission Viejo Lake. Josh paddled a rented kayak, gliding between the boats.

Steven fished his cell phone out of his pocket and checked the time.

"What? You late for a hot date?" I teased, scooting over to snuggle against his side.

"No. It's almost six and I'm just expecting a call from the...tile guy. He needs to drop off some...um...tile. At one of the job sites."

Josh paddled to shore, jumped out, and pulled the kayak onto the beach. "So, what's up?" he flopped onto the blanket beside us.

"Let me take your picture with the kayak." I dug the digital camera out of my beach bag and followed him to the waterline.

Josh posed holding the paddle with one foot on the edge of the bright yellow boat.

Steven's cell phone rang. He jumped up, took it from his pocket, and walked over to the deserted lifeguard stand to answer it.

When he finished the call, he pulled a one-dollar bill out of his wallet. "Josh, go to the snack bar and buy me a candy bar, please."

"What kind?" Josh asked.

"I don't care, whatever looks good." Steven pressed the money into Josh's hand, and Josh sprinted across the beach.

There was a faint rumble of a single-engine plane in the distance—a noise that usually blended into the sounds of calling seagulls and children's laughter.

Steven stepped beside me and whispered in my ear, "Annette, look up."

I dropped my head back and scanned the soft blue canvas. Filmy brush strokes of clouds dotted the sky; a thin sliver of pale moon hung in the distance.

Steven directed my gaze by pointing across the lake. A banner trailed on a short tether behind a small plane.

Instinctively, I knew what the words on the banner said. Through tears that suddenly blurred my vision, I turned to Steven in near panic and grasped his arm. "I have a feeling it says something really important, but I can't read it."

"Don't worry, it will come closer," he said.

The plane was almost directly overhead, but I still couldn't read the words on the banner. "What does it say?" I squinted through my tears.

He read it to me softly, leaning close. "It says, 'Annette will you marry me? Yours forever, Steven.'"

He took my hand and lowered himself onto one knee in the sand. "I want to spend the rest of my life with you. Will you marry me?"

A black velvet box appeared in his hand. Still so overwhelmed by the plane and banner, I didn't see where he had hidden it. Steven opened the box to and revealed a beautiful platinum ring: a princess cut diamond with two trillions, one on each side. The large facets of the center stone glittered in the sunlight.

"Yes!" I said. Tears ran down my face as Steven slid the ring onto my finger.

The plane banked and headed away from the beach. "The plane!" I grabbed the camera from atop the blanket and ran down the beach trying to take a picture of the banner.

"I ask you to marry me and now you're running away?" he called after me laughing.

I ran past a family playing a board game on a blanket, my feet spraying sand in my wake. "Congratulations!" they called out as I passed.

I followed the plane through the camera lens and snapped the picture. When I lowered the camera, Josh stood in front of me holding a Kit-Kat chocolate bar.

"Congratulations, Mom." He gave me a hug.

"Did you know about this?" I asked.

Josh nodded. "Steven asked me a couple weeks ago if he could marry you. He told me about the plane thing, but I didn't know he was going to do it today." He looked across the lake at the small plane banking for another lap. "It's pretty cool, huh?"

"Very cool," I said.

"Tell him I'm keeping the candy bar. Now I know he was just trying to get rid of me." Josh opened the wrapper and took a bite. "I'm going to return the kayak." He jogged over and pushed it into the water.

I walked back toward Steven. As I approached, I saw he had been watching Josh and me.

We curled up together on the blanket and watched the plane circle the lake a few more times until it disappeared into the setting sun.

Steven propped himself on an elbow. "So, are you sure you really want to marry me?"

It was like someone asking if I was sure I ever wanted to breathe again.

"Absolutely. I think I'm the luckiest girl in the world." I leaned to kiss him. He returned my nibbling kisses with a deeper press of passion.

When we pulled apart, his eyes danced. "If you're actually going to marry me, I hope you like to travel because I want to show you the world. Think you can handle that?" he said.

Steven reached into the back pocket of his jeans, withdrew an envelope, and handed it to me. I lifted the flap and pulled out a Continental Airlines flight itinerary with the final destination labeled CDG—Charles De Gaulle Airport: France.

"I want you to meet my parents. They bought a villa in Belcodene when they retired. We leave on Friday for three weeks. That is, if you're not too busy to go," he said.

I felt like I died and landed on Fantasy Island. The plane just left, and all I needed was Tattoo, the little guy in the white suit, to show me to my bungalow.

"What about Josh?" I asked.

"I want them to meet you both." Steven reached to fan out the pages in my hand: there were three.

My head spun. I'm a full-time writer. I'm in-love. The most amazing man in the world just asked me to marry him. And now I'm going to Europe. My fairy godmother out-did herself this time.

"I can't believe this is real," I said.

Steven tucked the pages into his pocket. "Believe it. This is as real as it gets," he said.

I was still stunned. "Are you sure you want to marry *me*?" I asked.

Steven cupped my face in his hands. His kiss was gentle and lingering. He whispered against my lips, "I'd marry you a hundred times just to show you how much I love you."

satisfaction soufflé

2 pure hearts
4 Tbsp. granulated joy
3/4 cup communication
1 tsp. comfort
3 Tbsp. enchantment
Tabs of mutual admiration

Cut away any old bruises from hearts, discard dark spots.

Whisk joy and communication to peaks of appreciation. Swirl enchantment together with comfort to form a glaze of harmony.

Fold hearts into above mixture to create trust. Simmer over consistent heat of intimacy.

In two soufflé dishes, butter the bottoms and sides with mutual admiration, paying special attention to the sides.

Spoon equal amounts of trust into the prepared dishes. Create a channel around the inside of each dish to allow for personal growth. Savor completely.

Yield: Eternal bliss. Unlimited servings.
Nutritional Value: None.
No Guaranteed weight loss.

The distinct possibility of weight gain. But who cares, I'm in-love!

part six

afterword

harmony in the universe

If someone had told me on the morning Kevin broke up with me that in twenty months I would be engaged to marry someone else—someone who really was my soul mate—I wouldn't have believed it. I would've insisted things like that only happened in the movies, not in real life. And definitely not to me.

Perhaps it was serendipity. Fate. Destiny. Faith. Chance. Karma. Whatever it's called, I realized it really does exist.

In the journal entry "Fortune Cookie Wisdom," there was a story about a wine party I attended. Well, it wasn't until six months into my engagement to Steven that I found out Lana, the hostess, was a remodeling client of his. Steven had been invited to that wine party, but didn't attend because he went out of town. Had he been there, I would've met him in June, before I was emotionally ready.

Was it coincidence that we both would've been in that exact place at that exact time? Was it coincidence that he didn't go? Steven and I have discovered many other places where we've crossed paths in the last ten years and never met. It just wasn't the right time.

It's funny to me now. Funny that I fought so hard against letting go and moving on, when all along, that was what I was supposed to do.

If I had a chance to say something to Kevin, it would be: Thank You. Thank you for knowing it wasn't right.

Because now I know what right feels like.

Dear Reader,

I'd love to hear from you. Please stop by *The Break-Up Diet* website at www.thebreak-updiet.com. I have a special gift for you—*The Break-Up Survival Guide*. It's a free, downloadable e-book that you can keep for yourself and forward to your friends, especially the ones who desperately need it!

At *The Break-Up Diet* website, you can also read and comment on the blog, share your break-up stories, and send me an email. For book clubs, you'll find a link to guided reading questions about compelling, woman-centric themes found in the book, and information about how to schedule a visit for me to speak with your group.

Thank you for supporting my tiny voice in such a noisy world.

Love, Peace, and Happiness,
Annette